SHORT DRAMAS FOR THE CHURCH

SHORT DRAMAS FOR THE CHURCH

DORCAS DIAZ SHANER

Judson Press ® Valley Forge

SHORT DRAMAS FOR THE CHURCH

Copyright © 1980
Judson Press, Valley Forge, PA 19482-0851

Third Printing, 1985

Unless otherwise indicated, Bible quotations in this volume are from the Revised Standard Version of the Bible, copyrighted 1946, 1952, 1971, 1973 © by the Division of Christian Education of the National Council of the Churches of Christ in the United States of America, and are used by permission.

Other versions of the Bible quoted in this book are:
The Living Bible. Tyndale House Publishers, Wheaton, Ill. Used by permission.
Today's English Version, the *Good News Bible*—Old Testament: Copyright © American Bible Society, 1976; New Testament: Copyright © American Bible Society, 1966, 1971, 1976. Used by permission.

Library of Congress Cataloging in Publication Data
Shaner, Dorcas Díaz.
  Short dramas for the church.

  1. Christian drama, American. I. Title.
PS3569.H3318S54   812'.54   80-19291
ISBN 0-8170-0883-7

The name JUDSON PRESS is registered as a trademark in the U.S. Patent Office. Printed in the U.S.A. ⊕

Acknowledgments

Much has been said about the loneliest of all professions—writing. However, many have accompanied me through the journey from the birth of the idea for this book to the complete fruition that is embodied here, and to them I am grateful.

I wish to thank those friends and actors who kindly performed my work so that I could see its strengths and weaknesses and smooth out the rough edges. I am especially grateful to Lawrence Janssen of Green Lake, Wisconsin, who throughout the years has been a constant source of encouragement. Some of the pieces in this book were originally prepared at his request. Some were a result of experiences shared with students while I was on the faculty of the Christian Writers Conference at Green Lake, Wisconsin.

Most of all, I owe a lifetime of gratitude to my husband, Donald, who has not only encouraged my writing but has also spent many hours laboriously reading the manuscript, making corrections and additions when necessary, and preparing the majority of the discussion questions. His love and affirmation are a gift that cannot be repaid.

Dorcas Díaz Shaner
Philadelphia, Pa.

Contents

Introduction

This book has been the direct leading of the Holy Spirit; God's love has made this work possible.

Drama is an intimate experience. Audiences attend the theater in order to escape, relate, and identify with the actors and the action. Hospitals use drama as therapy, and schools use it as a teaching technique. The author desires that her readers and potential audiences (through the presentation of these works) identify with the characters of the Bible and relate to the contemporary figures who appear in these pages. Through these characters God may be revealed to the reader-audience, and the reader-audience may also find fulfillment and identification with other seeking Christians and thus share in an intimate spiritual feast in God's agape.

Rationale for Writing This Book

Recently I was asked by some of my seminary students if any new dramatic material was available for a pastor or a lay person to use in a worship service. They wanted to try more creative approaches to the worship experience. Some of them had experimented with dramatic monologues and one-act plays, but most of these were too long and wordy for the average lay person to learn quickly. There seemed to be a genuine need for a resource which included material which could be presented simply but which would also include material for those who wished to present more ambitious productions. This was not an unusual request. For years pastors and others who attended my performances have asked for similar resources. It thus became evident that I would have to prepare a work which could meet the needs of as many persons as possible.

The works you find here include dramatic monologues, dramatic duets, trios, quartets, and readers theatre. Included are also some stingers. While most of these were prepared for presentation on a stage or platform, with little or no revision, these works can be easily adapted to the chancel area. Duplicate pages are included for each drama so that each participant has a copy. An extra copy is also included for the director.

When to Use This Book

The opportunities for use of the dramas in this book are myriad. The author has performed or directed these works in all of the following instances: as the morning and evening sermons, as an illustration of one of the points of the morning or evening sermon, as the anthem, as the benediction, and as the introit. They have been performed in colleges, high schools, churches, business meetings, youth groups, midweek services, conventions, conferences, workshops, and many other instances too numerous to list. Your choice of situation is limited only by your imagination.

What About Costumes?

The dramatic monologues are especially effective when a simple costume is used. For the biblical characters you would probably use garb typical of the time period. Your interpretation will be reflected in the clothing you select. Therefore, these pieces will have a different effect if you use contemporary dress. In all cases simplicity is the key. For many of the duets and trios, black shirt and skirt or pants are very effective. Again it is important to note that you may become as elaborate as your means and approach permit.

What About Staging?

In most instances no scenery is necessary. Simple staging with the effective use of lights should suffice to set the mood. A stool, a lectern when a reading is to be presented, a table or a chair can help to set the limits of the scene. A great deal of liberty may be taken with the scenery. But beware—if your stage is bare, you will need to convey a great deal more with the voice and body. Above all, keep the stage clear and clean. Curtains should work smoothly, and exits and entranceways must be easily accessible.

What About Lighting?

Let your imagination be your guide! These plays have been performed at different times with the aid of (1) candlelight, (2) floor lamps, (3) simple spotlights, or (4) elaborate stage lights. The most important thing to remember is the *mood* you are trying to generate.

A Note About Dramatic Monologues

In performing a monologue, the actor will want to keep in mind that while no one else actually speaks to him or her, he or she must give the audience the impression that the stage is filled with other characters. Thus, head and body movements should correspond with the dots (. . .), which indicate a pause, often followed by a line which is a *response* to another character in the scene.

What Is a Stinger?

A "stinger" is what the name implies. It is something that *stings*. It is intended to be abrasive, pungent, and pointed. Like a mosquito, which moves rather quickly to its target and then buzzes off, a good stinger moves quickly, delivers the punch line, and leaves its audience smarting in thought.

All parts of a stinger are vital, but the punch line is most important of all. The drama needs to set the stage—begin a process of hearing and reacting, and of anticipating—then make its point quickly and close. The real value lies in the use made of it from that point on. This use may be as the introduction to a sermon, to a group discussion, or to individual thought. Because the punch line is of primary importance, it will need to be delivered with clarity and good timing.

The Use of Probes

At the end of each of the pieces you will find questions which can be used to stimulate discussion. Sometimes the audience will not agree with the ending of a piece or with the author's interpretation of an incident. *Good*. Discussion should help them express these differences and perhaps engender a greater understanding of the theme of the piece. Some of the pieces will be *incomplete* unless discussion follows. Examples of these are "The Celebration," "The Dinner Party," and "Brothers." You will note that the latter has two endings. The discussion period might reveal a third possible ending to the dilemma presented in the parable.

It is suggested that discussion would best take place in small groups followed by a plenary session. It must be remembered, however, that these are only suggestions for the use of the material and that the best use is that which meets the needs of the participants.

A Word About Memorization

I have always felt that memorization frees the actor to interpret fully the character he or she is portraying. It allows the audience to see the character without anything coming between it and the actor. Unfortunately, it is not always feasible to expect amateurs to perform in this manner; therefore, these pieces have been prepared with the idea that they may be read if necessary. In any case, they should be so well learned that only an occasional glimpse at the script is necessary. Naturally, it is expected that readers theatre will be read. Even then, lines should be learned to such a degree that interpretation will not be impaired.

James
A Dramatic Monologue

SETTING: *The garden of Gethsemane. A young man is sitting on the ground. He pulls his robes closer around himself. He yawns loudly and expansively. He seems about to fall asleep but shakes himself awake.*

No, no! I mustn't fall asleep. The last thing he asked us to do was to stay awake. But I'm so tired. It's been a long day, or, rather, it's been a very long week; and this garden air may be refreshing, but it's also lulling me to sleep. . . . Yes, John, I was as startled as you when he told us of his plans to enter Jerusalem on a donkey. It didn't seem very kingly to me either, but the people certainly responded—all those palms and branches—and the singing and shouting—it was thrilling! It never ceases to amaze me how wonderful he can be with the crowds. Remember how he quieted those people who were stoning that person outside the city gates? . . . That's right. I had almost forgotten that time when he fed five thousand who had come to hear him speak. That could have turned into an ugly incident, but he knew just what to do to calm them and take care of their needs. Incredible, isn't it? *(Yawns again.)* Peter, why do you think the Master asked us to wait here like this? Do you suppose we'll get to see him as he was that time on the mountain with Moses and Elijah? . . . That had to be the most wonderful experience of my life. I would gladly have stayed there forever. . . . *(Tries to make himself more comfortable.)* Oh, the trunk of this tree is really digging into my back. *(Moving.)* There, that's better. . . . *(Stifles a yawn.)* John, you seem so much closer to Jesus than even Peter or I. Why do you think Jesus was so sad at the Passover dinner tonight? And all that business about betrayal. I don't mind admitting I was very confused. He seemed so—I don't know—*different* tonight. Do you know what I mean? It was almost as if he were expecting something to happen. . . . Yes, that's what I sensed; he was depressed. . . . Peter, do you understand what I'm talking about? Didn't he seem strange to you? . . . I'm glad you noticed it, too. It was almost as if he were saying good-bye when he said, "A little while and you will see me no more." Where could he be going that we wouldn't be able to follow? *(Exhausted now.)* Doesn't he ever tire? There he is, up there praying, and I can hardly keep my eyes open. *(Looking for a comfortable spot.)* I think I'll just lie down for a minute. It won't hurt to shut my eyes for a little minute. *(Falls asleep.)*

Probes

1. To what extent does this depict the modern church and church people: awake and alive when exciting things are happening, but asleep and inactive when deep, spiritual commitment is required?

2. How do Jesus' words in Matthew 26:40, "So, could you not watch with me one hour?" apply to us today?

James

A Dramatic Monologue

SETTING: *The garden of Gethsemane. A young man is sitting on the ground. He pulls his robes closer around himself. He yawns loudly and expansively. He seems about to fall asleep but shakes himself awake.*

No, no! I mustn't fall asleep. The last thing he asked us to do was to stay awake. But I'm so tired. It's been a long day, or, rather, it's been a very long week; and this garden air may be refreshing, but it's also lulling me to sleep. . . . Yes, John, I was as startled as you when he told us of his plans to enter Jerusalem on a donkey. It didn't seem very kingly to me either, but the people certainly responded—all those palms and branches—and the singing and shouting—it was thrilling! It never ceases to amaze me how wonderful he can be with the crowds. Remember how he quieted those people who were stoning that person outside the city gates? . . . That's right. I had almost forgotten that time when he fed five thousand who had come to hear him speak. That could have turned into an ugly incident, but he knew just what to do to calm them and take care of their needs. Incredible, isn't it? *(Yawns again.)* Peter, why do you think the Master asked us to wait here like this? Do you suppose we'll get to see him as he was that time on the mountain with Moses and Elijah? . . . That had to be the most wonderful experience of my life. I would gladly have stayed there forever. . . . *(Tries to make himself more comfortable.)* Oh, the trunk of this tree is really digging into my back. *(Moving.)* There, that's better. . . . *(Stifles a yawn.)* John, you seem so much closer to Jesus than even Peter or I. Why do you think Jesus was so sad at the Passover dinner tonight? And all that business about betrayal. I don't mind admitting I was very confused. He seemed so—I don't know—*different* tonight. Do you know what I mean? It was almost as if he were expecting something to happen. . . . Yes, that's what I sensed; he was depressed. . . . Peter, do you understand what I'm talking about? Didn't he seem strange to you? . . . I'm glad you noticed it, too. It was almost as if he were saying good-bye when he said, "A little while and you will see me no more." Where could he be going that we wouldn't be able to follow? *(Exhausted now.)* Doesn't he ever tire? There he is, up there praying, and I can hardly keep my eyes open. *(Looking for a comfortable spot.)* I think I'll just lie down for a minute. It won't hurt to shut my eyes for a little minute. *(Falls asleep.)*

Probes

1. To what extent does this depict the modern church and church people: awake and alive when exciting things are happening, but asleep and inactive when deep, spiritual commitment is required?

2. How do Jesus' words in Matthew 26:40, "So, could you not watch with me one hour?" apply to us today?

Peter
A Dramatic Monologue

SETTING: *A large man stumbles into view. He is obviously a laborer. His hands cover his eyes. He is in agony.*

What have I done? What have I done? The cock has crowed three times, and I have denied him just as he said I would. *(Angrily.)* I deserve to have my tongue cut out! . . . What's that I hear? Could it be the Roman soldiers looking for *me?* That woman did recognize me. What should I do? Where can I hide? *(Kneels.)* Here, this rock will give me some shelter. . . . *(Beseechingly.)* O Lord, don't let them find me. I'm so scared. Please, Lord, spare me. . . . Thank God they have gone the other way. But what am I saying? I don't sound like one of the Master's closest friends. I sound like a coward. Afraid for myself. Oh, agony, I never dreamed it would be like this! I was so sure I could stand up to anything that came our way—and look at me now: a spineless shell of a man. . . . And what did the others do? Did anyone stand up for him? I was willing to fight at first; I even used my sword, but he forbade me. Then why did I run? . . . Why can't I be the rock he named me? I was so proud to be among his special ones. If he could see me now, he would die of shame. . . . *(Stands.)* At least I must not cower. I will try not to act the fool. . . . *(Quietly.)* How could he have known I would deny him that way? *(Laughs a little to himself.)* Isn't it ironic that I, who have seen him perform countless miracles, should question how he could know what a dolt like I would do? He told me, and I didn't believe him. . . . I was so filled with foolish pride that I didn't even understand what he was trying to say to me. . . . When those people around the fire said they had seen me with Jesus, something inside me exploded. I wanted to admit that he was my friend, but I couldn't. Something stopped my mouth. It was as though my fear had paralyzed my brain so that I couldn't think straight. *(Covering his face.)* My shame is so great! Acting like this right after telling him I would follow him—oh, God, right after telling him I would gladly lay down my life for him. *(Kneels down again.)* Forgive me, Lord, oh, please forgive me. *(Bends his body over completely so that his face is hidden in his lap. Freeze.)*

Probes

1. Is the story of Peter the story of every person—full of pride and self-assurance but failing when total commitment is required?

2. In light of Peter's later dynamic and faithful leadership, are his words of contrition an accurate display of what you think his attitude would have been?

3. Does Peter's failure give us comfort when we fail or inspiration to remain faithful?

4. Is there always the temptation for those closest to the Lord to take him for granted?

Peter
A Dramatic Monologue

SETTING: *A large man stumbles into view. He is obviously a laborer. His hands cover his eyes. He is in agony.*

What have I done? What have I done? The cock has crowed three times, and I have denied him just as he said I would. *(Angrily.)* I deserve to have my tongue cut out! . . . What's that I hear? Could it be the Roman soldiers looking for *me?* That woman did recognize me. What should I do? Where can I hide? *(Kneels.)* Here, this rock will give me some shelter. . . . *(Beseechingly.)* O Lord, don't let them find me. I'm so scared. Please, Lord, spare me. . . . Thank God they have gone the other way. But what am I saying? I don't sound like one of the Master's closest friends. I sound like a coward. Afraid for myself. Oh, agony, I never dreamed it would be like this! I was so sure I could stand up to anything that came our way—and look at me now: a spineless shell of a man. . . . And what did the others do? Did anyone stand up for him? I was willing to fight at first; I even used my sword, but he forbade me. Then why did I run? . . . Why can't I be the rock he named me? I was so proud to be among his special ones. If he could see me now, he would die of shame. . . . *(Stands.)* At least I must not cower. I will try not to act the fool. . . . *(Quietly.)* How could he have known I would deny him that way? *(Laughs a little to himself.)* Isn't it ironic that I, who have seen him perform countless miracles, should question how he could know what a dolt like I would do? He told me, and I didn't believe him. . . . I was so filled with foolish pride that I didn't even understand what he was trying to say to me. . . . When those people around the fire said they had seen me with Jesus, something inside me exploded. I wanted to admit that he was my friend, but I couldn't. Something stopped my mouth. It was as though my fear had paralyzed my brain so that I couldn't think straight. *(Covering his face.)* My shame is so great! Acting like this right after telling him I would follow him—oh, God, right after telling him I would gladly lay down my life for him. *(Kneels down again.)* Forgive me, Lord, oh, please forgive me. *(Bends his body over completely so that his face is hidden in his lap. Freeze.)*

Probes

1. Is the story of Peter the story of every person—full of pride and self-assurance but failing when total commitment is required?

2. In light of Peter's later dynamic and faithful leadership, are his words of contrition an accurate display of what you think his attitude would have been?

3. Does Peter's failure give us comfort when we fail or inspiration to remain faithful?

4. Is there always the temptation for those closest to the Lord to take him for granted?

The Witness
A Dramatic Monologue

SETTING: *This character may be portrayed by either a man or a woman; so make the appropriate changes in reference to the husband and wife. A peasant moves to the center of the stage. He or she is in a courtroom. His or her speech should approximate that of an unschooled person.*

(Raising right hand.) I promise to tell da truth, da whole truth, and nothin' but da truth, so help me God. . . . I live in da city of Jerusalem with my wife and children. . . . Yeah, I was there *(defensively),* but so was a hundred others. I don' know why you hadda pick on me. . . . That's a lie, I ain't never seen him before in my life. I jus' heard all the screamin' and hollerin' and like everybody else wanted ta see what was happenin'. Is there any crime in that? . . . Like I said, I hear all this noise and I go see what it's all about. Everybody was crowdin' the sidewalk; so I decides ta try ta look from my balcony, but that ain't no good either 'cause we live too far back from that block; so I go back down again. . . . No, da kids had already left for my sister's house where we was all gonna celebrate da holidays; so it was just my wife and me. She said she didn' wanna be bothered with no crowds; she hates crowds, says they make her sick. *(Gossipy.)* She never goes out in a big group if she don' have ta. . . . *(Hurt.)* I'm sorry. I'll try ta stick to the point. Anyways, I go back down and I find my friend who always knows what's happenin' and he tells me all about it. It was still early; so I decides to see for myself. By that time da biggest part of da group passed by; so we follows up the hill where things was gettin' started. . . . *(Angrily.)* Are you callin' me a name? Well, just see you don't. I don't go lookin' for no gory scenes or get a thrill outa seein' blood an' all like that. Everybody was goin' up; I just didn' wanna miss nothin'. Besides, I heard there'd been this big parade da other day and that da same guy was in it and that it was *really* somethin' ta see. *(Turning.)* If you wanna know da truth, Your Honor, I was very disappointed. I mean, da way some of them was talkin' you'd think da Messiah had come. All I seen was this skinny man between two other guys, hangin' on a cross. So what's da big deal? When it started ta rain, I went home. Honest, Your Honor, I don' know why you hadda call me ta come here. There was a whole lot of other people there. What I seen, they seen, too. . . . So—I don't get it—what's all the fuss about? *(Freeze.)*

Probes

1. Have you ever wished that you had lived during the time of Christ and had seen him in person? Would your faith have been stronger than it is now?

2. If you had never heard Jesus' teachings but had witnessed his crucifixion, would your testimony be different from the person in the monologue?

3. Are those who have never seen Jesus and yet believe more blessed?

4. What other things do people refuse to make a "fuss" over but which are of great significance?

The Witness

A Dramatic Monologue

SETTING: *This character may be portrayed by either a man or a woman; so make the appropriate changes in reference to the husband and wife. A peasant moves to the center of the stage. He or she is in a courtroom. His or her speech should approximate that of an unschooled person.*

(Raising right hand.) I promise to tell da truth, da whole truth, and nothin' but da truth, so help me God. . . . I live in da city of Jerusalem with my wife and children. . . . Yeah, I was there *(defensively)*, but so was a hundred others. I don' know why you hadda pick on me. . . . That's a lie, I ain't never seen him before in my life. I jus' heard all the screamin' and hollerin' and like everybody else wanted ta see what was happenin'. Is there any crime in that? . . . Like I said, I hear all this noise and I go see what it's all about. Everybody was crowdin' the sidewalk; so I decides ta try ta look from my balcony, but that ain't no good either 'cause we live too far back from that block; so I go back down again. . . . No, da kids had already left for my sister's house where we was all gonna celebrate da holidays; so it was just my wife and me. She said she didn' wanna be bothered with no crowds; she hates crowds, says they make her sick. *(Gossipy.)* She never goes out in a big group if she don' have ta. . . . *(Hurt.)* I'm sorry. I'll try ta stick to the point. Anyways, I go back down and I find my friend who always knows what's happenin' and he tells me all about it. It was still early; so I decides to see for myself. By that time da biggest part of da group passed by; so we follows up the hill where things was gettin' started. . . . *(Angrily.)* Are you callin' me a name? Well, just see you don't. I don't go lookin' for no gory scenes or get a thrill outa seein' blood an' all like that. Everybody was goin' up; I just didn' wanna miss nothin'. Besides, I heard there'd been this big parade da other day and that da same guy was in it and that it was *really* somethin' ta see. *(Turning.)* If you wanna know da truth, Your Honor, I was very disappointed. I mean, da way some of them was talkin' you'd think da Messiah had come. All I seen was this skinny man between two other guys, hangin' on a cross. So what's da big deal? When it started ta rain, I went home. Honest, Your Honor, I don' know why you hadda call me ta come here. There was a whole lot of other people there. What I seen, they seen, too. . . . So—I don't get it—what's all the fuss about? *(Freeze.)*

Probes

1. Have you ever wished that you had lived during the time of Christ and had seen him in person? Would your faith have been stronger than it is now?

2. If you had never heard Jesus' teachings but had witnessed his crucifixion, would your testimony be different from the person in the monologue?

3. Are those who have never seen Jesus and yet believe more blessed?

4. What other things do people refuse to make a "fuss" over but which are of great significance?

Mary (The Mother of Jesus)

A Dramatic Monologue

SETTING: *MARY is lying in a heap, as though she has remained where she had fallen after a long, exhausting walk. She looks tired and worn. She is about middle aged, but suffering makes her seem older. She rises to her knees.*

(Crying.) My son, my first-born son, why has God brought you to this place? *(No longer crying, but lost in reverie.)* Kings came to your humble birth-place to give you tribute. Angels sang of your coming. . . . *(Looking up.)* And look at you now—hanging helpless and worn. What has happened to my baby, the blessed one? *(Angrily.)* Are your accusers so depraved that they cannot see what is before them? Didn't they understand what you were teaching them? Some of those who listened to you preach on the hills of Galilee are the very ones who are taunting you now. And where are those who followed you and said they loved you? *(Sadly.)* All gone—save John. Dear John. He is like another son to me. His sweetness is so com-forting. . . . *(Cheered by a remembrance.)* My dear boy Jesus. You were such a rascal—getting away from me and I thinking you were lost—always wanting to be with the elders, talking and asking questions. And *such* questions! The rabbis were really impressed with your knowledge. Coming from a carpenter's home—they couldn't believe such wisdom. But you and I know the truth. You were not from a carpenter's home. No, my son,

you are not even really my son. Born of my body, perhaps, but still not flesh of man's flesh or bone of man's bone. Who could understand? Who could I tell? Indeed, who would listen? I guess they would think me mad, or a fool. . . . All these years, watching you grow, I've known that you were mine for only a little while. But, son, why so cruel a death? My heart breaks and wants to shatter the skies with its screams. . . . I waited all these years to see you crowned king. My darling, the *sign* reads "King of the Jews," but the Jews don't know you. Your poor crown holds blood rather than rubies. *(Stands as if to come closer to cross.)* . . . Dear, dear son. What can I do to make it easier for you? If I could take your place and bear your pain, I would gladly give my body for you. . . . *(Trying to be reasonable.)* But you have your work. You always said you had your work. When will I see its fruits, dear one? When will I know with all my soul that those dreams were visions and those voices were from God? . . . What was that you said? "It is finished?" *(Looking around.)* O Lord, what is finished? Surely not your work that has just begun? Your life? My precious, inside of me you will never die. You will live as long as this poor body can move. And, somehow, I know you will live even beyond me and all the others who are here. So, my dear son, try not to hurt too much. Until this pain is all over, Mother will stay with you. *(Takes one step forward and then freez-es.)*

Probes

1. What thoughts have passed through your mind as you have experienced the death of a loved one?

2. Do Mary's words accurately portray what you think her attitude would have been?

3. Has the Protestant church given less emphasis to Mary than she should have received? What view of Mary should the church set forth today?

4. To what extent are Mary's words the expression of a grieving mother or of a faithful disciple?

Mary (The Mother of Jesus)
A Dramatic Monologue

SETTING: *MARY is lying in a heap, as though she has remained where she had fallen after a long, exhausting walk. She looks tired and worn. She is about middle aged, but suffering makes her seem older. She rises to her knees.*

(Crying.) My son, my first-born son, why has God brought you to this place? *(No longer crying, but lost in reverie.)* Kings came to your humble birthplace to give you tribute. Angels sang of your coming. . . . *(Looking up.)* And look at you now—hanging helpless and worn. What has happened to my baby, the blessed one? *(Angrily.)* Are your accusers so depraved that they cannot see what is before them? Didn't they understand what you were teaching them? Some of those who listened to you preach on the hills of Galilee are the very ones who are taunting you now. And where are those who followed you and said they loved you? *(Sadly.)* All gone—save John. Dear John. He is like another son to me. His sweetness is so comforting. . . . *(Cheered by a remembrance.)* My dear boy Jesus. You were such a rascal—getting away from me and I thinking you were lost—always wanting to be with the elders, talking and asking questions. And *such* questions! The rabbis were really impressed with your knowledge. Coming from a carpenter's home—they couldn't believe such wisdom. But you and I know the truth. You were not from a carpenter's home. No, my son, you are not even really my son. Born of my body, perhaps, but still not flesh of man's flesh or bone of man's bone. Who could understand? Who could I tell? Indeed, who would listen? I guess they would think me mad, or a fool. . . . All these years, watching you grow, I've known that you were mine for only a little while. But, son, why so cruel a death? My heart breaks and wants to shatter the skies with its screams. . . . I waited all these years to see you crowned king. My darling, the *sign* reads "King of the Jews," but the Jews don't know you. Your poor crown holds blood rather than rubies. *(Stands as if to come closer to cross.)* . . . Dear, dear son. What can I do to make it easier for you? If I could take your place and bear your pain, I would gladly give my body for you. . . . *(Trying to be reasonable.)* But you have your work. You always said you had your work. When will I see its fruits, dear one? When will I know with all my soul that those dreams were visions and those voices were from God? . . . What was that you said? "It is finished?" *(Looking around.)* O Lord, what is finished? Surely not your work that has just begun? Your life? My precious, inside of me you will never die. You will live as long as this poor body can move. And, somehow, I know you will live even beyond me and all the others who are here. So, my dear son, try not to hurt too much. Until this pain is all over, Mother will stay with you. *(Takes one step forward and then freezes.)*

Probes

1. What thoughts have passed through your mind as you have experienced the death of a loved one?

2. Do Mary's words accurately portray what you think her attitude would have been?

3. Has the Protestant church given less emphasis to Mary than she should have received? What view of Mary should the church set forth today?

4. To what extent are Mary's words the expression of a grieving mother or of a faithful disciple?

Mary Magdalene
A Dramatic Monologue

SETTING: *A young woman moves to center stage. She has been running and is out of breath. She pantomimes knocking on a door. When no one answers, she bangs desperately.*

Let me in, let me in. . . . It's me, Mary. Hurry, please hurry. . . . Oh, thank you. *(Enters room.)* I ran all the way. . . . I'm all out of breath. I don't know how to tell you this. . . . No, I'm all right, at least I think I am. *(Breathlessly.)* It's happened. Oh, I can't believe it, but it's happened just as he said it would. . . . No, I don't think anyone followed me; you are all quite safe. . . . I was very careful. But, please, let me tell you. . . . What's the matter with you? . . . I am *not* hysterical; I'm just out of breath from running. . . . Thank you, but I'd rather stand. I mustn't stay long; there are others to tell. . . . Yes, I'll start from the beginning. . . . This morning I was taking the oils to the tomb; and when I got there, it was empty. I screamed, "Robbers, robbers!" but of course no one heard me. I couldn't believe my eyes. Why should anyone want to steal my master's body? I just fell down sobbing. Then—then I *saw* him. . . . He was so beautiful. . . . Yes, you understood me. That's where I was. . . . I am *not* losing my mind. He asked me why I was crying and I told him that someone had stolen my master's body. You see, I didn't recognize him right away. Then he said my name. Oh, Peter, you know how he can do that. . . . Why shouldn't I have recognized him then? Haven't I spent these many years with him? Haven't I come to know his face as well as I know my own? . . . No, he didn't let me touch him even though I tried. He said he had to ascend to his father and that I should come and tell you; so I just got up and ran, and here I am. . . . What do you mean the tension of the past few days has been too much for me? I know what I heard; I know what I saw. . . . Oh, Peter, John, it was so wonderful; I don't think I can stand it. But . . . where are you going? . . . Come back. . . . Don't you believe me? *(Crying out to heaven.)* Dear God, why don't they believe me? *(Freeze.)*

Probes

1. How would your own reaction to the resurrection differ from that of Mary Magdalene? How *does* it differ in your own life today?

2. What does the reaction of the apostles to Mary's news tell of their attitude toward women? See Luke 24:10-11. Would it have made a difference if men had brought the word? See Luke 24:33-34.

3. Do the spirit and faith of Mary Magdalene have implications for the proclamation of the Good News by women in the modern church?

4. How does the recognition that "the Lord has risen indeed" change one's life and behavior?

Mary Magdalene
A Dramatic Monologue

SETTING: *A young woman moves to center stage. She has been running and is out of breath. She pantomimes knocking on a door. When no one answers, she bangs desperately.*

Let me in, let me in. . . . It's me, Mary. Hurry, please hurry. . . . Oh, thank you. *(Enters room.)* I ran all the way. . . . I'm all out of breath. I don't know how to tell you this. . . . No, I'm all right, at least I think I am. *(Breathlessly.)* It's happened. Oh, I can't believe it, but it's happened just as he said it would. . . . No, I don't think anyone followed me; you are all quite safe. . . . I was very careful. But, please, let me tell you. . . . What's the matter with you? . . . I am *not* hysterical; I'm just out of breath from running. . . . Thank you, but I'd rather stand. I mustn't stay long; there are others to tell. . . . Yes, I'll start from the beginning. . . . This morning I was taking the oils to the tomb; and when I got there, it was empty. I screamed, "Robbers, robbers!" but of course no one heard me. I couldn't believe my eyes. Why should anyone want to steal my master's body? I just fell down sobbing. Then—then I *saw* him. . . . He was so beautiful. . . . Yes, you understood me. That's where I was. . . . I am *not* losing my mind. He asked me why I was crying and I told him that someone had stolen my master's body. You see, I didn't recognize him right away. Then he said my name. Oh, Peter, you know how he can do that. . . . Why shouldn't I have recognized him then? Haven't I spent these many years with him? Haven't I come to know his face as well as I know my own? . . . No, he didn't let me touch him even though I tried. He said he had to ascend to his father and that I should come and tell you; so I just got up and ran, and here I am. . . . What do you mean the tension of the past few days has been too much for me? I know what I heard; I know what I saw. . . . Oh, Peter, John, it was so wonderful; I don't think I can stand it. But . . . where are you going? . . . Come back. . . . Don't you believe me? *(Crying out to heaven.)* Dear God, why don't they believe me? *(Freeze.)*

Probes

1. How would your own reaction to the resurrection differ from that of Mary Magdalene? How *does* it differ in your own life today?

2. What does the reaction of the apostles to Mary's news tell of their attitude toward women? See Luke 24:10-11. Would it have made a difference if men had brought the word? See Luke 24:33-34.

3. Do the spirit and faith of Mary Magdalene have implications for the proclamation of the Good News by women in the modern church?

4. How does the recognition that "the Lord has risen indeed" change one's life and behavior?

Patience

A Stinger in the Form of a Dramatic Monologue

SETTING: *Early morning in the kitchen. A young woman is preparing breakfast. As she pantomimes setting the table and serving the eggs, she hums "Take Time to Be Holy." She seems very happy.*

(Calling out loudly.) Come on down, you guys; breakfast is ready. . . . What? . . . Yes, I'm just putting the eggs on the table; so please hurry down. . . . *(Humming, but not as gaily.)* . . . Hey, fellers, will you please get down here? Breakfast is getting cold. . . . *(More loudly.)* What? . . . Wherever you put them when you took them off. . . . Well, then, come down without them. . . . I don't care if the chair *is* cold; my eggs are getting cold, too. . . . *(Humming same tune, angrily now.)* . . . Well, it's about time. Sit down. Jim, it's your turn to say grace. . . . No, you didn't; Carl did. . . . Well, say it anyway. . . . Jim, if you don't hurry up and say grace, I'm going to . . . good. *(Bows head with a smug smile.)* Now, that wasn't so hard, was it? Please pass the butter. . . . No, Carl, you cannot keep your Sunday school offering to put toward a new book. . . . You are not going to become an illiterate. You get enough allowance not to

(screaming) Jim! Don't do that with your dirty hands; why do you think I gave you a napkin? . . . Carl, watch out for your milk. . . . *(Banging on table.)* Now, you just get up and clean that yourself, young man. . . . No, I will not help you. . . . *(To husband.)* Please, Ron, I'm having enough trouble keeping these boys in line without your arguing with me. . . . Look, boys, couldn't we just have one nice morning for a change? Let's all try being nice, OK? Thank you. . . . *(Shrieking.)* Jim! I warned you before. Now, you get yourself upstairs and change your shirt. . . . I can't help it if you've not finished eating; you are as far as I'm concerned. . . . *(Barely controlling her rage.)* Well, if he would stop wiping his hands on his clean shirt and use his napkin. . . . *(Stony silence while she continues eating.)* . . . Have you all finished? Hurry up and finish dressing while I put the dishes in the sink. *(Pantomimes action while humming "Take Time to Be Holy" loudly through her teeth.)* . . . Let's go, boys; we're late. . . . Will you please hurry up? You know I have to teach Sunday school today. . . . Look, wise guy, so what if the lesson *is* on *patience?* One more crack out of you and you're grounded for a week! *(Freeze.)*

Probes

1. Discuss the problem of "practicing what you preach" in regard to family life.

2. How frequently do you think similar incidents occur in families prior to going to church or Sunday school? Give personal examples.

3. People may attend church to receive help for personal problems, but to what extent do personal and family problems keep them from adequate preparation to be helped?

Patience

A Stinger in the Form of a Dramatic Monologue

SETTING: *Early morning in the kitchen. A young woman is preparing breakfast. As she pantomimes setting the table and serving the eggs, she hums "Take Time to Be Holy." She seems very happy.*

(Calling out loudly.) Come on down, you guys; breakfast is ready. ... What? ... Yes, I'm just putting the eggs on the table; so please hurry down. ... *(Humming, but not as gaily.)* ... Hey, fellers, will you please get down here? Breakfast is getting cold. ... *(More loudly.)* What? ... Wherever you put them when you took them off. ... Well, then, come down without them. ... I don't care if the chair *is* cold; my eggs are getting cold, too. ... *(Humming same tune, angrily now.)* ... Well, it's about time. Sit down. Jim, it's your turn to say grace. ... No, you didn't; Carl did. ... Well, say it anyway. ... Jim, if you don't hurry up and say grace, I'm going to ... good. *(Bows head with a smug smile.)* Now, that wasn't so hard, was it? Please pass the butter. ... No, Carl, you cannot keep your Sunday school offering to put toward a new book. ... You are not going to become an illiterate. You get enough allowance not to

(screaming) Jim! Don't do that with your dirty hands; why do you think I gave you a napkin? ... Carl, watch out for your milk. ... *(Banging on table.)* Now, you just get up and clean that yourself, young man. ... No, I will not help you. ... *(To husband.)* Please, Ron, I'm having enough trouble keeping these boys in line without your arguing with me. ... Look, boys, couldn't we just have one nice morning for a change? Let's all try being nice, OK? Thank you. ... *(Shrieking.)* Jim! I warned you before. Now, you get yourself upstairs and change your shirt. ... I can't help it if you've not finished eating; you are as far as I'm concerned. ... *(Barely controlling her rage.)* Well, if he would stop wiping his hands on his clean shirt and use his napkin. ... *(Stony silence while she continues eating.)* ... Have you all finished? Hurry up and finish dressing while I put the dishes in the sink. *(Pantomimes action while humming "Take Time to Be Holy" loudly through her teeth.)* ... Let's go, boys; we're late. ... Will you please hurry up? You know I have to teach Sunday school today. ... Look, wise guy, so what if the lesson *is* on *patience?* One more crack out of you and you're grounded for a week! *(Freeze.)*

Probes

1. Discuss the problem of "practicing what you preach" in regard to family life.

2. How frequently do you think similar incidents occur in families prior to going to church or Sunday school? Give personal examples.

3. People may attend church to receive help for personal problems, but to what extent do personal and family problems keep them from adequate preparation to be helped?

The Press Conference
A Dramatic Monologue

SETTING: *A bare stage with a lectern in the center. A spotlight is focused on the lectern. A person (sex and age are not important), obviously very nervous, enters, fidgets with clothing, goes to lectern, and clears throat.*

Ladies and gentlemen of the press, thank you for your time and attention. Please bear with me if I seem a little nervous, but this is my first press conference, and . . . *(clears throat again)* you may begin your questions. *(Pointing.)* Yes? . . . There were hundreds of people there, from all over the world, in fact. . . . No, we were not planning anything; this experience was all absolutely new to *me,* and I'd say it was a miracle. . . . Yes, I said miracle. That's why I called this meeting. I thought if I could tell you about it, you could tell the rest of the world. *(Holding up hands as a call for silence.)* Please, one at a time. . . . This is exactly what happened. My brother and I had just come to that area to do some business and visit some family and friends. We were discussing rising costs when suddenly we heard this great noise. Naturally our curiosity was aroused; so we went over to see what was causing the disturbance. Just then a group of men and women came pouring out of a small building, laughing and shouting. At first we assumed that they were drunk and wondered that they could be so jovial so early in the day. But when we looked more closely, we realized that they were not drunk. Some were crying and others were laughing, but they were all *happy.* And this is when the miracle began. One of them began to speak to the crowd. Now my brother and I speak five languages between us, and *he* heard him in Greek, and *I* heard him in Aramaic! . . . No, I am absolutely sure. The man next to me spoke only Hebrew, and he swore that *that's* what was being spoken. But even more exciting was the *feeling* we all had. The man spoke of love and forgiveness of sin, and of a man called Jesus who can save us from our sins. And as he spoke, it was as if only *I* were there, and as if he were speaking only to me. I, too, was filled with this incredible spirit. I, too, wanted to praise this man Jesus. . . . *(Pointing to newsperson.)* . . . Yes, later I talked with the leader, and he admitted that the Jesus of whom he spoke was the same man who was executed during this last Passover season. . . . *(Answering someone on right.)* How can I believe that this dead Jesus can save? Well, because his death was part of God's plan. God raised him from the dead on the third day and. . . . No, this is *not* a ridiculous idea. I tell you his rising and this experience we had yesterday were a miracle. . . . Is it mad to say that my life has been changed? I'm filled with a peace and joy I've never known before. . . . *(Answering a question.)* No one is paying me to say these things. . . . I am not ignorant. I am an educated. . . . Well, I can see that I will not be able to count on you to help me. I will just have to go myself and tell to everyone I meet this story. *(Exits.)*

Probes

1. How do you suppose an event like Pentecost would be handled by the news media if it occurred today?

2. The message of the gospel is transmitted by many means: preaching, tracts, radio, television, and books. Is the primary method, however, still what was concluded: "I will just have to go myself and tell to everyone I meet this story"?

3. What miracles of faith still happen today? Are they related to Pentecost?

The Press Conference
A Dramatic Monologue

SETTING: *A bare stage with a lectern in the center. A spotlight is focused on the lectern. A person (sex and age are not important), obviously very nervous, enters, fidgets with clothing, goes to lectern, and clears throat.*

Ladies and gentlemen of the press, thank you for your time and attention. Please bear with me if I seem a little nervous, but this is my first press conference, and . . . *(clears throat again)* you may begin your questions. *(Pointing.)* Yes? . . . There were hundreds of people there, from all over the world, in fact. . . . No, we were not planning anything; this experience was all absolutely new to *me,* and I'd say it was a miracle. . . . Yes, I said miracle. That's why I called this meeting. I thought if I could tell you about it, you could tell the rest of the world. *(Holding up hands as a call for silence.)* Please, one at a time. . . . This is exactly what happened. My brother and I had just come to that area to do some business and visit some family and friends. We were discussing rising costs when suddenly we heard this great noise. Naturally our curiosity was aroused; so we went over to see what was causing the disturbance. Just then a group of men and women came pouring out of a small building, laughing and shouting. At first we assumed that they were drunk and wondered that they could be so jovial so early in the day. But when we looked more closely, we realized that they were not drunk. Some were crying and others were laughing, but they were all *happy.* And this is when the miracle began. One of them began to speak to the crowd. Now my brother and I speak five languages between us, and *he* heard him in Greek, and *I* heard him in Aramaic! . . . No, I am absolutely sure. The man next to me spoke only Hebrew, and he swore that *that's* what was being spoken. But even more exciting was the *feeling* we all had. The man spoke of love and forgiveness of sin, and of a man called Jesus who can save us from our sins. And as he spoke, it was as if only *I* were there, and as if he were speaking only to me. I, too, was filled with this incredible spirit. I, too, wanted to praise this man Jesus. . . . *(Pointing to newsperson.)* . . . Yes, later I talked with the leader, and he admitted that the Jesus of whom he spoke was the same man who was executed during this last Passover season. . . . *(Answering someone on right.)* How can I believe that this dead Jesus can save? Well, because his death was part of God's plan. God raised him from the dead on the third day and. . . . No, this is *not* a ridiculous idea. I tell you his rising and this experience we had yesterday were a miracle. . . . Is it mad to say that my life has been changed? I'm filled with a peace and joy I've never known before. . . . *(Answering a question.)* No one is paying me to say these things. . . . I am not ignorant. I am an educated. . . . Well, I can see that I will not be able to count on you to help me. I will just have to go myself and tell to everyone I meet this story. *(Exits.)*

Probes

1. How do you suppose an event like Pentecost would be handled by the news media if it occurred today?

2. The message of the gospel is transmitted by many means: preaching, tracts, radio, television, and books. Is the primary method, however, still what was concluded: "I will just have to go myself and tell to everyone I meet this story"?

3. What miracles of faith still happen today? Are they related to Pentecost?

Dorcas
A Dramatic Monologue

SETTING: *A dark stage with a spotlight on center stage. We are in DORCAS'S bedroom. When spotlight comes on, DORCAS is lying on a cot. She is asleep. As she wakens, she stretches widely and emits a loud and healthy yawn.*

Ah, that feels good. *(Rubs eyes.)* Why, hello, Peter. What are you doing here? . . . I thought I heard your voice in my dreams. . . . But it's strange because I don't really remember dreaming at all. . . . *(Frightened.)* Peter, what are you doing here by my bed? Does my husband know that you are in my room? . . . *(Happy laughter at the answer.)* Of course, he does. I'm sorry. . . . *(Still happy.)* What's that? . . . Oh, I feel fine. In fact, I feel magnificent, almost like a young girl, though goodness knows I'm far from being that, aren't I? . . . What? . . . Yes, now that you mention it, I guess I was sick. . . . Yes, I do remember that. But I don't feel a thing. . . . Peter, what's that noise outside? . . . They're mourning? But that's impossible; I feel just fine. Look. *(Stands.)* I can walk, and the way I feel, I can probably run. . . . But if what you are saying is true, then I was—dare I say it—dead! But that's absurd, isn't it? *(For a moment she is concerned, then begins to remember.)* Wait! I remember now. I said good-bye to my children and family; so I must have known I was dying. But I didn't die; I mean I couldn't have, because here I am. . . . This is incredible. It's all coming back to me. . . . Praise God, I'm alive! I really am alive. . . . It's an indescribable feeling. I'm born anew. I have my life again. . . . God bless you, Peter. God's given me back my health and family through you. . . . Call them all in; I want to tell them how much I love them. I want to praise God *for* them. I want to praise God *with* them. . . . *(Calling to family and friends off stage.)* Phoebe, Mary, come in and see. I'm back! I'm back!

—curtain—

Probes

1. Does the evidence of modern people suffering clinical death and returning to life give more or less credibility to the story of Dorcas?

2. Do we take life for granted? Do you suppose Dorcas did after her experience? How would her life have changed?

3. To what extent should the church be concerned with "saving souls" as compared to ministering to the whole person, to his or her physical and spiritual needs?

Dorcas

A Dramatic Monologue

SETTING: *A dark stage with a spotlight on center stage. We are in DORCAS'S bedroom. When spotlight comes on, DORCAS is lying on a cot. She is asleep. As she wakens, she stretches widely and emits a loud and healthy yawn.*

Ah, that feels good. *(Rubs eyes.)* Why, hello, Peter. What are you doing here? ... I thought I heard your voice in my dreams. ... But it's strange because I don't really remember dreaming at all. ... *(Frightened.)* Peter, what are you doing here by my bed? Does my husband know that you are in my room? ... *(Happy laughter at the answer.)* Of course, he does. I'm sorry. ... *(Still happy.)* What's that? ... Oh, I feel fine. In fact, I feel magnificent, almost like a young girl, though goodness knows I'm far from being that, aren't I? ... What? ... Yes, now that you mention it, I guess I was sick. ... Yes, I do remember that. But I don't feel a thing. ... Peter, what's that noise outside? ... They're mourning? But that's impossible; I feel just fine. Look. *(Stands.)* I can walk, and the way I feel, I can probably run. ... But if what you are saying is true, then I was—dare I say it—*dead!* But that's absurd, isn't it? *(For a moment she is concerned, then begins to remember.)* Wait! I remember now. I said good-bye to my children and family; so I must have known I was dying. But I didn't die; I mean I couldn't have, because here I am. ... This is incredible. It's all coming back to me. ... Praise God, I'm alive! I really am alive. ... It's an indescribable feeling. I'm born anew. I have my life again. ... God bless you, Peter. God's given me back my health and family through you. ... Call them all in; I want to tell them how much I love them. I want to praise God *for* them. I want to praise God *with* them. ... *(Calling to family and friends off stage.)* Phoebe, Mary, come in and see. I'm back! I'm back!

—curtain—

Probes

1. Does the evidence of modern people suffering clinical death and returning to life give more or less credibility to the story of Dorcas?

2. Do we take life for granted? Do you suppose Dorcas did after her experience? How would her life have changed?

3. To what extent should the church be concerned with "saving souls" as compared to ministering to the whole person, to his or her physical and spiritual needs?

The Sister
A Dramatic Monologue

SETTING: *A young woman enters. She is carrying a large basket.*

Remember, you promised to do what I said if I let you come along. Now wait for me here and don't make any noise. Let me go and put him down, and I'll come back and sit by you. *(Moves downstage and pantomimes action.)* There, he's perfectly safe now, poor dear. Mother and Father are so worried about him. . . . *(Returns to center stage.)* No, I don't mind taking care of him. If I didn't do it, something awful might happen, and I'd never forgive myself. I saw Sara after little Dan—you know—I can't even say it. It was horrible, her watching them do it and all. I thought she would go crazy. All she could say was, "It's my fault. Why didn't I *do* something?" But there was nothing she could do then. There's nothing anyone can do when the soldiers come. Now, no one can get her to talk or anything, not even her husband. He doesn't know what to do to help her. . . . Oh, Rebecca, why should anyone want to kill little babies? They haven't hurt anyone. *(Pause.)* Oh, well. *(With a sigh takes out a small bundle.)* Here, have a piece of cheese and bread. I know it's not much, but it's all I have. . . . I'm not sure what Mother will do next. He's already three months old and big and pretty noisy. She just can't take the chance of keeping him at home any longer. She thought of this on the spur of the moment, and it seems to be working out well. I guess we'll have to wait and see what happens. Father spends all night trying to get a minion together so he can have special prayers said for his safety, but he almost never is able to get more than two or three to come. It's not that they don't want to—at least that's what Father says—it's just they have so much to worry about themselves. You're lucky, Rebecca, you know that? . . . Yes, you are. You don't have any baby brothers. I never thought I'd live to hear a Hebrew say that; but here I am, saying it. . . . I don't know the answer to that question. We've waited all these years, and nothing has changed. People laugh at Mother and Father because they haven't lost faith. Live for now as best you can because all we'll ever have is mud, straw, and brick to build the Pharaoh's tomb. That's what the others think: mud, straw, and brick—that's all. But not . . . *(frightened)* Rebecca, look! Who's that? . . . *It can't* be her. I was sure she never came this far. I told Mother I knew it would be safe here. What shall I do? I don't have time to get him without being seen. . . . Oh, no! He's starting to cry; she's sure to hear him. . . . She's going to him. What shall I do? *(Pleading.)* Please, God, don't let Pharaoh's daughter kill my baby brother! *(Freeze.)*

Probes

1. When things look the darkest, does God often appear to work in some entirely unexpected way to bring God's plan, if not ours, to fruition? Give examples.

2. In times of crises, what is the place of faith and works, hope and courage, thought and action?

3. Discuss the suffering of the Jews in modern times, seeking to discover how God's plan and purpose may be operative.

The Sister
A Dramatic Monologue

SETTING: *A young woman enters. She is carrying a large basket.*

Remember, you promised to do what I said if I let you come along. Now wait for me here and don't make any noise. Let me go and put him down, and I'll come back and sit by you. *(Moves downstage and pantomimes action.)* There, he's perfectly safe now, poor dear. Mother and Father are so worried about him. . . . *(Returns to center stage.)* No, I don't mind taking care of him. If I didn't do it, something awful might happen, and I'd never forgive myself. I saw Sara after little Dan—you know—I can't even say it. It was horrible, her watching them do it and all. I thought she would go crazy. All she could say was, "It's my fault. Why didn't I *do* something?" But there was nothing she could do then. There's nothing anyone can do when the soldiers come. Now, no one can get her to talk or anything, not even her husband. He doesn't know what to do to help her. . . . Oh, Rebecca, why should anyone want to kill little babies? They haven't hurt anyone. *(Pause.)* Oh, well. *(With a sigh takes out a small bundle.)* Here, have a piece of cheese and bread. I know it's not much, but it's all I have. . . . I'm not sure what Mother will do next. He's already three months old and big and pretty noisy. She just can't take the chance of keeping him at home any longer. She thought of this on the spur of the moment, and it seems to be working out well. I guess we'll have to wait and see what happens. Father spends all night trying to get a minion together so he can have special prayers said for his safety, but he almost never is able to get more than two or three to come. It's not that they don't want to—at least that's what Father says—it's just they have so much to worry about themselves. You're lucky, Rebecca, you know that? . . . Yes, you are. You don't have any baby brothers. I never thought I'd live to hear a Hebrew say that; but here I am, saying it. . . . I don't know the answer to that question. We've waited all these years, and nothing has changed. People laugh at Mother and Father because they haven't lost faith. Live for now as best you can because all we'll ever have is mud, straw, and brick to build the Pharaoh's tomb. That's what the others think: mud, straw, and brick—that's all. But not . . . *(frightened)* Rebecca, look! Who's that? . . . *It can't* be her. I was sure she never came this far. I told Mother I knew it would be safe here. What shall I do? I don't have time to get him without being seen. . . . Oh, no! He's starting to cry; she's sure to hear him. . . . She's going to him. What shall I do? *(Pleading.)* Please, God, don't let Pharaoh's daughter kill my baby brother! *(Freeze.)*

Probes

1. When things look the darkest, does God often appear to work in some entirely unexpected way to bring God's plan, if not ours, to fruition? Give examples.

2. In times of crises, what is the place of faith and works, hope and courage, thought and action?

3. Discuss the suffering of the Jews in modern times, seeking to discover how God's plan and purpose may be operative.

Litany for the Breath of Life

A Dramatic Monologue

SETTING: *A woman, noticeably pregnant, is seated and is speaking on the telephone.*

Oh, Mike, don't worry, I'm OK; just get home from work and get me to the hospital, all right? . . . And I love *you.* Bye, darling. *(Hangs up.)* . . . *(Pats her stomach.)* So, you're giving notice that you're ready to be born, are you? I do hope *we're* ready for *you.* Let me see: Mom's getting us the bassinet; Mike's folks bought us the playpen; we've got plenty of disposable diapers; and the room is painted and decorated. What else is there? Hmm . . . *(Almost under her breath.)* bottles, nipples, formula, clothes . . . yep, I think we've got it all. *(Pats stomach again.)* When you get home, you'll have everything you need. *(Stands awkwardly.)* You know, this may seem silly, talking to an unborn baby this way, but now that it's almost time for you to come, I feel, well, that you're not *just* a part of me anymore. Why, we've been calling you "It" for such a long time that it's strange thinking of you as an independent person. But that's just what you are. *Someone,* a person who will have a name all your own. You know, I'm really looking forward to meeting you. . . . Oh, oh, I'd better sit down. Listen, don't get too impatient; please wait for your father to get home. I'm not that anxious to meet you that I want to greet you alone. Just hold on, OK? *(Sits.)* Even so, it's hard to believe that you are going to be a regular human being. I guess we've been thinking so hard of all the *things* we had to do and get for you that we forgot to spend time thinking what we would like you to be like. . . . Sounds silly, doesn't it? But I guess most parents have dreams for their children long before they are even born. . . . So what are you? A boy? A girl? . . . Is our world ready to give you a fair chance at life if you *are* a girl and you decide you want to be something that boys usually are? . . . Will you want to be the president of the United States? . . . If you are a boy, will someone try to make you go off to war and maybe be killed? . . . O God, please help me to stop thinking like this. . . . *(Picks up a picture album from table.)* Well, your picture will soon be in here, too. Oh, yes, I must make sure Mike takes the camera to the hospital. So, will you be tall like your father *(Turns page of album.),* or will you be short like me? . . . *(Closes album.)* Dear baby, will your father and I be able to give you enough love so you won't feel we've neglected you? . . . Bringing up children today is so difficult. There is so much to watch for. Will we be able to protect you from drugs and all the things young people are using as substitutes for living? . . . It must be foolish to carry on like this, but I can't help it. I love you already, and I am worried about you already. . . . Goodness, I didn't realize there was so much to having a baby. These pains I'm having right now may only be the beginning. Little one, we don't want to fail you. What are the things you'll think about? Will you learn to love people? That's so important. . . . Will you ever think about God? *(Anxiously.)* Will you even *believe* in God? Oh, dear, we've spent so much time concerning ourselves with your physical needs that we haven't even stopped to think about your spiritual needs. . . . *(Stops, thinks for a minute, then places hands on stomach again.)* Dear God, I thank you for this new life that is about to come into your world. Please forgive Mike and me for not thinking of you first, but help us now to keep this little life very close to you. O God, I don't care if my little someone becomes a doctor or a lawyer or the president of the United States. Just take care of him or her; hold that life in your warm arms; and let him or her come closer to you and come to know and love you. Dear God, I promise today, even before I deliver this life to the world, to yield this person to you. Hear my prayer. . . . *(In the midst of her prayer a door is heard to open and close and from the wings the audience hears a man say, "Angela, are you all right? I'm home.")* . . . Mike, oh, Mike, thank God you are home. Yes, I am all right and finally ready to have this child of God.

—curtain—

47

Probes

1. Do most parents really appreciate their unique place in God's plan as creators of new life?

2. What do you suppose Mary thought about before the birth of her son, Jesus? (See Luke 1:46-55.)

3. How should parents treat their children in regard to sex roles, equality, and opportunity?

Litany for the Breath of Life

A Dramatic Monologue

SETTING: *A woman, noticeably pregnant, is seated and is speaking on the telephone.*

Oh, Mike, don't worry, I'm OK; just get home from work and get me to the hospital, all right? . . . And I love *you*. Bye, darling. *(Hangs up.)* . . . *(Pats her stomach.)* So, you're giving notice that you're ready to be born, are you? I do hope *we're* ready for *you*. Let me see: Mom's getting us the bassinet; Mike's folks bought us the playpen; we've got plenty of disposable diapers; and the room is painted and decorated. What else is there? Hmm . . . *(Almost under her breath.)* bottles, nipples, formula, clothes . . . yep, I think we've got it all. *(Pats stomach again.)* When you get home, you'll have everything you need. *(Stands awkwardly.)* You know, this may seem silly, talking to an unborn baby this way, but now that it's almost time for you to come, I feel, well, that you're not *just* a part of me anymore. Why, we've been calling you "It" for such a long time that it's strange thinking of you as an independent person. But that's just what you are. *Someone,* a person who will have a name all your own. You know, I'm really looking forward to meeting you. . . . Oh, oh, I'd better sit down. Listen, don't get too impatient; please wait for your father to get home. I'm not that anxious to meet you that I want to greet you alone. Just hold on, OK? *(Sits.)* Even so, it's hard to believe that you are going to be a regular human being. I guess we've been thinking so hard of all the *things* we had to do and get for you that we forgot to spend time thinking what we would like you to be like. . . . Sounds silly, doesn't it? But I guess most parents have dreams for their children long before they are even born. . . . So what are you? A boy? A girl? . . . Is our world ready to give you a fair chance at life if you *are* a girl and you decide you want to be something that boys usually are? . . . Will you want to be the president of the United States? . . . If you are a boy, will someone try to make you go off to war and maybe be killed? . . . O God, please help me to stop thinking like this. . . . *(Picks up a picture album from table.)* Well, your picture will soon be in here, too. Oh, yes, I must make sure Mike takes the camera to the hospital. So, will you be tall like your father *(Turns page of album.)*, or will you be short like me? . . . *(Closes album.)* Dear baby, will your father and I be able to give you enough love so you won't feel we've neglected you? . . . Bringing up children today is so difficult. There is so much to watch for. Will we be able to protect you from drugs and all the things young people are using as substitutes for living? . . . It must be foolish to carry on like this, but I can't help it. I love you already, and I am worried about you already. . . . Goodness, I didn't realize there was so much to having a baby. These pains I'm having right now may only be the beginning. Little one, we don't want to fail you. What are the things you'll think about? Will you learn to love people? That's so important. . . . Will you ever think about God? *(Anxiously.)* Will you even *believe* in God? Oh, dear, we've spent so much time concerning ourselves with your physical needs that we haven't even stopped to think about your spiritual needs. . . . *(Stops, thinks for a minute, then places hands on stomach again.)* Dear God, I thank you for this new life that is about to come into your world. Please forgive Mike and me for not thinking of you first, but help us now to keep this little life very close to you. O God, I don't care if my little someone becomes a doctor or a lawyer or the president of the United States. Just take care of him or her; hold that life in your warm arms; and let him or her come closer to you and come to know and love you. Dear God, I promise today, even before I deliver this life to the world, to yield this person to you. Hear my prayer. . . . *(In the midst of her prayer a door is heard to open and close and from the wings the audience hears a man say, "Angela, are you all right? I'm home.")* . . . Mike, oh, Mike, thank God you are home. Yes, I am all right and finally ready to have this child of God.

—*curtain*—

Probes

1. Do most parents really appreciate their unique place in God's plan as creators of new life?

2. What do you suppose Mary thought about before the birth of her son, Jesus? (See Luke 1:46-55.)

3. How should parents treat their children in regard to sex roles, equality, and opportunity?

Martha
A Dramatic Monologue

SETTING: *A woman is busy in the kitchen. She moves hurriedly from one thing to another while speaking to her unseen companion.*

But, Master, it isn't fair. I only have two hands, and the work is just too much for me. . . . Why must I work so hard? *(Fast and all in one breath.)* Well, simply because the bread won't bake itself, and the lamb refuses to roast itself, and who else is going to feed all the people who come to hear you speak, and there are still the sweet courses to *(She is interrupted.)* . . . I'm sorry I carry on so, but I know Mary better than you do, Master, and let me tell you—since we were little girls, she's always been doing things like this to me. She always seems to find some excuse to leave me with all the work. This time she said I was planning and fussing with too many things. . . . No, she's just lazy, that's all. . . . But how can you say that? I know my responsibilities and fulfill them; isn't that important anymore? . . . I'll *tell* you what I'd like you to do. I'd like you to tell her to get in here and help me with all this work. She should at least be willing to do her fair share. . . . Master, she's not doing anything but sitting on the floor listening to you and the men, and you say she's doing something important? . . . Of course, I love her. Lazarus and the two of us have always been very close; you know that, Master. . . . Perhaps I did sound a little bitter, but it's just that even when we were little kids, Mary, being the baby, was always spoiled. First Mother and Father treated her carefully because she was so sickly as a child. She had them so wrapped around her little finger that she got her way in all things. Now it's the same thing with Lazarus. He's kind to both of us, but he's always worried that something might be too much for her or that she might catch a chill and get the lung disease. Our brother pampers her as if she were still a child. It isn't fair, that's all. . . . I know, but I'm tired, Teacher— plain tired. . . . How can you say that? I've worked so hard to please you. I've cooked all your favorite things. It's the nicest and most splendid meal I've ever prepared, and you say it is too much? . . . *(Incredulously.)* You think Mary is the wiser? I don't understand. . . . Please, Master, I told you why I can't come out and sit with the rest of you. There is simply too much to do. Please, won't you tell Mary to come in here and give me a little help?

—*curtain*—

Probes

1. Do you think Martha's complaints were at all justified? Why or why not?

2. In spite of Martha's practicality, see and discuss her profound declaration of faith in John 11:27.

3. Are you primarily a Martha or a Mary at home? In the church?

4. Is there a place for both Marthas and Marys in the world? In the church?

Martha
A Dramatic Monologue

SETTING: *A woman is busy in the kitchen. She moves hurriedly from one thing to another while speaking to her unseen companion.*

But, Master, it isn't fair. I only have two hands, and the work is just too much for me. . . . Why must I work so hard? *(Fast and all in one breath.)* Well, simply because the bread won't bake itself, and the lamb refuses to roast itself, and who else is going to feed all the people who come to hear you speak, and there are still the sweet courses to *(She is interrupted.)* . . . I'm sorry I carry on so, but I know Mary better than you do, Master, and let me tell you—since we were little girls, she's always been doing things like this to me. She always seems to find some excuse to leave me with all the work. This time she said I was planning and fussing with too many things. . . . No, she's just lazy, that's all. . . . But how can you say that? I know my responsibilities and fulfill them; isn't that important anymore? . . . I'll *tell* you what I'd like you to do. I'd like you to tell her to get in here and help me with all this work. She should at least be willing to do her fair share. . . . Master, she's not doing anything but sitting on the floor listening to you and the men, and you say she's doing something important? . . . Of course, I love her. Lazarus and the two of us have always been very close; you know that, Master. . . . Perhaps I did sound a little bitter, but it's just that even when we were little kids, Mary, being the baby, was always spoiled. First Mother and Father treated her carefully because she was so sickly as a child. She had them so wrapped around her little finger that she got her way in all things. Now it's the same thing with Lazarus. He's kind to both of us, but he's always worried that something might be too much for her or that she might catch a chill and get the lung disease. Our brother pampers her as if she were still a child. It isn't fair, that's all. . . . I know, but I'm tired, Teacher—plain tired. . . . How can you say that? I've worked so hard to please you. I've cooked all your favorite things. It's the nicest and most splendid meal I've ever prepared, and you say it is too much? . . . *(Incredulously.)* You think Mary is the wiser? I don't understand. . . . Please, Master, I told you why I can't come out and sit with the rest of you. There is simply too much to do. Please, won't you tell Mary to come in here and give me a little help?

—curtain—

Probes

1. Do you think Martha's complaints were at all justified? Why or why not?

2. In spite of Martha's practicality, see and discuss her profound declaration of faith in John 11:27.

3. Are you primarily a Martha or a Mary at home? In the church?

4. Is there a place for both Marthas and Marys in the world? In the church?

The Woman at the Well

A Dramatic Monologue

SETTING: *A woman enters carrying a water jar on her head. She moves downstage center and pantomimes the drawing of water from the well and pouring it into her water jar. She is tired, and so after completing her chore, she sits and cups her hands to drink some water from her jar. She looks up and sees someone else arrive.*

Hello, Rachel, how are you? . . . Yes, it has been a very busy week. I always feel this way just before the high holy days—so much cooking and preparing. And I haven't been able to sleep very much lately. I've been so excited about my experience last week. . . . Didn't I tell you about it? I thought I had told everyone. . . . That's right, you were gone last week. Oh, Rachel, something wonderful has happened to me. I feel it will change my whole life. . . . I'm deadly serious. Have you ever felt lonely when you were surrounded by a lot of people, or sad when you should have felt happy, empty when you should have felt full? . . . I know everyone feels that way sometimes, but I'm talking about feeling like this often, more often than not. . . . *(Becoming very animated.)* I know it's hard for you to imagine someone like me talking like this, but that's one of the things that is going to change. I'm going to be honest with people and honest with myself for a change. I've been fooling myself all these years, making everyone think I was happy with my life. But not anymore. I found something new and exciting, and I'll never be the same again. . . . Last week I met a man who understood how I feel without my ever saying a word to him. . . . *(Turning away.)* That's very unkind of you, Rachel. I know that there have been many men in my life, but this time it is different. . . . You're not the only one who has reacted like that to my story; but if you'll hear me out, you may understand. . . . *(Pauses as if trying to find the right words.)* I came to the well to get the afternoon water last week, and I saw this man sitting right here where I am now. He looked as if he had been on a long journey. He asked me for a drink, and from the way that he

spoke I knew that he was a Jew. . . . I was surprised that he spoke to me, too, but it was what he said that surprised me most. He said that he had a well from which sprang living water. . . . Yes, I agree. At one point I wondered if he might be a little crazy. But, Rachel, he knew all about me. He started to tell me about my life and husbands—and Daniel—yes, he knew that Daniel isn't my husband. I don't know how he knew. He just looked at me, and it was as if he had known me all my life. I couldn't believe what I was hearing. And he knew what was in my heart as well. . . . It couldn't have been an accident or a trick. He didn't dwell on my past; he just knew about it. Then he said something I'll never forget. He said, "Whoever drinks this water will get thirsty again. The water that I will give him will become in him a spring which will provide him with life-giving water and give him eternal life!" [John 4:13, 14*b*, TEV]. . . . that's exactly what he said. Here, let me help you with your jar. *(Pantomimes helping Rachel fill her water jar, but continues talking throughout.)* I was so confused I didn't know how to deal with this person who must be a prophet of some kind; so I said the first thing that came into my mind. I said, "I know that the Messiah will come, and when he comes, he will tell us everything" [John 4:25, TEV]. Rachel, you won't believe what he said next. He said, "I am he, I who am talking with you" [John 4:26, TEV]. . . . Don't be ridiculous; why should I make up a story like this? That is the way it really happened. . . . I don't know what to make of it. All I know is that talking to him made me feel complete and full. For the first time in my life my *soul* felt nourished. I've been looking for spiritual food and drink, thinking I could find it through physical fulfillment. He comes from God, of that there is no doubt, and he can fill my life and yours. He *must* be the Christ, don't you think? Rachel, I want to stop looking for illusive joys. I want to rest and drink from the living water of Christ. . . . There, your jar is full. Let's go home. Perhaps there are some others who haven't heard the story yet. *(Exits.)*

Probes

1. The biblical story of Jesus' meeting with the Samaritan woman at the well is found in John 4:7-30. In light of the biblical events, does the monologue represent what her likely attitude and spirit would be? Why or why not?

2. When one first meets Jesus, the Messiah, is one's life always radically changed? Does it always involve the impulse to tell others about it?

3. Is it the prevailing attitude that the church is only for the "good" and "right kind" of people? Does this differ from the spirit of Jesus?

The Woman at the Well

A Dramatic Monologue

SETTING: *A woman enters carrying a water jar on her head. She moves downstage center and pantomimes the drawing of water from the well and pouring it into her water jar. She is tired, and so after completing her chore, she sits and cups her hands to drink some water from her jar. She looks up and sees someone else arrive.*

Hello, Rachel, how are you? . . . Yes, it has been a very busy week. I always feel this way just before the high holy days—so much cooking and preparing. And I haven't been able to sleep very much lately. I've been so excited about my experience last week. . . . Didn't I tell you about it? I thought I had told everyone. . . . That's right, you were gone last week. Oh, Rachel, something wonderful has happened to me. I feel it will change my whole life. . . . I'm deadly serious. Have you ever felt lonely when you were surrounded by a lot of people, or sad when you should have felt happy, empty when you should have felt full? . . . I know everyone feels that way sometimes, but I'm talking about feeling like this often, more often than not. . . . *(Becoming very animated.)* I know it's hard for you to imagine someone like me talking like this, but that's one of the things that is going to change. I'm going to be honest with people and honest with myself for a change. I've been fooling myself all these years, making everyone think I was happy with my life. But not anymore. I found something new and exciting, and I'll never be the same again. . . . Last week I met a man who understood how I feel without my ever saying a word to him. . . . *(Turning away.)* That's very unkind of you, Rachel. I know that there have been many men in my life, but this time it is different. . . . You're not the only one who has reacted like that to my story; but if you'll hear me out, you may understand. . . . *(Pauses as if trying to find the right words.)* I came to the well to get the afternoon water last week, and I saw this man sitting right here where I am now. He looked as if he had been on a long journey. He asked me for a drink, and from the way that he spoke I knew that he was a Jew. . . . I was surprised that he spoke to me, too, but it was what he said that surprised me most. He said that he had a well from which sprang living water. . . . Yes, I agree. At one point I wondered if he might be a little crazy. But, Rachel, he knew all about me. He started to tell me about my life and husbands—and Daniel—yes, he knew that Daniel isn't my husband. I don't know how he knew. He just looked at me, and it was as if he had known me all my life. I couldn't believe what I was hearing. And he knew what was in my heart as well. . . . It couldn't have been an accident or a trick. He didn't dwell on my past; he just knew about it. Then he said something I'll never forget. He said, "Whoever drinks this water will get thirsty again. The water that I will give him will become in him a spring which will provide him with life-giving water and give him eternal life!" [John 4:13, 14b, TEV]. . . . that's exactly what he said. Here, let me help you with your jar. *(Pantomimes helping Rachel fill her water jar, but continues talking throughout.)* I was so confused I didn't know how to deal with this person who must be a prophet of some kind; so I said the first thing that came into my mind. I said, "I know that the Messiah will come, and when he comes, he will tell us everything" [John 4:25, TEV]. Rachel, you won't believe what he said next. He said, "I am he, I who am talking with you" [John 4:26, TEV]. . . . Don't be ridiculous; why should I make up a story like this? That is the way it really happened. . . . I don't know what to make of it. All I know is that talking to him made me feel complete and full. For the first time in my life my *soul* felt nourished. I've been looking for spiritual food and drink, thinking I could find it through physical fulfillment. He comes from God, of that there is no doubt, and he can fill my life and yours. He *must* be the Christ, don't you think? Rachel, I want to stop looking for illusive joys. I want to rest and drink from the living water of Christ. . . . There, your jar is full. Let's go home. Perhaps there are some others who haven't heard the story yet. *(Exits.)*

Probes

1. The biblical story of Jesus' meeting with the Samaritan woman at the well is found in John 4:7-30. In light of the biblical events, does the monologue represent what her likely attitude and spirit would be? Why or why not?

2. When one first meets Jesus, the Messiah, is one's life always radically changed? Does it always involve the impulse to tell others about it?

3. Is it the prevailing attitude that the church is only for the "good" and "right kind" of people? Does this differ from the spirit of Jesus?

The Celebration
A Dramatic Monologue

SETTING: *The speaker—either a man or a woman—is dressed in bright "party clothes." He or she walks to the podium at center stage.*

Good morning, ladies and gentlemen. Welcome to our celebration. This is a wonderful day, and we are so glad that you could come and share it with us. I have been asked by our hosts to act as a master [or mistress] of ceremonies. I have never done this kind of thing before; so I hope you will bear with me if I make some mistakes.

(Clears throat.) Oh, yes, our hostess was concerned that you all have a good time today. She planned this occasion carefully and wanted to be sure you were all comfortable and relaxed. Please let one of the family know if there is anything you need or want. The Glad Tidings Players are here for your entertainment, as is the "Hallelujah Chorus."

(Takes out some notes, shifts them around, smooths them on the podium. It is best if the following is memorized and not read. Notes, however, may be used as an aid to memory.)

Grace, the woman we are here to honor today, was born more than eighty-five years ago. Her mother died when she was only eight, and her father died when she was thirteen. She then went to live with relatives who allowed her to work for her keep. On her eighteenth birthday Grace left home. She had saved enough to pay for a third-class ticket aboard a ship which took her to the United States. She had heard wonderful stories about that place. She knew that everyone was rich there and that if you looked carefully, you could find gold coins lying right in the middle of the streets. All you had to do was bend down and take them; no one cared; there was plenty for all. But when she got off the ship, she found that it was nothing like she had expected. Tall, ugly, gray buildings towered over her. There was a great deal of refuse and litter on the streets, but no gold.

Instead, Grace found a job in a factory. She sewed the band on the inside of men's hats. She had to be very careful because the sewing machines were not too safe; there was little light, and sometimes after working for twelve hours with only a short break for lunch a girl could get very tired and make a mistake. Worse still, she could have a serious accident which could cripple her for life. Grace lost two fingers in five years.

(Looks up from notes, leans on podium, and continues in a more conversational tone.) I remember the first time I met Grace. I was ten years old, and my Sunday school teacher was dear old Miss Elsie. Miss Elsie was seventy-five when she finally allowed the Sunday school superintendent to retire her. *(He chuckles at the memory.)* One day Grace walked into the classroom to take Miss Elsie's place as our teacher. She was young and pretty and full of interesting ideas and stories about places where none of us had ever been. She was wonderful, like a breath of fresh air. We all fell in love with her. Soon after that, Grace met a gentleman named Ralph. Soon they were married and later had three children.

Growing up with Grace and Ralph was really wonderful. Ralph treated all the boys like sons and took us to picnics and to the ball game. But the most exciting activity we did on Sundays after church services. Sometimes he would have us bring our lunch, and then with his family we would all eat together in the classroom. Then we were ready for the afternoon's adventure. All of us would walk the many miles across town until we came to a large building. In that old church Grace and Ralph had begun a local congregation of persons from their native country. When I was thirteen, they put me to work with the smaller boys since they spoke English. Ralph led the services and preached the sermon; Grace played the piano for the hymns.

When the church membership reached one hundred, Ralph and Grace helped them call an ordained pastor. Then the two of them went to another area where they helped another group start and build a congregation. This pattern continued for many years. When Ralph finally retired from the post office, they were able to accept a full-time call to a small church.

To many, these lives sound dull and uneventful, but to us who knew them, Grace and Ralph led exciting and dynamic lives which influenced many others beyond their circle. Listen to something that Grace wrote several years ago. *(Reading from a card.)*

"When I die, I don't want anyone to grieve. Instead I want you to celebrate my life and my going to be with the Lord. Make it a joyful day with a lot of laughter and singing. I want trumpets to play and choirs to sing. Greet one another with love and cheerfulness. Please, don't look at my body; I won't be there. My spirit will be rejoicing with God and sharing with you in the great celebration of life.

"When you lower my body into the earth, don't let anyone be afraid or cry. The shell I borrowed for these few years will be returning to its source. The darkness of the burial box will not entomb me, but it will serve as a human necessity of life. I will be with you, near you always, as long as you remember me."

(Looking up from notes.) So, friends, let's follow her wishes. You see, there is no casket here today. Ralph and his children and his grandchildren are here to help us celebrate the joy of Grace's salvation. *(In the distance the soft introduction to the "Hallelujah Chorus" by Handel may be heard. As the speech continues, the volume is raised, and at the speech's conclusion it is up to an appropriate level.)* Let the trumpet sound; let the chorus swell and sing aloud the praises of God and his majesty. Praise the Lord, for one more soul has gone to be with him. *(Allow record to play the "Hallelujah Chorus" in its entirety.)*

Probes

1. Which best depicts the Christian spirit in funeral or memorial services—the celebration of life or the sorrow over death? Explain your answer.

2. Discuss the appropriateness of such things as viewings, open or closed caskets, memorial services, expensive funerals, and music in regard to the burial of the dead.

3. Death and dying consist of a central emphasis in the ministry of the church. To what extent have funeral homes taken over this function? Is this desirable?

4. Is the funeral service primarily for the departed or for those who remain? Discuss.

The Celebration
A Dramatic Monologue

SETTING: *The speaker—either a man or a woman—is dressed in bright "party clothes." He or she walks to the podium at center stage.*

Good morning, ladies and gentlemen. Welcome to our celebration. This is a wonderful day, and we are so glad that you could come and share it with us. I have been asked by our hosts to act as a master [or mistress] of ceremonies. I have never done this kind of thing before; so I hope you will bear with me if I make some mistakes.

(Clears throat.) Oh, yes, our hostess was concerned that you all have a good time today. She planned this occasion carefully and wanted to be sure you were all comfortable and relaxed. Please let one of the family know if there is anything you need or want. The Glad Tidings Players are here for your entertainment, as is the "Hallelujah Chorus."

(Takes out some notes, shifts them around, smooths them on the podium. It is best if the following is memorized and not read. Notes, however, may be used as an aid to memory.)

Grace, the woman we are here to honor today, was born more than eighty-five years ago. Her mother died when she was only eight, and her father died when she was thirteen. She then went to live with relatives who allowed her to work for her keep. On her eighteenth birthday Grace left home. She had saved enough to pay for a third-class ticket aboard a ship which took her to the United States. She had heard wonderful stories about that place. She knew that everyone was rich there and that if you looked carefully, you could find gold coins lying right in the middle of the streets. All you had to do was bend down and take them; no one cared; there was plenty for all. But when she got off the ship, she found that it was nothing like she had expected. Tall, ugly, gray buildings towered over her. There was a great deal of refuse and litter on the streets, but no gold.

Instead, Grace found a job in a factory. She sewed the band on the inside of men's hats. She had to be very careful because the sewing machines were not too safe; there was little light, and sometimes after working for twelve hours with only a short break for lunch a girl could get very tired and make a mistake. Worse still, she could have a serious accident which could cripple her for life. Grace lost two fingers in five years.

(Looks up from notes, leans on podium, and continues in a more conversational tone.) I remember the first time I met Grace. I was ten years old, and my Sunday school teacher was dear old Miss Elsie. Miss Elsie was seventy-five when she finally allowed the Sunday school superintendent to retire her. *(He chuckles at the memory.)* One day Grace walked into the classroom to take Miss Elsie's place as our teacher. She was young and pretty and full of interesting ideas and stories about places where none of us had ever been. She was wonderful, like a breath of fresh air. We all fell in love with her. Soon after that, Grace met a gentleman named Ralph. Soon they were married and later had three children.

Growing up with Grace and Ralph was really wonderful. Ralph treated all the boys like sons and took us to picnics and to the ball game. But the most exciting activity we did on Sundays after church services. Sometimes he would have us bring our lunch, and then with his family we would all eat together in the classroom. Then we were ready for the afternoon's adventure. All of us would walk the many miles across town until we came to a large building. In that old church Grace and Ralph had begun a local congregation of persons from their native country. When I was thirteen, they put me to work with the smaller boys since they spoke English. Ralph led the services and preached the sermon; Grace played the piano for the hymns.

When the church membership reached one hundred, Ralph and Grace helped them call an ordained pastor. Then the two of them went to another area where they helped another group start and build a congregation. This pattern continued for many years. When Ralph finally retired from the post office, they were able to accept a full-time call to a small church.

To many, these lives sound dull and uneventful, but to us who knew them, Grace and Ralph led exciting and dynamic lives which influenced many others beyond their circle. Listen to something that Grace wrote several years ago. *(Reading from a card.)*

"When I die, I don't want anyone to grieve. Instead I want you to celebrate my life and my going to be with the Lord. Make it a joyful day with a lot of laughter and singing. I want trumpets to play and choirs to sing. Greet one another with love and cheerfulness. Please, don't look at my body; I won't be there. My spirit will be rejoicing with God and sharing with you in the great celebration of life.

"When you lower my body into the earth, don't let anyone be afraid or cry. The shell I borrowed for these few years will be returning to its source. The darkness of the burial box will not entomb me, but it will serve as a human necessity of life. I will be with you, near you always, as long as you remember me."

(Looking up from notes.) So, friends, let's follow her wishes. You see, there is no casket here today. Ralph and his children and his grandchildren are here to help us celebrate the joy of Grace's salvation. *(In the distance the soft introduction to the "Hallelujah Chorus" by Handel may be heard. As the speech continues, the volume is raised, and at the speech's conclusion it is up to an appropriate level.)* Let the trumpet sound; let the chorus swell and sing aloud the praises of God and his majesty. Praise the Lord, for one more soul has gone to be with him. *(Allow record to play the "Hallelujah Chorus" in its entirety.)*

Probes

1. Which best depicts the Christian spirit in funeral or memorial services—the celebration of life or the sorrow over death? Explain your answer.

2. Discuss the appropriateness of such things as viewings, open or closed caskets, memorial services, expensive funerals, and music in regard to the burial of the dead.

3. Death and dying consist of a central emphasis in the ministry of the church. To what extent have funeral homes taken over this function? Is this desirable?

4. Is the funeral service primarily for the departed or for those who remain? Discuss.

A Husband's Liberation
A Stinger in the Form of a Dramatic Duet

APPLICATION: To help persons think deeply about the similarities and differences between people and about how the church should react to social change in the contemporary situation. This could be used effectively with a number of types of programs with a "family" emphasis.

SETTING: *A man is setting the table for dinner. He's angry and bangs the plates and silverware as he works. (A door is heard to open and close.)*

MAC: Is that you, Rose?

ROSE *(entering):* Sure is, honey, how are you?

MAC: Rotten!

ROSE: Aw, I'm sorry. How's about a kiss? *(MAC moves away.)* Hey, what's eating you?

MAC: Nothing. I just don't feel like kissing, and if you'd had a day like mine, you wouldn't feel like it either.

ROSE: OK, what did the kids do now? *(Sits and takes out newspaper.)*

MAC: It's not just the kids. I have to do everything around here. All I see are dirty dishes, kids' bottoms, and a grumpy wife at the end of the day.

ROSE: Grumpy? I'm the one who was denied a simple kiss.

MAC *(contritely):* I know, and I'm sorry. *(Gives ROSE a peck on the cheek.)* Today was just one of "those" days.

ROSE: Why don't you tell me about it, honey? *(Opens paper and begins to read.)*

MAC: Well, for starters, having to get up twice in the middle of the night, once to give Timmy his four o'clock feeding and earlier to make sure Susie used the bathroom, didn't help me feel rested this morning.

ROSE *(looking up):* I'm sorry. *(Returns to newspaper.)*

MAC: And what really bugs me is that you lie there all the while, snoring away without a care in the world. Then this morning just when I thought I would be able to get the house vacuumed, Jimmie's teacher called to say he had thrown up, and would I come over and get him at school.

ROSE *(still reading):* How is he now?

MAC: Oh, he's all right, just a touch of the flu. But he's kept me running all afternoon taking him things so he won't get lonely.

ROSE: That's Jimmie, all right.

MAC: But that was just today; meanwhile, there are a million other things that I don't even get to.

ROSE *(turning a page):* That's the way it goes.

MAC: Look, Rose, I don't mind this kind of work. I know it's all part of my job. But when you get home at five, it's all over for you. But the day is only half over for me. It's not fair. I need help!

ROSE: I'm sorry, Mac, but I'm tired. I've got a lot of responsibilities at work. I need time to unwind and renew myself.

MAC: And when do I get a chance to renew myself . . . to say nothing of occasionally having a little fun?

ROSE *(condescendingly):* I don't think it's the same. You don't need to be especially refreshed to take care of a couple of kids and keep a house clean. You just don't have the same kind of responsibilities.

MAC: Is that so? I suppose the lives of three little kids are not an important responsibility?

ROSE *(annoyed, puts down the paper):* Of course it is. I didn't mean that. But when we first talked about this arrangement, you said you would welcome the change from all the tension at the office. You said that since you wouldn't have outside employment, taking care of the kids and the house would be your job and that you would not mind handling it all.

MAC: But you didn't tell me it would be like *this!!*

ROSE: Yes I did! I told you just what being a homemaker would be like.

MAC: BUT I DIDN'T BELIEVE YOU!!!!

Probes

1. Is this sort of family arrangement such a rare situation in today's society?

2. What compromises would you recommend for this couple? Would you be willing to make the same compromises if the wife were staying at home?

3. How are sex-related roles changing in the modern church?

4. Is there such a thing as "the woman's place" in the church family?

5. How should we interpret what the Bible says about the relationship of men and women?

A Husband's Liberation
A Stinger in the Form of a Dramatic Duet

APPLICATION: To help persons think deeply about the similarities and differences between people and about how the church should react to social change in the contemporary situation. This could be used effectively with a number of types of programs with a "family" emphasis.

SETTING: *A man is setting the table for dinner. He's angry and bangs the plates and silverware as he works. (A door is heard to open and close.)*

MAC: Is that you, Rose?

ROSE *(entering)*: Sure is, honey, how are you?

MAC: Rotten!

ROSE: Aw, I'm sorry. How's about a kiss? *(MAC moves away.)* Hey, what's eating you?

MAC: Nothing. I just don't feel like kissing, and if you'd had a day like mine, you wouldn't feel like it either.

ROSE: OK, what did the kids do now? *(Sits and takes out newspaper.)*

MAC: It's not just the kids. I have to do everything around here. All I see are dirty dishes, kids' bottoms, and a grumpy wife at the end of the day.

ROSE: Grumpy? I'm the one who was denied a simple kiss.

MAC *(contritely)*: I know, and I'm sorry. *(Gives ROSE a peck on the cheek.)* Today was just one of "those" days.

ROSE: Why don't you tell me about it, honey? *(Opens paper and begins to read.)*

MAC: Well, for starters, having to get up twice in the middle of the night, once to give Timmy his four o'clock feeding and earlier to make sure Susie used the bathroom, didn't help me feel rested this morning.

ROSE *(looking up)*: I'm sorry. *(Returns to newspaper.)*

MAC: And what really bugs me is that you lie there all the while, snoring away without a care in the world. Then this morning just when I thought I would be able to get the house vacuumed, Jimmie's teacher called to say he had thrown up, and would I come over and get him at school.

ROSE *(still reading)*: How is he now?

MAC: Oh, he's all right, just a touch of the flu. But he's kept me running all afternoon taking him things so he won't get lonely.

ROSE: That's Jimmie, all right.

MAC: But that was just today; meanwhile, there are a million other things that I don't even get to.

ROSE *(turning a page)*: That's the way it goes.

MAC: Look, Rose, I don't mind this kind of work. I know it's all part of my job. But when you get home at five, it's all over for you. But the day is only half over for me. It's not fair. I need help!

ROSE: I'm sorry, Mac, but I'm tired. I've got a lot of responsibilities at work. I need time to unwind and renew myself.

MAC: And when do I get a chance to renew myself ... to say nothing of occasionally having a little fun?

ROSE *(condescendingly)*: I don't think it's the same. You don't need to be especially refreshed to take care of a couple of kids and keep a house clean. You just don't have the same kind of responsibilities.

MAC: Is that so? I suppose the lives of three little kids are not an important responsibility?

ROSE *(annoyed, puts down the paper)*: Of course it is. I didn't mean that. But when we first talked about this arrangement, you said you would welcome the change from all the tension at the office. You said that since you wouldn't have outside employment, taking care of the kids and the house would be your job and that you would not mind handling it all.

MAC: But you didn't tell me it would be like *this!!*

ROSE: Yes I did! I told you just what being a homemaker would be like.

MAC: BUT I DIDN'T BELIEVE YOU!!!!

Probes

1. Is this sort of family arrangement such a rare situation in today's society?

2. What compromises would you recommend for this couple? Would you be willing to make the same compromises if the wife were staying at home?

3. How are sex-related roles changing in the modern church?

4. Is there such a thing as "the woman's place" in the church family?

5. How should we interpret what the Bible says about the relationship of men and women?

A Husband's Liberation
A Stinger in the Form of a Dramatic Duet

APPLICATION: To help persons think deeply about the similarities and differences between people and about how the church should react to social change in the contemporary situation. This could be used effectively with a number of types of programs with a "family" emphasis.

SETTING: *A man is setting the table for dinner. He's angry and bangs the plates and silverware as he works. (A door is heard to open and close.)*

MAC: Is that you, Rose?

ROSE *(entering):* Sure is, honey, how are you?

MAC: Rotten!

ROSE: Aw, I'm sorry. How's about a kiss? *(MAC moves away.)* Hey, what's eating you?

MAC: Nothing. I just don't feel like kissing, and if you'd had a day like mine, you wouldn't feel like it either.

ROSE: OK, what did the kids do now? *(Sits and takes out newspaper.)*

MAC: It's not just the kids. I have to do everything around here. All I see are dirty dishes, kids' bottoms, and a grumpy wife at the end of the day.

ROSE: Grumpy? I'm the one who was denied a simple kiss.

MAC *(contritely):* I know, and I'm sorry. *(Gives ROSE a peck on the cheek.)* Today was just one of "those" days.

ROSE: Why don't you tell me about it, honey? *(Opens paper and begins to read.)*

MAC: Well, for starters, having to get up twice in the middle of the night, once to give Timmy his four o'clock feeding and earlier to make sure Susie used the bathroom, didn't help me feel rested this morning.

ROSE *(looking up):* I'm sorry. *(Returns to newspaper.)*

MAC: And what really bugs me is that you lie there all the while, snoring away without a care in the world. Then this morning just when I thought I would be able to get the house vacuumed, Jimmie's teacher called to say he had thrown up, and would I come over and get him at school.

ROSE *(still reading):* How is he now?

MAC: Oh, he's all right, just a touch of the flu. But he's kept me running all afternoon taking him things so he won't get lonely.

ROSE: That's Jimmie, all right.

MAC: But that was just today; meanwhile, there are a million other things that I don't even get to.

ROSE *(turning a page):* That's the way it goes.

MAC: Look, Rose, I don't mind this kind of work. I know it's all part of my job. But when you get home at five, it's all over for you. But the day is only half over for me. It's not fair. I need help!

ROSE: I'm sorry, Mac, but I'm tired. I've got a lot of responsibilities at work. I need time to unwind and renew myself.

MAC: And when do I get a chance to renew myself ... to say nothing of occasionally having a little fun?

ROSE *(condescendingly):* I don't think it's the same. You don't need to be especially refreshed to take care of a couple of kids and keep a house clean. You just don't have the same kind of responsibilities.

MAC: Is that so? I suppose the lives of three little kids are not an important responsibility?

ROSE *(annoyed, puts down the paper):* Of course it is. I didn't mean that. But when we first talked about this arrangement, you said you would welcome the change from all the tension at the office. You said that since you wouldn't have outside employment, taking care of the kids and the house would be your job and that you would not mind handling it all.

MAC: But you didn't tell me it would be like *this!!*

ROSE: Yes I did! I told you just what being a homemaker would be like.

MAC: BUT I DIDN'T BELIEVE YOU!!!!

Probes

1. Is this sort of family arrangement such a rare situation in today's society?

2. What compromises would you recommend for this couple? Would you be willing to make the same compromises if the wife were staying at home?

3. How are sex-related roles changing in the modern church?

4. Is there such a thing as "the woman's place" in the church family?

5. How should we interpret what the Bible says about the relationship of men and women?

Man on a Tightrope
A Stinger in the Form of a Dramatic Duet

APPLICATION: To help persons see the dimension of Christian life that calls for total dedication in the face of danger, opposition, criticism, and unconcern.

SETTING: *Two persons are standing close to each other center stage. They are engrossed in something they see above them.*

WOMAN: You think he'll make it?

MAN: I don't know. It sure looks windy up there.

WOMAN: I sure hope he doesn't fall. I couldn't stand to watch it.

MAN: Well, don't look then.

WOMAN: My goodness, he's actually skipping across.

MAN: What a jerk!

WOMAN: What do you mean?

MAN: Who else but a fool would get himself in such a predicament?

WOMAN: I think he's brave. It takes guts to do what he's doing.

MAN: It takes more than guts to keep from falling.

WOMAN: That's just it. He's also talented; otherwise he'd never make it.

MAN: He's not finished yet.

WOMAN: No, but I think he's going to be OK. *(Screams.)*

MAN: See what I told you? It was almost curtains for him that time.

WOMAN: He's got to make it; he's just got to.

MAN: I hope he falls; it'll serve him right!

WOMAN: What?

MAN: Sure. Anyone dumb enough to take such a chance with his life deserves to fail.

Probes

1. Discuss: "Faith is leaping into the dark of uncertainty as well as running the risk of getting hurt to find out the truth."

2. Are there times when it is best to "play it safe" in the work of the church? When is it right to take chances in undertaking some innovative change that may bring criticism to you and to the church?

3. Do we like to see other people fail? What are our feelings when others fail in both large and small undertakings?

Man on a Tightrope

A Stinger in the Form of a Dramatic Duet

APPLICATION: To help persons see the dimension of Christian life that calls for total dedication in the face of danger, opposition, criticism, and unconcern.

SETTING: *Two persons are standing close to each other center stage. They are engrossed in something they see above them.*

WOMAN: You think he'll make it?
MAN: I don't know. It sure looks windy up there.
WOMAN: I sure hope he doesn't fall. I couldn't stand to watch it.
MAN: Well, don't look then.
WOMAN: My goodness, he's actually skipping across.
MAN: What a jerk!

WOMAN: What do you mean?
MAN: Who else but a fool would get himself in such a predicament?
WOMAN: I think he's brave. It takes guts to do what he's doing.
MAN: It takes more than guts to keep from falling.
WOMAN: That's just it. He's also talented; otherwise he'd never make it.
MAN: He's not finished yet.
WOMAN: No, but I think he's going to be OK. *(Screams.)*
MAN: See what I told you? It was almost curtains for him that time.
WOMAN: He's got to make it; he's just got to.
MAN: I hope he falls; it'll serve him right!
WOMAN: What?
MAN: Sure. Anyone dumb enough to take such a chance with his life deserves to fail.

Probes

1. Discuss: "Faith is leaping into the dark of uncertainty as well as running the risk of getting hurt to find out the truth."

2. Are there times when it is best to "play it safe" in the work of the church? When is it right to take chances in undertaking some innovative change that may bring criticism to you and to the church?

3. Do we like to see other people fail? What are our feelings when others fail in both large and small undertakings?

Man on a Tightrope
A Stinger in the Form of a Dramatic Duet

APPLICATION: To help persons see the dimension of Christian life that calls for total dedication in the face of danger, opposition, criticism, and unconcern.

SETTING: *Two persons are standing close to each other center stage. They are engrossed in something they see above them.*

WOMAN: You think he'll make it?
MAN: I don't know. It sure looks windy up there.
WOMAN: I sure hope he doesn't fall. I couldn't stand to watch it.
MAN: Well, don't look then.
WOMAN: My goodness, he's actually skipping across.
MAN: What a jerk!

WOMAN: What do you mean?
MAN: Who else but a fool would get himself in such a predicament?
WOMAN: I think he's brave. It takes guts to do what he's doing.
MAN: It takes more than guts to keep from falling.
WOMAN: That's just it. He's also talented; otherwise he'd never make it.
MAN: He's not finished yet.
WOMAN: No, but I think he's going to be OK. *(Screams.)*
MAN: See what I told you? It was almost curtains for him that time.
WOMAN: He's got to make it; he's just got to.
MAN: I hope he falls; it'll serve him right!
WOMAN: What?
MAN: Sure. Anyone dumb enough to take such a chance with his life deserves to fail.

Probes

1. Discuss: "Faith is leaping into the dark of uncertainty as well as running the risk of getting hurt to find out the truth."

2. Are there times when it is best to "play it safe" in the work of the church? When is it right to take chances in undertaking some innovative change that may bring criticism to you and to the church?

3. Do we like to see other people fail? What are our feelings when others fail in both large and small undertakings?

Eeney—Meeney—Miney—Moe

A Stinger in the Form of a Dramatic Duet
(Based on a True Story)

APPLICATION: To assist persons to examine their attitudes toward people who are different and to examine the implications of having stereotypes in creating attitudes on which relationships are built or by which they are destroyed.

SETTING: *Two people meet on the sidewalk in front of their garden apartment, or two people (back to back) are talking on the telephone.*

CHRIS: Hi there, stranger. I haven't seen you in a long time.

MARY: Hi, Chris, I guess it has been some time. But I warned you that once I started school, I wouldn't be able to see you too often.

CHRIS: I know, but this is ridiculous. We live on the same floor, and Tim and I haven't seen you and Dan for almost a month. Why don't we plan to get together at our place for dinner sometime this week?

MARY: We'd really love to, but right now it's the end of the first marking period, and that means tests to grade, parent-teacher conferences to schedule, ad infinitum.

CHRIS: That's really too bad. You sure do work hard, especially when you consider the class of people you have to deal with—all those Puerto Ricans. It turns my stomach just to think about it.

MARY: I don't understand. I enjoy teaching at the Franklin School.

CHRIS: You do? I couldn't take it. All those P.R.s do is pollute the town. They come into this country, get on welfare, and live lazy, dirty, and happily ever after.

MARY: But, Chris, surely you don't believe that *all* Puerto Ricans are dirty and lazy.

CHRIS: Absolutely! I've never met one yet who could speak good American. They're just stupid foreigners. Really, Mary, I can't understand why you stand up for them. If they are so good, then why don't they get out of the ghetto and live decently?

MARY: What do you know about the city? You've always lived in the suburbs. You don't know how hard it is for someone to escape from that kind of prison.

CHRIS: Well, one thing's for sure: I can spot a Puerto Rican a mile away, and I wouldn't get that close to one if I could help it.

MARY: Is that so? What happened to your missionary zeal? In church you're always saying that we have a responsibility to bring Christ to the "heathen."

CHRIS: That's something completely different. I wouldn't want them to die without being saved.

MARY: But if you don't intend to get within a mile of them, how are you going to take them the gospel?

CHRIS: That's what *missionaries* are for.

MARY: So—once you give your money for missions, your responsibility is over.

CHRIS: Well, not exactly. I do think we should *pray* for them.

MARY: I think you need to read the thirteenth chapter of First Corinthians.

CHRIS *(beginning to feel uncomfortable):* Let's stop this nonsense. *(Nervous giggle.)* My father was right—one should never discuss politics or religion. You always end up arguing.

MARY *(sarcastically):* A shame—I was just beginning to enjoy myself.

CHRIS: I'll tell you what. Why don't you and Dan come over on Saturday for dinner? We'll have one of our lovely times together again and forget all this unpleasant business.

MARY: I don't know, Chris. You may not be able to entertain when you have so much packing to do.

CHRIS: Packing? What for?

MARY: Well, you are going to move now, aren't you?

CHRIS: Don't be silly, Mary. Why should we move? Tim and I love it here.

MARY: It's just that I thought you could identify us from a mile away. You see, Chris, *I* am a Puerto Rican. *Hasta la vista. (Exits.)*

Probes

1. To what degree is acceptance (affirmation) based on likeness?

2. Is there a sense in which some people insist that acceptance must be earned? What does this say about "grace" as Christians understand it?

3. How would you deal with stereotypes such as were set forth by Chris?

4. To what degree is support of missions motivated by guilt for refusal to accept as neighbors people who are different? Can you apply Jesus' definition of "neighbor" to this stinger?

Eeney—Meeney—Miney—Moe

A Stinger in the Form of a Dramatic Duet
(Based on a True Story)

APPLICATION: To assist persons to examine their attitudes toward people who are different and to examine the implications of having stereotypes in creating attitudes on which relationships are built or by which they are destroyed.

SETTING: *Two people meet on the sidewalk in front of their garden apartment, or two people (back to back) are talking on the telephone.*

CHRIS: Hi there, stranger. I haven't seen you in a long time.

MARY: Hi, Chris, I guess it has been some time. But I warned you that once I started school, I wouldn't be able to see you too often.

CHRIS: I know, but this is ridiculous. We live on the same floor, and Tim and I haven't seen you and Dan for almost a month. Why don't we plan to get together at our place for dinner sometime this week?

MARY: We'd really love to, but right now it's the end of the first marking period, and that means tests to grade, parent-teacher conferences to schedule, ad infinitum.

CHRIS: That's really too bad. You sure do work hard, especially when you consider the class of people you have to deal with—all those Puerto Ricans. It turns my stomach just to think about it.

MARY: I don't understand. I enjoy teaching at the Franklin School.

CHRIS: You do? I couldn't take it. All those P.R.s do is pollute the town. They come into this country, get on welfare, and live lazy, dirty, and happily ever after.

MARY: But, Chris, surely you don't believe that *all* Puerto Ricans are dirty and lazy.

CHRIS: Absolutely! I've never met one yet who could speak good American. They're just stupid foreigners. Really, Mary, I can't understand why you stand up for them. If they are so good, then why don't they get out of the ghetto and live decently?

MARY: What do you know about the city? You've always lived in the suburbs. You don't know how hard it is for someone to escape from that kind of prison.

CHRIS: Well, one thing's for sure: I can spot a Puerto Rican a mile away, and I wouldn't get that close to one if I could help it.

MARY: Is that so? What happened to your missionary zeal? In church you're always saying that we have a responsibility to bring Christ to the "heathen."

CHRIS: That's something completely different. I wouldn't want them to die without being saved.

MARY: But if you don't intend to get within a mile of them, how are you going to take them the gospel?

CHRIS: That's what *missionaries* are for.

MARY: So—once you give your money for missions, your responsibility is over.

CHRIS: Well, not exactly. I do think we should *pray* for them.

MARY: I think you need to read the thirteenth chapter of First Corinthians.

CHRIS *(beginning to feel uncomfortable):* Let's stop this nonsense. *(Nervous giggle.)* My father was right—one should never discuss politics or religion. You always end up arguing.

MARY *(sarcastically):* A shame—I was just beginning to enjoy myself.

CHRIS: I'll tell you what. Why don't you and Dan come over on Saturday for dinner? We'll have one of our lovely times together again and forget all this unpleasant business.

MARY: I don't know, Chris. You may not be able to entertain when you have so much packing to do.

CHRIS: Packing? What for?

MARY: Well, you are going to move now, aren't you?

CHRIS: Don't be silly, Mary. Why should we move? Tim and I love it here.

MARY: It's just that I thought you could identify us from a mile away. You see, Chris, *I* am a Puerto Rican. *Hasta la vista. (Exits.)*

Probes

1. To what degree is acceptance (affirmation) based on likeness?

2. Is there a sense in which some people insist that acceptance must be earned? What does this say about "grace" as Christians understand it?

3. How would you deal with stereotypes such as were set forth by Chris?

4. To what degree is support of missions motivated by guilt for refusal to accept as neighbors people who are different? Can you apply Jesus' definition of "neighbor" to this stinger?

Eeney—Meeney—Miney—Moe

A Stinger in the Form of a Dramatic Duet
(Based on a True Story)

APPLICATION: To assist persons to examine their attitudes toward people who are different and to examine the implications of having stereotypes in creating attitudes on which relationships are built or by which they are destroyed.

SETTING: *Two people meet on the sidewalk in front of their garden apartment, or two people (back to back) are talking on the telephone.*

CHRIS: Hi there, stranger. I haven't seen you in a long time.

MARY: Hi, Chris, I guess it has been some time. But I warned you that once I started school, I wouldn't be able to see you too often.

CHRIS: I know, but this is ridiculous. We live on the same floor, and Tim and I haven't seen you and Dan for almost a month. Why don't we plan to get together at our place for dinner sometime this week?

MARY: We'd really love to, but right now it's the end of the first marking period, and that means tests to grade, parent-teacher conferences to schedule, ad infinitum.

CHRIS: That's really too bad. You sure do work hard, especially when you consider the class of people you have to deal with—all those Puerto Ricans. It turns my stomach just to think about it.

MARY: I don't understand. I enjoy teaching at the Franklin School.

CHRIS: You do? I couldn't take it. All those P.R.s do is pollute the town. They come into this country, get on welfare, and live lazy, dirty, and happily ever after.

MARY: But, Chris, surely you don't believe that *all* Puerto Ricans are dirty and lazy.

CHRIS: Absolutely! I've never met one yet who could speak good American. They're just stupid foreigners. Really, Mary, I can't understand why you stand up for them. If they are so good, then why don't they get out of the ghetto and live decently?

MARY: What do you know about the city? You've always lived in the suburbs. You don't know how hard it is for someone to escape from that kind of prison.

CHRIS: Well, one thing's for sure: I can spot a Puerto Rican a mile away, and I wouldn't get that close to one if I could help it.

MARY: Is that so? What happened to your missionary zeal? In church you're always saying that we have a responsibility to bring Christ to the "heathen."

CHRIS: That's something completely different. I wouldn't want them to die without being saved.

MARY: But if you don't intend to get within a mile of them, how are you going to take them the gospel?

CHRIS: That's what *missionaries* are for.

MARY: So—once you give your money for missions, your responsibility is over.

CHRIS: Well, not exactly, I do think we should *pray* for them.

MARY: I think you need to read the thirteenth chapter of First Corinthians.

CHRIS *(beginning to feel uncomfortable)*: Let's stop this nonsense. *(Nervous giggle.)* My father was right—one should never discuss politics or religion. You always end up arguing.

MARY *(sarcastically)*: A shame—I was just beginning to enjoy myself.

CHRIS: I'll tell you what. Why don't you and Dan come over on Saturday for dinner? We'll have one of our lovely times together again and forget all this unpleasant business.

MARY: I don't know, Chris. You may not be able to entertain when you have so much packing to do.

CHRIS: Packing? What for?

MARY: Well, you are going to move now, aren't you?

CHRIS: Don't be silly, Mary. Why should we move? Tim and I love it here.

MARY: It's just that I thought you could identify us from a mile away. You see, Chris, *I* am a Puerto Rican. *Hasta la vista. (Exits.)*

Probes

1. To what degree is acceptance (affirmation) based on likeness?

2. Is there a sense in which some people insist that acceptance must be earned? What does this say about "grace" as Christians understand it?

3. How would you deal with stereotypes such as were set forth by Chris?

4. To what degree is support of missions motivated by guilt for refusal to accept as neighbors people who are different? Can you apply Jesus' definition of "neighbor" to this stinger?

Encounter in the Park

A Modern Parable in the Form of a Dramatic Duet
(Stinger)

SETTING: *A well-dressed woman (W#1) is seated on a park bench. She is feeding pigeons. She is murmuring to the birds and does not notice when another woman (W#2) sits down next to her. W#2 is disheveled and dirty.*

W#1 *(speaking to the birds):* There, there, you dears, you'll all get your share. Don't push so much. Hey, you—big one. Let the little ones eat. Don't hog all the peanuts for yourself.

W#2: They know how to take care of Number One.

W#1: Well, they should share.

W#2: Why should they? It's every bird for itself in this world. They know if they don't scramble for their food, they are going to end up hungry.

W#1: No, they won't. I'll give them all some. Can't you see me trying to be fair to all of them?

W#2: You see that little one over there, the one with some bare spots on his coat?

W#1: Poor baby—looks like he's got something wrong with him.

W#2: You'd better believe it. Those bare spots probably came from other birds pecking at him. He's the weak one of the crowd, or maybe he's sick. *(Knowingly.)* They'll peck at him until he dies.

W#1 *(sitting up straight, no longer feeding the birds):* The callous little beasts. Why should they be so mean to each other?

W#2: Why not? They know how the world runs. They know that if they let the weak ones live, there won't be as much for the rest of them. You know, survival of the fittest.

W#1: That's a terrible philosophy of life.

W#2: So what's so different from the way people treat one another?

W#1 *(suddenly noticing the other woman's appearance):* Quite a bit I think. *(Moves away from her just a little.)* People don't turn on their brothers and sisters when they are hurt.

W#2: Oh, don't they? What do you call war—playtime? Who wants to take in refugees? No one!

W#1 *(warming up to the argument):* Ah, but the *church*—the church has always been ready to help the needy. Sweaters for Britain, CARE packages, White Cross bandages and dressings . . .

W#2: Do tell. And where was the church during the Second World War when Hitler was butchering all those Jews? Some members were horrified, but where was the church as a *body?* Did it cry out against this horror? What about the boat people from Vietnam—who wanted them? No one, that's who. (W#1 *begins to protest, but W#2 continues.)* Oh, I know, many churches adopted Vietnamese families. Earlier, some had adopted Cuban families. And some even sent money for relief work. But where was the *indignity*, the *outcry* from the church, the *ultimatums* it ought to have been making to the government?

W#1: It's hard to do things for *all* the people; we helped the few we could. We heard from many churches.

W#2: SILENCE—that's all we heard. If the body of believers had united the way they say they are united, the hew and cry over these injustices would have been heard around the world.

W#1 *(standing):* Ma'am, I think you are being unfair and rude. I won't sit here and listen to your diatribe.

W#2: Fine, run away if you like. But tell me, could you please give me a dollar? I haven't had anything to eat in a long time, and I could use a good meal.

W#1: A *dollar?* Is that what you panhandlers are asking for now? It's not enough that I have to sit here and be insulted by someone who is probably living off my taxes already! Am I also expected to give her money? Not on your life—*sister!*

W#2: Oh, is that what you are—my *sister?*

—curtain—

Probes

1. Are we our brother's—and sister's—keeper? What does this mean in the modern world?

2. What place does power and success play in living out the Christian gospel?

3. Is the church to be concerned about the hungry and poor throughout the world or only those in the local community?

Encounter in the Park

A Modern Parable in the Form of a Dramatic Duet
(Stinger)

SETTING: *A well-dressed woman (W#1) is seated on a park bench. She is feeding pigeons. She is murmuring to the birds and does not notice when another woman (W#2) sits down next to her. W#2 is disheveled and dirty.*

W#1 *(speaking to the birds):* There, there, you dears, you'll all get your share. Don't push so much. Hey, you—big one. Let the little ones eat. Don't hog all the peanuts for yourself.

W#2: They know how to take care of Number One.

W#1: Well, they should share.

W#2: Why should they? It's every bird for itself in this world. They know if they don't scramble for their food, they are going to end up hungry.

W#1: No, they won't. I'll give them all some. Can't you see me trying to be fair to all of them?

W#2: You see that little one over there, the one with some bare spots on his coat?

W#1: Poor baby—looks like he's got something wrong with him.

W#2: You'd better believe it. Those bare spots probably came from other birds pecking at him. He's the weak one of the crowd, or maybe he's sick. *(Knowingly.)* They'll peck at him until he dies.

W#1 *(sitting up straight, no longer feeding the birds):* The callous little beasts. Why should they be so mean to each other?

W#2: Why not? They know how the world runs. They know that if they let the weak ones live, there won't be as much for the rest of them. You know, survival of the fittest.

W#1: That's a terrible philosophy of life.

W#2: So what's so different from the way people treat one another?

W#1 *(suddenly noticing the other woman's appearance):* Quite a bit I think. *(Moves away from her just a little.)* People don't turn on their brothers and sisters when they are hurt.

W#2: Oh, don't they? What do you call war—

playtime? Who wants to take in refugees? No one!

W#1 *(warming up to the argument):* Ah, but the *church*—the church has always been ready to help the needy. Sweaters for Britain, CARE packages, White Cross bandages and dressings . . .

W#2: Do tell. And where was the church during the Second World War when Hitler was butchering all those Jews? Some members were horrified, but where was the church as a *body?* Did it cry out against this horror? What about the boat people from Vietnam—who wanted them? No one, that's who. *(W#1 begins to protest, but W#2 continues.)* Oh, I know, many churches adopted Vietnamese families. Earlier, some had adopted Cuban families. And some even sent money for relief work. But where was the *indignity,* the *outcry* from the church, the *ultimatums* it ought to have been making to the government?

W#1: It's hard to do things for *all* the people; we helped the few we could. We heard from many churches.

W#2: SILENCE—that's all we heard. If the body of believers had united the way they say they are united, the hew and cry over these injustices would have been heard around the world.

W#1 *(standing):* Ma'am, I think you are being unfair and rude. I won't sit here and listen to your diatribe.

W#2: Fine, run away if you like. But tell me, could you please give me a dollar? I haven't had anything to eat in a long time, and I could use a good meal.

W#1: A *dollar?* Is that what you panhandlers are asking for now? It's not enough that I have to sit here and be insulted by someone who is probably living off my taxes already! Am I also expected to give her money? Not on your life—*sister!*

W#2: Oh, is that what you are—my *sister?*

—curtain—

Probes

1. Are we our brother's—and sister's—keeper? What does this mean in the modern world?

2. What place does power and success play in living out the Christian gospel?

3. Is the church to be concerned about the hungry and poor throughout the world or only those in the local community?

Encounter in the Park

A Modern Parable in the Form of a Dramatic Duet
(Stinger)

SETTING: *A well-dressed woman (W#1) is seated on a park bench. She is feeding pigeons. She is murmuring to the birds and does not notice when another woman (W#2) sits down next to her. W#2 is disheveled and dirty.*

W#1 *(speaking to the birds):* There, there, you dears, you'll all get your share. Don't push so much. Hey, you—big one. Let the little ones eat. Don't hog all the peanuts for yourself.

W#2: They know how to take care of Number One.

W#1: Well, they should share.

W#2: Why should they? It's every bird for itself in this world. They know if they don't scramble for their food, they are going to end up hungry.

W#1: No, they won't. I'll give them all some. Can't you see me trying to be fair to all of them?

W#2: You see that little one over there, the one with some bare spots on his coat?

W#1: Poor baby—looks like he's got something wrong with him.

W#2: You'd better believe it. Those bare spots probably came from other birds pecking at him. He's the weak one of the crowd, or maybe he's sick. *(Knowingly.)* They'll peck at him until he dies.

W#1 *(sitting up straight, no longer feeding the birds):* The callous little beasts. Why should they be so mean to each other?

W#2: Why not? They know how the world runs. They know that if they let the weak ones live, there won't be as much for the rest of them. You know, survival of the fittest.

W#1: That's a terrible philosophy of life.

W#2: So what's so different from the way people treat one another?

W#1 *(suddenly noticing the other woman's appearance):* Quite a bit I think. *(Moves away from her just a little.)* People don't turn on their brothers and sisters when they are hurt.

W#2: Oh, don't they? What do you call war—

playtime? Who wants to take in refugees? No one!

W#1 *(warming up to the argument):* Ah, but the church—the church has always been ready to help the needy. Sweaters for Britain, CARE packages, White Cross bandages and dressings . . .

W#2: Do tell. And where was the church during the Second World War when Hitler was butchering all those Jews? Some members were horrified, but where was the church as a *body?* Did it cry out against this horror? What about the boat people from Vietnam—who wanted them? No one, that's who. (W#1 *begins to protest, but W#2 continues.)* Oh, I know, many churches adopted Vietnamese families. Earlier, some had adopted Cuban families. And some even sent money for relief work. But where was the *indignity,* the *outcry* from the church, the *ultimatums* it ought to have been making to the government?

W#1: It's hard to do things for *all* the people; we helped the few we could. We heard from many churches.

W#2: SILENCE—that's all we heard. If the body of believers had united the way they say they are united, the hew and cry over these injustices would have been heard around the world.

W#1 *(standing):* Ma'am, I think you are being unfair and rude. I won't sit here and listen to your diatribe.

W#2: Fine, run away if you like. But tell me, could you please give me a dollar? I haven't had anything to eat in a long time, and I could use a good meal.

W#1: A *dollar?* Is that what you panhandlers are asking for now? It's not enough that I have to sit here and be insulted by someone who is probably living off my taxes already! Am I also expected to give her money? Not on your life—*sister!*

W#2: Oh, is that what you are—my *sister?*

—curtain—

Probes

1. Are we our brother's—and sister's—keeper? What does this mean in the modern world?

2. What place does power and success play in living out the Christian gospel?

3. Is the church to be concerned about the hungry and poor throughout the world or only those in the local community?

Who Chose You?

A Dramatic Duet

APPLICATION: To help persons to discover the grace of God that is operative in the building of community based on mutual acceptance and the need to affirm and to be affirmed.

SETTING: *Two persons are on the telephone.*

JOAN: Hi, Alice. How are you?

ALICE: Great! What's new?

JOAN: Have you heard about the Hamiltons?

ALICE *(excited):* You mean they finally got their baby?

JOAN: That's right.

ALICE: How marvelous! I think they were on the waiting list for two years. They must be very excited.

JOAN: That's putting it mildly. Jack is so proud he can hardly talk about anything else.

ALICE: What is it?

JOAN: A girl. They named her Clara. Oh, it's a wonderful thing they're doing. You know, Alice, I believe that when a couple adopts a baby, the Lord blesses them with a child of their own.

ALICE: But, Joan, this baby is their own, or it will be as soon as the court hearing is final, and that's only a formality. In their hearts that baby is already a part of them.

JOAN: Maybe, but it's not the same. After all, this child is not their own flesh and blood.

ALICE: That doesn't make the child any less theirs.

JOAN: I know they love this baby as if it *were* their own, but let's face it—two other people are her *real* parents.

ALICE: Joan, do you consider yourself a child of God?

JOAN: Of course, but what does that have to do with anything?

ALICE: Was God *your* biological father?

JOAN: Don't be ridiculous!

ALICE: Well, if you aren't God's biological child, what makes you think you're a child of God at all?

JOAN: Because it says so in the Bible. Something to do with the fact that in Christ we are all sons of God.

ALICE: That's right. One place is in Galatians 4:4-5 where it says, "When the time had fully come, God sent forth his Son . . . to redeem those who were under the law, so that we might receive adoption as sons."

JOAN: I've never thought of myself as *adopted.*

ALICE: And yet those are the very words Paul uses in his epistles. In fact, in Romans 8:17 he says, "If children, then heirs, heirs of God and fellow heirs with Christ. . . ." When Jack and Carol go before the judge in six months to finalize the adoption, Clara will legally become *their* heir.

JOAN: And I'm *God's* heir through Jesus Christ?

ALICE: That's right.

JOAN *(thoughtfully):* You know, I've never considered myself a member of God's family quite this way before. . . . So we're all adopted. . . . I guess I've always taken being God's child sort of for granted.

ALICE: Yes, I suppose we all have. But you know, Joan, something else Carol told me made me think just as much.

JOAN: Oh?

ALICE: She said, "Not only have we adopted Clara, but Jack and I have adopted each other. Our most fervent prayer is that someday Jack and I will be adopted by Clara."

JOAN: I'd say that is every parent's prayer.

—curtain—

Probes

1. What values are operative in the Christian community in regard to the differences between acceptance by adoption (deliberate choice) and being "born" into the relationship?

2. Who benefits from "adoption"? The adopted one? The adopters? Both? Why?

3. Discuss the need of every person for affirmation. Is affirmation more than acceptance?

4. Discuss the subtle differences in the terms "given up for adoption," "put up for adoption," and "chosen through adoption."

Who Chose You?

A Dramatic Duet

APPLICATION: To help persons to discover the grace of God that is operative in the building of community based on mutual acceptance and the need to affirm and to be affirmed.

SETTING: *Two persons are on the telephone.*

JOAN: Hi, Alice. How are you?

ALICE: Great! What's new?

JOAN: Have you heard about the Hamiltons?

ALICE *(excited):* You mean they finally got their baby?

JOAN: That's right.

ALICE: How marvelous! I think they were on the waiting list for two years. They must be very excited.

JOAN: That's putting it mildly. Jack is so proud he can hardly talk about anything else.

ALICE: What is it?

JOAN: A girl. They named her Clara. Oh, it's a wonderful thing they're doing. You know, Alice, I believe that when a couple adopts a baby, the Lord blesses them with a child of their own.

ALICE: But, Joan, this baby is their own, or it will be as soon as the court hearing is final, and that's only a formality. In their hearts that baby is already a part of them.

JOAN: Maybe, but it's not the same. After all, this child is not their own flesh and blood.

ALICE: That doesn't make the child any less theirs.

JOAN: I know they love this baby as if it *were* their own, but let's face it—two other people are her *real* parents.

ALICE: Joan, do you consider yourself a child of God?

JOAN: Of course, but what does that have to do with anything?

ALICE: Was God *your* biological father?

JOAN: Don't be ridiculous!

ALICE: Well, if you aren't God's biological child, what makes you think you're a child of God at all?

JOAN: Because it says so in the Bible. Something to do with the fact that in Christ we are all sons of God.

ALICE: That's right. One place is in Galatians 4:4-5 where it says, "When the time had fully come, God sent forth his Son . . . to redeem those who were under the law, so that we might receive adoption as sons."

JOAN: I've never thought of myself as *adopted.*

ALICE: And yet those are the very words Paul uses in his epistles. In fact, in Romans 8:17 he says, "If children, then heirs, heirs of God and fellow heirs with Christ. . . ." When Jack and Carol go before the judge in six months to finalize the adoption, Clara will legally become *their* heir.

JOAN: And I'm *God's* heir through Jesus Christ?

ALICE: That's right.

JOAN *(thoughtfully):* You know, I've never considered myself a member of God's family quite this way before. . . . So we're all adopted. . . . I guess I've always taken being God's child sort of for granted.

ALICE: Yes, I suppose we all have. But you know, Joan, something else Carol told me made me think just as much.

JOAN: Oh?

ALICE: She said, "Not only have we adopted Clara, but Jack and I have adopted each other. Our most fervent prayer is that someday Jack and I will be adopted by Clara."

JOAN: I'd say that is every parent's prayer.

—curtain—

Probes

1. What values are operative in the Christian community in regard to the differences between acceptance by adoption (deliberate choice) and being "born" into the relationship?

2. Who benefits from "adoption"? The adopted one? The adopters? Both? Why?

3. Discuss the need of every person for affirmation. Is affirmation more than acceptance?

4. Discuss the subtle differences in the terms "given up for adoption," "put up for adoption," and "chosen through adoption."

Who Chose You?

A Dramatic Duet

APPLICATION: To help persons to discover the grace of God that is operative in the building of community based on mutual acceptance and the need to affirm and to be affirmed.

SETTING: *Two persons are on the telephone.*

JOAN: Hi, Alice. How are you?

ALICE: Great! What's new?

JOAN: Have you heard about the Hamiltons?

ALICE *(excited):* You mean they finally got their baby?

JOAN: That's right.

ALICE: How marvelous! I think they were on the waiting list for two years. They must be very excited.

JOAN: That's putting it mildly. Jack is so proud he can hardly talk about anything else.

ALICE: What is it?

JOAN: A girl. They named her Clara. Oh, it's a wonderful thing they're doing. You know, Alice, I believe that when a couple adopts a baby, the Lord blesses them with a child of their own.

ALICE: But, Joan, this baby is their own, or it will be as soon as the court hearing is final, and that's only a formality. In their hearts that baby is already a part of them.

JOAN: Maybe, but it's not the same. After all, this child is not their own flesh and blood.

ALICE: That doesn't make the child any less theirs.

JOAN: I know they love this baby as if it *were* their own, but let's face it—two other people are her *real* parents.

ALICE: Joan, do you consider yourself a child of God?

JOAN: Of course, but what does that have to do with anything?

ALICE: Was God *your* biological father?

JOAN: Don't be ridiculous!

ALICE: Well, if you aren't God's biological child, what makes you think you're a child of God at all?

JOAN: Because it says so in the Bible. Something to do with the fact that in Christ we are all sons of God.

ALICE: That's right. One place is in Galatians 4:4-5 where it says, "When the time had fully come, God sent forth his Son . . . to redeem those who were under the law, so that we might receive adoption as sons."

JOAN: I've never thought of myself as *adopted.*

ALICE: And yet those are the very words Paul uses in his epistles. In fact, in Romans 8:17 he says, "If children, then heirs, heirs of God and fellow heirs with Christ. . . ." When Jack and Carol go before the judge in six months to finalize the adoption, Clara will legally become *their* heir.

JOAN: And I'm *God's* heir through Jesus Christ?

ALICE: That's right.

JOAN *(thoughtfully):* You know, I've never considered myself a member of God's family quite this way before. . . . So we're all adopted. . . . I guess I've always taken being God's child sort of for granted.

ALICE: Yes, I suppose we all have. But you know, Joan, something else Carol told me made me think just as much.

JOAN: Oh?

ALICE: She said, "Not only have we adopted Clara, but Jack and I have adopted each other. Our most fervent prayer is that someday Jack and I will be adopted by Clara."

JOAN: I'd say that is every parent's prayer.

—curtain—

Probes

1. What values are operative in the Christian community in regard to the differences between acceptance by adoption (deliberate choice) and being "born" into the relationship?

2. Who benefits from "adoption"? The adopted one? The adopters? Both? Why?

3. Discuss the need of every person for affirmation. Is affirmation more than acceptance?

4. Discuss the subtle differences in the terms "given up for adoption," "put up for adoption," and "chosen through adoption."

The Dinner Party

A Parable in the Form of a Dramatic Duet

SETTING: *Two men servants, dressed in formal wear, are on stage. (If formal wear is not available, dark blue or black suits with white shirts and black bow ties would be appropriate.) SERVANT I is obviously the head butler and SERVANT II is a servant of lesser standing. S I is pacing back and forth in front of a desk. S II is seated at the desk and is going over a list of RSVPs.*

SERVANT I: What do you mean they can't come? That's impossible! Those invitations to His Majesty's dinner party were sent out months ago.

SERVANT II: I know, but what can I do about it? They all had good excuses.

S I: I don't believe it. This is the most important event of the year, and they have the nerve to say that they can't come? Who do they think they are? What kind of excuses could they possibly have given?

S II *(defensively)*: They all seemed legitimate to me, sir. *(Checking his list.)* Lord and Lady Tepid had to make settlement on their property in the country.

S I: Oh, dear, His Majesty is not going to like that. They knew well enough in advance and could have scheduled the settlement for another time.

S II: Mrs. Warm's thoroughbred just had a new foal, and she feels that she needs to be near the horses tonight.

S I: Surely she realizes that this is not just *any* dinner. She could afford to be away from her animals for a short time.

S II: Those are only two of the guests invited, but most of the responses were in that vein. Oh, yes, the Lukes can't come because they were just married. They felt certain that His Majesty would understand.

S I: How many responses did you get so far?

S II: All one hundred of them, sir.

S I *(pulling at his hair)*: I *don't* believe this! You mean *NO* one is coming?

S II: That's right, sir.

S I: I don't know what to tell him. What do you suggest, Smythe?

S II *(standing and coming out from behind the desk)*: I certainly don't know, sir. That's not my responsibility, thank goodness. I just do my job as best I can.

S I *(regaining control of himself)*: Of course, you do. I didn't mean to burden you with my problems. I'll just have to speak to His Majesty myself. Wait for me here. *(He brushes imaginary dust from his suit, straightens his tie, pauses for a deep breath, and walks as though about to meet a king. Exits stage right.)*

(S II brings chair around from behind desk. He sits, looks at his watch frequently, and waits impatiently. When S I enters, he rises quickly in deference.)

S I *(enters slowly, shaking his head in disbelief)*: If I hadn't been there, I wouldn't have believed it.

S II *(goes to him)*: What happened? You look stunned.

S I: I guess that's what I am. A good word for it, Smythe—stunned.

S II: But, sir, what happened when you told him no one was coming to his dinner party?

S I: He laughed!

S II: He laughed? He hadn't been drinking, had he, sir?

S I *(indignantly)*: Of course not! I tell you, he just laughed.

S II: *Then* what did he do? Surely he did more than laugh.

S I: Well, that's the curious thing. It was only a soft laugh. Then he seemed to become thoughtful and a little angry. He looked into space for some time. Then, as though waking from a dream, he said, "Go out into the streets and alleys of the town, and bring here the poor and crippled and blind and lame. Tell them all to come inside so that my house may be full."

S II: Are you going to do it?

S I: Absolutely! I'm going to do it; and you are going to help me.

S II: Me?

S I: That's right, Smythe—YOU! Now come along; we have a lot of work to do.

(They come downstage and move among the audience. They stop, shake hands with members of the audience, speaking to each person they meet.*)

S I and S II: Our Master would like you to come to his banquet tonight. Everything is

93

ready. He is waiting for you. All you need
to do is come.

*(When they have each spoken to several people,
they exit through the back of the auditorium.)*

—*blackout*—

* Effective use of the voices may be made by S
II *echoing* each statement made by S I.

Probes

1. Are there any legitimate excuses for not answering God's invitation for full discipleship in God's kingdom?

2. Discuss the modern theological concept that "God is on the side of the poor." Is this a valid biblical idea? (See the prophets, especially Amos, for a call for social justice to the poor and a denunciation of the wealthy rulers.)

The Dinner Party

A Parable in the Form of a Dramatic Duet

SETTING: *Two men servants, dressed in formal wear, are on stage. (If formal wear is not available, dark blue or black suits with white shirts and black bow ties would be appropriate.) SERVANT I is obviously the head butler and SERVANT II is a servant of lesser standing. S I is pacing back and forth in front of a desk. S II is seated at the desk and is going over a list of RSVPs.*

SERVANT I: What do you mean they can't come? That's impossible! Those invitations to His Majesty's dinner party were sent out months ago.

SERVANT II: I know, but what can I do about it? They all had good excuses.

S I: I don't believe it. This is the most important event of the year, and they have the nerve to say that they can't come? Who do they think they are? What kind of excuses could they possibly have given?

S II *(defensively):* They all seemed legitimate to me, sir. *(Checking his list.)* Lord and Lady Tepid had to make settlement on their property in the country.

S I: Oh, dear, His Majesty is not going to like that. They knew well enough in advance and could have scheduled the settlement for another time.

S II: Mrs. Warm's thoroughbred just had a new foal, and she feels that she needs to be near the horses tonight.

S I: Surely she realizes that this is not just *any* dinner. She could afford to be away from her animals for a short time.

S II: Those are only two of the guests invited, but most of the responses were in that vein. Oh, yes, the Lukes can't come because they were just married. They felt certain that His Majesty would understand.

S I: How many responses did you get so far?

S II: All one hundred of them, sir.

S I *(pulling at his hair):* I *don't* believe this! You mean *NO* one is coming?

S II: That's right, sir.

S I: I don't know what to tell him. What do you suggest, Smythe?

S II *(standing and coming out from behind desk):* I certainly don't know, sir. That's not my responsibility, thank goodness. I just do my job as best I can.

S I *(regaining control of himself):* Of course, you do. I didn't mean to burden you with my problems. I'll just have to speak to His Majesty myself. Wait for me here. *(He brushes imaginary dust from his suit, straightens his tie, pauses for a deep breath, and walks as though about to meet a king. Exits stage right.)*

(S II brings chair around from behind desk. He sits, looks at his watch frequently, and waits impatiently. When S I enters, he rises quickly in deference.)

S I *(enters slowly, shaking his head in disbelief):* If I hadn't been there, I wouldn't have believed it.

S II *(goes to him):* What happened? You look stunned.

S I: I guess that's what I am. A good word for it, Smythe—stunned.

S II: But, sir, what happened when you told him no one was coming to his dinner party?

S I: He laughed!

S II: He laughed? He hadn't been drinking, had he, sir?

S I *(indignantly):* Of course not! I tell you, he just laughed.

S II: *Then* what did he do? Surely he did more than laugh.

S I: Well, that's the curious thing. It was only a soft laugh. Then he seemed to become thoughtful and a little angry. He looked into space for some time. Then, as though waking from a dream, he said, "Go out into the streets and alleys of the town, and bring here the poor and crippled and blind and lame. Tell them all to come inside so that my house may be full."

S II: Are you going to do it?

S I: Absolutely! I'm going to do it; and you are going to help me.

S II: Me?

S I: That's right, Smythe—YOU! Now come along; we have a lot of work to do.

(They come downstage and move among the audience. They stop, shake hands with members of the audience, speaking to each person they meet.)*

S I and S II: Our Master would like you to come to his banquet tonight. Everything is

95

ready. He is waiting for you. All you need
to do is come.

*(When they have each spoken to several people,
they exit through the back of the auditorium.)*

—*blackout*—

* Effective use of the voices may be made by S
II *echoing* each statement made by S I.

Probes

1. Are there any legitimate excuses for not answering God's invitation for
full discipleship in God's kingdom?

2. Discuss the modern theological concept that "God is on the side of the
poor." Is this a valid biblical idea? (See the prophets, especially Amos, for a
call for social justice to the poor and a denunciation of the wealthy rulers.)

The Dinner Party

A Parable in the Form of a Dramatic Duet

SETTING: *Two men servants, dressed in formal wear, are on stage. (If formal wear is not available, dark blue or black suits with white shirts and black bow ties would be appropriate.) SERVANT I is obviously the head butler and SERVANT II is a servant of lesser standing. S I is pacing back and forth in front of a desk. S II is seated at the desk and is going over a list of RSVPs.*

SERVANT I: What do you mean they can't come? That's impossible! Those invitations to His Majesty's dinner party were sent out months ago.

SERVANT II: I know, but what can I do about it? They all had good excuses.

S I: I don't believe it. This is the most important event of the year, and they have the nerve to say that they can't come? Who do they think they are? What kind of excuses could they possibly have given?

S II *(defensively)*: They all seemed legitimate to me, sir. *(Checking his list.)* Lord and Lady Tepid had to make settlement on their property in the country.

S I: Oh, dear, His Majesty is not going to like that. They knew well enough in advance and could have scheduled the settlement for another time.

S II: Mrs. Warm's thoroughbred just had a new foal, and she feels that she needs to be near the horses tonight.

S I: Surely she realizes that this is not just *any* dinner. She could afford to be away from her animals for a short time.

S II: Those are only two of the guests invited, but most of the responses were in that vein. Oh, yes, the Lukes can't come because they were just married. They felt certain that His Majesty would understand.

S I: How many responses did you get so far?

S II: All one hundred of them, sir.

S I *(pulling at his hair)*: I *don't* believe this! You mean *NO* one is coming?

S II: That's right, sir.

S I: I don't know what to tell him. What do you suggest, Smythe?

S II *(standing and coming out from behind the desk)*: I certainly don't know, sir. That's not my responsibility, thank goodness. I just do my job as best I can.

S I *(regaining control of himself)*: Of course, you do. I didn't mean to burden you with my problems. I'll just have to speak to His Majesty myself. Wait for me here. *(He brushes imaginary dust from his suit, straightens his tie, pauses for a deep breath, and walks as though about to meet a king. Exits stage right.)*

(S II brings chair around from behind desk. He sits, looks at his watch frequently, and waits impatiently. When S I enters, he rises quickly in deference.)

S I *(enters slowly, shaking his head in disbelief)*: If I hadn't been there, I wouldn't have believed it.

S II *(goes to him)*: What happened? You look stunned.

S I: I guess that's what I am. A good word for it, Smythe—stunned.

S II: But, sir, what happened when you told him no one was coming to his dinner party?

S I: He laughed!

S II: He laughed? He hadn't been drinking, had he, sir?

S I *(indignantly)*: Of course not! I tell you, he just laughed.

S II: *Then* what did he do? Surely he did more than laugh.

S I: Well, that's the curious thing. It was only a soft laugh. Then he seemed to become thoughtful and a little angry. He looked into space for some time. Then, as though waking from a dream, he said, "Go out into the streets and alleys of the town, and bring here the poor and crippled and blind and lame. Tell them all to come inside so that my house may be full."

S II: Are you going to do it?

S I: Absolutely! I'm going to do it; and you are going to help me.

S II: Me?

S I: That's right, Smythe—YOU! Now come along; we have a lot of work to do.

(They come downstage and move among the audience. They stop, shake hands with members of the audience, speaking to each person they meet.)*

S I and S II: Our Master would like you to come to his banquet tonight. Everything is

ready. He is waiting for you. All you need ——
to do is come.

(When they have each spoken to several people, they exit through the back of the auditorium.)

—*blackout*—

* Effective use of the voices may be made by S
II *echoing* each statement made by S I.

Probes

1. Are there any legitimate excuses for not answering God's invitation for full discipleship in God's kingdom?

2. Discuss the modern theological concept that "God is on the side of the poor." Is this a valid biblical idea? (See the prophets, especially Amos, for a call for social justice to the poor and a denunciation of the wealthy rulers.)

The Beginning

A Stinger in the Form of a Dramatic Duet

SETTING: *Two persons are seated back to back on a bare stage.*

VOICE 1 *(loud yawn):* Ah, well, I guess I should get up. It's getting late, and I have a lot to do.

VOICE 2 *(unenthusiastically):* Yeah, me too. *(Doesn't move.)*

VOICE 1: Think it'll rain today?

VOICE 2: Nah, report said sunny today.

VOICE 1: Good. I've got a lot to do today, and rain would only make it uncomfortable.

VOICE 2: Yeah, rain would be no good. *(Pause.)* You know what?

VOICE 1: What? *(Still not turning around.)*

VOICE 2: I can't remember what it was I was supposed to do today. I think it was something important, but I can't remember what it was or why it was important.

VOICE 1 *(a little angry):* Yes, it was important. You are supposed to be helping *me.*

VOICE 2: That's right. Well, that's a relief. At least now I know what it is I'm supposed to be doing.

VOICE 1: Are you ready then?

VOICE 2: No, I still have to put on my shoes.

VOICE 1: Well, do it, stupid! I don't have all day.

VOICE 2 *(putting on shoes):* You don't have to get nasty. *(Takes some time and makes great effort and mutterings while putting on shoes.)* There, I'm ready. *(Quiet—neither move.)*

VOICE 1 *(loud yawn):* Ah, well, I guess I should get up. It's getting late and I have a lot to do. *(Still leaning on back of VOICE 2.)*

VOICE 2: Yeah, me too. *(Pause.)* Hey, just what am I supposed to be helping you do, anyway?

VOICE 1 *(finally turning):* Boy, are you dumb! The boss told us to tell everyone we see the Good News of the age.

VOICE 2: Oh, yeah, go tell everyone we see *(Short pause.)* what Good News?

VOICE 1: *The* Good News.

VOICE 2: So? What is it?

VOICE 1: What's what? Will you make sense?

VOICE 2: What's the Good News we're supposed to tell everyone we see?

VOICE 1: *(turning to VOICE 2):* I already told you.

VOICE 2: No, you didn't.

VOICE 1: I did so!

VOICE 2 *(yelling):* But I don't know what you are talking about!

VOICE 1: Then why should I bother? Even if I gave you a long speech, you wouldn't know what I was talking about. Why don't you just leave me alone? *(Turns from VOICE 2. There is a long, sullen pause. They return to original positions leaning against each other.)* Look, it's getting late. I'd better get up. I've got a lot to do.

VOICE 2: Yeah, me too.

(They slide down to the floor, lying with their heads together, though still facing in opposite directions.)

—curtain—

Probes

1. To what extent do the two participants express the attitude of the modern church? Does the whole church or simply do some church members hold this attitude?

2. Is the work of evangelism the job only of pastors and missionaries, or is it the responsibility of every believer?

3. Is the reluctance to witness based on the lack of knowledge of the Good News or of how to express it? Do you think the participants would be reluctant if the news they had was a bit of gossip or a fresh rumor?

The Beginning
A Stinger in the Form of a Dramatic Duet

SETTING: *Two persons are seated back to back on a bare stage.*

VOICE 1 *(loud yawn):* Ah, well, I guess I should get up. It's getting late, and I have a lot to do.

VOICE 2 *(unenthusiastically):* Yeah, me too. *(Doesn't move.)*

VOICE 1: Think it'll rain today?

VOICE 2: Nah, report said sunny today.

VOICE 1: Good. I've got a lot to do today, and rain would only make it uncomfortable.

VOICE 2: Yeah, rain would be no good. *(Pause.)* You know what?

VOICE 1: What? *(Still not turning around.)*

VOICE 2: I can't remember what it was I was supposed to do today. I think it was something important, but I can't remember what it was or why it was important.

VOICE 1 *(a little angry):* Yes, it was important. You are supposed to be helping *me.*

VOICE 2: That's right. Well, that's a relief. At least now I know what it is I'm supposed to be doing.

VOICE 1: Are you ready then?

VOICE 2: No, I still have to put on my shoes.

VOICE 1: Well, do it, stupid! I don't have all day.

VOICE 2 *(putting on shoes):* You don't have to get nasty. *(Takes some time and makes great effort and mutterings while putting on shoes.)* There, I'm ready. *(Quiet—neither move.)*

VOICE 1 *(loud yawn):* Ah, well, I guess I should get up. It's getting late and I have a lot to do. *(Still leaning on back of VOICE 2.)*

VOICE 2: Yeah, me too. *(Pause.)* Hey, just what am I supposed to be helping you do, anyway?

VOICE 1 *(finally turning):* Boy, are you dumb! The boss told us to tell everyone we see the Good News of the age.

VOICE 2: Oh, yeah, go tell everyone we see *(Short pause.)* what Good News?

VOICE 1: *The* Good News.

VOICE 2: So? What is it?

VOICE 1: What's what? Will you make sense?

VOICE 2: What's the Good News we're supposed to tell everyone we see?

VOICE 1: *(turning to VOICE 2):* I already told you.

VOICE 2: No, you didn't.

VOICE 1: I did so!

VOICE 2 *(yelling):* But I don't know what you are talking about!

VOICE 1: Then why should I bother? Even if I gave you a long speech, you wouldn't know what I was talking about. Why don't you just leave me alone? *(Turns from VOICE 2. There is a long, sullen pause. They return to original positions leaning against each other.)* Look, it's getting late. I'd better get up. I've got a lot to do.

VOICE 2: Yeah, me too.

(They slide down to the floor, lying with their heads together, though still facing in opposite directions.)

—curtain—

Probes

1. To what extent do the two participants express the attitude of the modern church? Does the whole church or simply do some church members hold this attitude?

2. Is the work of evangelism the job only of pastors and missionaries, or is it the responsibility of every believer?

3. Is the reluctance to witness based on the lack of knowledge of the Good News or of how to express it? Do you think the participants would be reluctant if the news they had was a bit of gossip or a fresh rumor?

The Beginning
A Stinger in the Form of a Dramatic Duet

SETTING: *Two persons are seated back to back on a bare stage.*

VOICE 1 *(loud yawn):* Ah, well, I guess I should get up. It's getting late, and I have a lot to do.

VOICE 2 *(unenthusiastically):* Yeah, me too. *(Doesn't move.)*

VOICE 1: Think it'll rain today?

VOICE 2: Nah, report said sunny today.

VOICE 1: Good. I've got a lot to do today, and rain would only make it uncomfortable.

VOICE 2: Yeah, rain would be no good. *(Pause.)* You know what?

VOICE 1: What? *(Still not turning around.)*

VOICE 2: I can't remember what it was I was supposed to do today. I think it was something important, but I can't remember what it was or why it was important.

VOICE 1 *(a little angry):* Yes, it was important. You are supposed to be helping *me.*

VOICE 2: That's right. Well, that's a relief. At least now I know what it is I'm supposed to be doing.

VOICE 1: Are you ready then?

VOICE 2: No, I still have to put on my shoes.

VOICE 1: Well, do it, stupid! I don't have all day.

VOICE 2 *(putting on shoes):* You don't have to get nasty. *(Takes some time and makes great effort and mutterings while putting on shoes.)* There, I'm ready. *(Quiet—neither move.)*

VOICE 1 *(loud yawn):* Ah, well, I guess I should get up. It's getting late and I have a lot to do. *(Still leaning on back of VOICE 2.)*

VOICE 2: Yeah, me too. *(Pause.)* Hey, just what am I supposed to be helping you do, anyway?

VOICE 1 *(finally turning):* Boy, are you dumb! The boss told us to tell everyone we see the Good News of the age.

VOICE 2: Oh, yeah, go tell everyone we see *(Short pause.)* what Good News?

VOICE 1: *The* Good News.

VOICE 2: So? What is it?

VOICE 1: What's what? Will you make sense?

VOICE 2: What's the Good News we're supposed to tell everyone we see?

VOICE 1: *(turning to VOICE 2):* I already told you.

VOICE 2: No, you didn't.

VOICE 1: I did so!

VOICE 2 *(yelling):* But I don't know what you are talking about!

VOICE 1: Then why should I bother? Even if I gave you a long speech, you wouldn't know what I was talking about. Why don't you just leave me alone? *(Turns from VOICE 2. There is a long, sullen pause. They return to original positions leaning against each other.)* Look, it's getting late. I'd better get up. I've got a lot to do.

VOICE 2: Yeah, me too.

(They slide down to the floor, lying with their heads together, though still facing in opposite directions.)

—curtain—

Probes

1. To what extent do the two participants express the attitude of the modern church? Does the whole church or simply do some church members hold this attitude?

2. Is the work of evangelism the job only of pastors and missionaries, or is it the responsibility of every believer?

3. Is the reluctance to witness based on the lack of knowledge of the Good News or of how to express it? Do you think the participants would be reluctant if the news they had was a bit of gossip or a fresh rumor?

Brothers

A Stinger in the Form of a Dramatic Trio

SETTING: *A living room in a modest home. A young woman is singing along with the music coming from a radio as she works cleaning the house. A man enters, slams the door shut, and, without asking the woman, turns off the radio.*

JEAN: Hey, I was listening to that program.

FRANK: It's nothing but a lot of junk; I hate it!

JEAN: What's gotten into you? You know I work best with a little music for background.

FRANK: Well, I'm home now and I want it quiet. Can't a man find a little peace in his own house?

JEAN *(concerned):* Something's wrong, Frank; I can tell. This is not like you. Are you OK?

FRANK *(pacing):* Sure, sure, good old Frank is just fine!

JEAN: Calm down, honey; you know you shouldn't get so excited. Remember your blood pressure.

FRANK *(sits down on edge of sofa):* I know I'm acting crazy, but I can't help it. I've had it up to here with that kid.

JEAN: What kid? Did something happen at work today?

FRANK: Did it ever! What would you say if I told you that Jake is back?

JEAN: I'd say that's great. I'll bet your father was happy to see him again.

FRANK *(sullen):* Oh, he was happy all right. Couldn't leave him alone. It was "My son Jake this" and "My son Jake that" and "Get a chair for good old Jake" and "Look, guys, my son is back." His *son* is back, like I haven't been here all the time. What does that make *me?*

JEAN: Come on, Frank, honey, you're not jealous . . . are you?

FRANK: Jealous has nothing to do with it! I've worked my head off for that man, and I stuck it out when things weren't going so well. What did "Good old Jake" do? Oh—he had to have his cut of the business right away—even before the old man died.

JEAN: We've been through all this before. I thought you had worked it out in your head. Your share is still in the business; so it's growing. Jake can't take that away from you.

FRANK: Sure, my share is in the business, and I work and slave for Dad, and what do I get as a reward? *(Double meaning.)* The *business!* That's what I get.

JEAN *(kindly):* Why are you so worked up? Jake came back and your father made a big fuss over him; so what?

FRANK *(exploding):* So what? *(Stands.)* After three years without sending us so much as a postcard, that rat brother of mine comes into the factory this afternoon looking like a Bowery bum—no—worse. He looked like he'd been on a bender for months. Sure—he'd been living on Easy Street and when his money runs out, what does he do? He comes begging and crawling, knowing that Dad won't be able to resist him. And what *does* Dad do? Doesn't even yell at him or cuss him out for making the family suffer all these years. Oh, no—he puts his arms around the kid, like nothing ever happened. *(Someone knocks on the door.)*

JEAN: Try to control yourself, dear; I'll see who it is. *(Goes to door. Audience cannot see who it is. She gasps.)* Oh—hello, uh, uh—do you want to come in? *(Muffled answer.)* No, it's OK. Maybe it's better this way. *(Turns to let JAKE in. His clothes are old, dirty, and disheveled. He is unshaven, but his hair is combed neatly. He looks tired and worn, and although he is a young man, he looks old. He is obviously an alcoholic.)*

FRANK *(standing):* What do *you* want? You're not getting the same treatment here that you conned Dad into giving you at the plant this afternoon. So just get out!

JEAN: Frank! Please!

JAKE: That's OK, Jean. I deserve it. I don't want to bother you, Frank. I just want to talk to you.

FRANK: I tried to talk to you before you left. The time for talk is over.

JAKE: It doesn't have to be.

FRANK: Look, I tried to get you to listen before. I begged you to talk to me for just one minute. But no—you didn't have any time for me then; you didn't want any part of what I had to say.

JAKE: I'm older now . . .

FRANK: Well, isn't that too bad? I'm older, too,

Jake—and wiser!

JAKE: Believe it or not, so am I. I learned a lot while I was gone . . .

FRANK: Sure you did. You learned how to spend a small fortune on those so-called friends of yours. You learned how to play the horses, roulette, and what else? Did you learn how to play with dope and booze and women?

JAKE: That's right. I learned all those things and more—worse things than you can imagine. I learned what it feels like to sleep in the gutter because you don't have the money for a bed in a flophouse. I learned what it's like to be hungry and to fight the dogs for the garbage that someone else throws out. *(Comes closer to FRANK.)* I learned what it's like to be without a home, without a father. *(Puts his arm on FRANK'S shoulder.)* Frank, I learned what it means to be without a brother.

FRANK *(afraid to look JAKE in the face; speaks softly; is still hurt and a little angry):* OK. So what do you want *me* to do?

JAKE: I know I hurt you and Dad, and I hurt a lot of other people, too. You were right, you know. Before I left, I didn't want you to talk to me, but I heard you. I heard you so well that when I was lying on the streets, I could hear your voice as close to me as you are now. Remember some of the things you said then?

FRANK *(turns away, visibly moved but still not yielding; sits on the sofa and puts his head in his hands; in a loud, tortured whisper):* Go away!

JAKE: I'll go away, Frank, but not until I've said all I came here to say. I know how you feel about me. Dad told me of your talk at the plant. I can't say I blame you. I'd probably feel the same way if I were you. But what I want you to know is that not only have I *changed*—a lot—but I've also come to appreciate you and Dad and all the things you do. I just want to work at the plant like any other hired hand. *(FRANK looks at him incredulously.)* Really—that's all I want—a job. At least here I'd know what I was doing. And maybe while I'm working, I can do something to make up for all the suffering I've caused you and Dad. I'm truly sorry for what I've done, and I need you to forgive me.

FRANK *(looking up at JAKE):* Me? Forgive you?

JAKE: That's right, Frank. I need *you* to forgive me. Will you? *(Extends his hand for his brother to shake.)*

First Ending

(FRANK, standing, puts his hands in his pockets. He looks carefully at JAKE.)

JEAN: Please, Frank . . .

FRANK: I don't know if I can.

JEAN: Try, Frank, try for your own sake as well as his.

FRANK *(shyly takes his brother's hand. They shake quietly, then in a burst of emotion they hug one another tightly.):* Welcome back, brother. Welcome back.

—curtain—

Second Ending

(FRANK remains seated. He looks up at his brother. He is bewildered.)

JEAN: Please, Frank . . .

FRANK: I don't know if I can.

JEAN: Try, Frank, try for your own sake as well as his.

(FRANK puts his head in his hands and silently sobs.)

—curtain—

Probes

1. Do the endings of the play reflect the spirit of the Christian gospel? How else might the play have ended?

2. Jesus' parable of the prodigal son is a story of forgiveness. Is it easier to forgive or to seek forgiveness? Why?

3. What does the play have to say about the forgiveness of God and human forgiveness?

Brothers

A Stinger in the Form of a Dramatic Trio

SETTING: *A living room in a modest home. A young woman is singing along with the music coming from a radio as she works cleaning the house. A man enters, slams the door shut, and, without asking the woman, turns off the radio.*

JEAN: Hey, I was listening to that program.

FRANK: It's nothing but a lot of junk; I hate it!

JEAN: What's gotten into you? You know I work best with a little music for background.

FRANK: Well, I'm home now and I want it quiet. Can't a man find a little peace in his own house?

JEAN *(concerned):* Something's wrong, Frank; I can tell. This is not like you. Are you OK?

FRANK *(pacing):* Sure, sure, good old Frank is just fine!

JEAN: Calm down, honey; you know you shouldn't get so excited. Remember your blood pressure.

FRANK *(sits down on edge of sofa):* I know I'm acting crazy, but I can't help it. I've had it up to here with that kid.

JEAN: What kid? Did something happen at work today?

FRANK: Did it ever! What would you say if I told you that Jake is back?

JEAN: I'd say that's great. I'll bet your father was happy to see him again.

FRANK *(sullen):* Oh, he was happy all right. Couldn't leave him alone. It was "My son Jake this" and "My son Jake that" and "Get a chair for good old Jake" and "Look, guys, my son is back." His *son* is back, like I haven't been here all the time. What does that make *me*?

JEAN: Come on, Frank, honey, you're not jealous . . . are you?

FRANK: Jealous has nothing to do with it! I've worked my head off for that man, and I stuck it out when things weren't going so well. What did "Good old Jake" do? Oh—he had to have his cut of the business right away—even before the old man died.

JEAN: We've been through all this before. I thought you had worked it out in your head. Your share is still in the business; so it's growing. Jake can't take that away from you.

FRANK: Sure, my share is in the business, and I work and slave for Dad, and what do I get as a reward? *(Double meaning.)* The *business!* That's what I get.

JEAN *(kindly):* Why are you so worked up? Jake came back and your father made a big fuss over him; so what?

FRANK *(exploding):* So what? *(Stands.)* After three years without sending us so much as a postcard, that rat brother of mine comes into the factory this afternoon looking like a Bowery bum—no—worse. He looked like he'd been on a bender for months. Sure—he'd been living on Easy Street and when his money runs out, what does he do? He comes begging and crawling, knowing that Dad won't be able to resist him. And what *does* Dad do? Doesn't even yell at him or cuss him out for making the family suffer all these years. Oh, no—he puts his arms around the kid, like nothing ever happened. *(Someone knocks on the door.)*

JEAN: Try to control yourself, dear; I'll see who it is. *(Goes to door. Audience cannot see who it is. She gasps.)* Oh—hello, uh, uh—do you want to come in? *(Muffled answer.)* No, it's OK. Maybe it's better this way. *(Turns to let JAKE in. His clothes are old, dirty, and disheveled. He is unshaven, but his hair is combed neatly. He looks tired and worn, and although he is a young man, he looks old. He is obviously an alcoholic.)*

FRANK *(standing):* What do *you* want? You're not getting the same treatment here that you conned Dad into giving you at the plant this afternoon. So just get out!

JEAN: Frank! Please!

JAKE: That's OK, Jean. I deserve it. I don't want to bother you, Frank. I just want to talk to you.

FRANK: I tried to talk to you before you left. The time for talk is over.

JAKE: It doesn't have to be.

FRANK: Look, I tried to get you to listen before. I begged you to talk to me for just one minute. But no—you didn't have any time for me then; you didn't want any part of what I had to say.

JAKE: I'm older now . . .

FRANK: Well, isn't that too bad? I'm older, too,

Jake—and wiser!

JAKE: Believe it or not, so am I. I learned a lot while I was gone . . .

FRANK: Sure you did. You learned how to spend a small fortune on those so-called friends of yours. You learned how to play the horses, roulette, and what else? Did you learn how to play with dope and booze and women?

JAKE: That's right. I learned all those things and more—worse things than you can imagine. I learned what it feels like to sleep in the gutter because you don't have the money for a bed in a flophouse. I learned what it's like to be hungry and to fight the dogs for the garbage that someone else throws out. *(Comes closer to FRANK.)* I learned what it's like to be without a home, without a father. *(Puts his arm on FRANK'S shoulder.)* Frank, I learned what it means to be without a brother.

FRANK *(afraid to look JAKE in the face; speaks softly; is still hurt and a little angry):* OK. So what do you want *me* to do?

JAKE: I know I hurt you and Dad, and I hurt a lot of other people, too. You were right, you know. Before I left, I didn't want you to talk to me, but I heard you. I heard you so well that when I was lying on the streets, I could hear your voice as close to me as you are now. Remember some of the things you said then?

FRANK *(turns away, visibly moved but still not yielding; sits on the sofa and puts his head in his hands; in a loud, tortured whisper):* Go away!

JAKE: I'll go away, Frank, but not until I've said all I came here to say. I know how you feel about me. Dad told me of your talk at the plant. I can't say I blame you. I'd probably feel the same way if I were you. But what I want you to know is that not only have I *changed*—a lot—but I've also come to appreciate you and Dad and all the things you do. I just want to work at the plant like any other hired hand. *(FRANK looks at him incredulously.)* Really—that's all I want—a job. At least here I'd know what I was doing. And maybe while I'm working, I can do something to make up for all the suffering I've caused you and Dad. I'm truly sorry for what I've done, and I need you to forgive me.

FRANK *(looking up at JAKE):* Me? Forgive you?

JAKE: That's right, Frank. I need *you* to forgive me. Will you? *(Extends his hand for his brother to shake.)*

First Ending

(FRANK, standing, puts his hands in his pockets. He looks carefully at JAKE.)

JEAN: Please, Frank . . .

FRANK: I don't know if I can.

JEAN: Try, Frank, try for your own sake as well as his.

FRANK *(shyly takes his brother's hand. They shake quietly, then in a burst of emotion they hug one another tightly.):* Welcome back, brother. Welcome back.

—curtain—

Second Ending

(FRANK remains seated. He looks up at his brother. He is bewildered.)

JEAN: Please, Frank . . .

FRANK: I don't know if I can.

JEAN: Try, Frank, try for your own sake as well as his.

(FRANK puts his head in his hands and silently sobs.)

—curtain—

Probes

1. Do the endings of the play reflect the spirit of the Christian gospel? How else might the play have ended?

2. Jesus' parable of the prodigal son is a story of forgiveness. Is it easier to forgive or to seek forgiveness? Why?

3. What does the play have to say about the forgiveness of God and human forgiveness?

Brothers

A Stinger in the Form of a Dramatic Trio

SETTING: *A living room in a modest home. A young woman is singing along with the music coming from a radio as she works cleaning the house. A man enters, slams the door shut, and, without asking the woman, turns off the radio.*

JEAN: Hey, I was listening to that program.

FRANK: It's nothing but a lot of junk; I hate it!

JEAN: What's gotten into you? You know I work best with a little music for background.

FRANK: Well, I'm home now and I want it quiet. Can't a man find a little peace in his own house?

JEAN (*concerned*): Something's wrong, Frank; I can tell. This is not like you. Are you OK?

FRANK (*pacing*): Sure, sure, good old Frank is just fine!

JEAN: Calm down, honey; you know you shouldn't get so excited. Remember your blood pressure.

FRANK (*sits down on edge of sofa*): I know I'm acting crazy, but I can't help it. I've had it up to here with that kid.

JEAN: What kid? Did something happen at work today?

FRANK: Did it ever! What would you say if I told you that Jake is back?

JEAN: I'd say that's great. I'll bet your father was happy to see him again.

FRANK (*sullen*): Oh, he was happy all right. Couldn't leave him alone. It was "My son Jake this" and "My son Jake that" and "Get a chair for good old Jake" and "Look, guys, my son is back." His *son* is back, like I haven't been here all the time. What does that make *me*?

JEAN: Come on, Frank, honey, you're not jealous . . . are you?

FRANK: Jealous has nothing to do with it! I've worked my head off for that man, and I stuck it out when things weren't going so well. What did "Good old Jake" do? Oh—he had to have his cut of the business right away—even before the old man died.

JEAN: We've been through all this before. I thought you had worked it out in your head. Your share is still in the business; so it's growing. Jake can't take that away from you.

FRANK: Sure, my share is in the business, and I work and slave for Dad, and what do I get as a reward? (*Double meaning.*) The *business!* That's what I get.

JEAN (*kindly*): Why are you so worked up? Jake came back and your father made a big fuss over him; so what?

FRANK (*exploding*): So what? (*Stands.*) After three years without sending us so much as a postcard, that rat brother of mine comes into the factory this afternoon looking like a Bowery bum—no—worse. He looked like he'd been on a bender for months. Sure— he'd been living on Easy Street and when his money runs out, what does he do? He comes begging and crawling, knowing that Dad won't be able to resist him. And what *does* Dad do? Doesn't even yell at him or cuss him out for making the family suffer all these years. Oh, no—he puts his arms around the kid, like nothing ever happened. (*Someone knocks on the door.*)

JEAN: Try to control yourself, dear; I'll see who it is. (*Goes to door. Audience cannot see who it is. She gasps.*) Oh—hello, uh, uh—do you want to come in? (*Muffled answer.*) No, it's OK. Maybe it's better this way. (*Turns to let JAKE in. His clothes are old, dirty, and disheveled. He is unshaven, but his hair is combed neatly. He looks tired and worn, and although he is a young man, he looks old. He is obviously an alcoholic.*)

FRANK (*standing*): What do *you* want? You're not getting the same treatment here that you conned Dad into giving you at the plant this afternoon. So just get out!

JEAN: Frank! Please!

JAKE: That's OK, Jean. I deserve it. I don't want to bother you, Frank. I just want to talk to you.

FRANK: I tried to talk to you before you left. The time for talk is over.

JAKE: It doesn't have to be.

FRANK: Look, I tried to get you to listen before. I begged you to talk to me for just one minute. But no—you didn't have any time for me then; you didn't want any part of what I had to say.

JAKE: I'm older now . . .

FRANK: Well, isn't that too bad? I'm older, too,

Jake—and wiser!

JAKE: Believe it or not, so am I. I learned a lot while I was gone . . .

FRANK: Sure you did. You learned how to spend a small fortune on those so-called friends of yours. You learned how to play the horses, roulette, and what else? Did you learn how to play with dope and booze and women?

JAKE: That's right. I learned all those things and more—worse things than you can imagine. I learned what it feels like to sleep in the gutter because you don't have the money for a bed in a flophouse. I learned what it's like to be hungry and to fight the dogs for the garbage that someone else throws out. *(Comes closer to FRANK.)* I learned what it's like to be without a home, without a father. *(Puts his arm on FRANK'S shoulder.)* Frank, I learned what it means to be without a brother.

FRANK *(afraid to look JAKE in the face; speaks softly; is still hurt and a little angry)*: OK. So what do you want *me* to do?

JAKE: I know I hurt you and Dad, and I hurt a lot of other people, too. You were right, you know. Before I left, I didn't want you to talk to me, but I heard you. I heard you so well that when I was lying on the streets, I could hear your voice as close to me as you are now. Remember some of the things you said then?

FRANK *(turns away, visibly moved but still not yielding; sits on the sofa and puts his head in his hands; in a loud, tortured whisper)*: Go away!

JAKE: I'll go away, Frank, but not until I've said all I came here to say. I know how you feel about me. Dad told me of your talk at the plant. I can't say I blame you. I'd probably feel the same way if I were you. But what I want you to know is that not only have I *changed*—a lot—but I've also come to appreciate you and Dad and all the things you do. I just want to work at the plant like any other hired hand. *(FRANK looks at him incredulously.)* Really—that's all I want—a job. At least here I'd know what I was doing. And maybe while I'm working, I can do something to make up for all the suffering I've caused you and Dad. I'm truly sorry for what I've done, and I need you to forgive me.

FRANK *(looking up at JAKE)*: Me? Forgive you?

JAKE: That's right, Frank. I need *you* to forgive me. Will you? *(Extends his hand for his brother to shake.)*

First Ending

(FRANK, standing, puts his hands in his pockets. He looks carefully at JAKE.)

JEAN: Please, Frank . . .

FRANK: I don't know if I can.

JEAN: Try, Frank, try for your own sake as well as his.

FRANK *(shyly takes his brother's hand. They shake quietly, then in a burst of emotion they hug one another tightly.)*: Welcome back, brother. Welcome back.

—curtain—

Second Ending

(FRANK remains seated. He looks up at his brother. He is bewildered.)

JEAN: Please, Frank . . .

FRANK: I don't know if I can.

JEAN: Try, Frank, try for your own sake as well as his.

(FRANK puts his head in his hands and silently sobs.)

—curtain—

Probes

1. Do the endings of the play reflect the spirit of the Christian gospel? How else might the play have ended?

2. Jesus' parable of the prodigal son is a story of forgiveness. Is it easier to forgive or to seek forgiveness? Why?

3. What does the play have to say about the forgiveness of God and human forgiveness?

110

Good News

A Dramatic Duet

SETTING: *Any room in a middle-class home.*

JOAN *(enters room, calling loudly):* Tommie! *(No answer.)* Hey, Tommie, where are you?

TOMMIE *(offstage; irritated):* Quit hollerin', will ya? I'm down here in the basement. What do you want?

JOAN *(taking off coat and putting down purse):* Can you come up here a minute? I've got some great news!

TOMMIE: Later, I'm busy.

JOAN: But it's important. Come on, please?

TOMMIE *(nearer):* OK, OK. But you'll have to make it short. I'm right in the middle of something. *(Now close to JOAN.)* So—what *is* it?

JOAN: It's just something that happened to me today while I was at Bible study class at Ethel's. Come on, sit down. I can't talk to you when you're standing up like that.

TOMMIE *(angrily sits):* Man, this had better be good, 'cause I just left a pile of work down there, and I haven't got all day to sit around and chat about your coffee klatches.

JOAN: Look, I'm trying to tell you something that's very important to me, and you're making it very hard.

TOMMIE: Well, I asked you to wait until later.

JOAN: But I told you this is important. You don't just wait until later when it's something important.

TOMMIE *(angrily):* All right; so I'm listening.

JOAN: No, you're not! It's not that easy to tell you right out what I have to tell you. *(Almost in tears.)* After all, I came in here all excited about some GOOD NEWS I wanted to share, and you don't even want to hear it.

TOMMIE: For Pete's sake, Joan, I came up here, didn't I?

JOAN: Yes, but look at your attitude. You take all the fun out of it for me.

TOMMIE *(standing):* That does it! I'm going back.

JOAN *(grabs him by the sleeve):* Look, I've got this GOOD NEWS to tell you, and you're going to listen whether you like it or not.

TOMMIE *(yelling):* Well, tell me already!!!!

JOAN *(looks up at him):* Oh, oh *(Gives up.),* FORGET IT! *(As she says this, she hits him on the arm and stalks out.)*

Probes

1. Does modern family life basically consist of each individual doing as he or she pleases with little regard for the feelings or interests of others?

2. What implications does the problem in the first question have for evangelism? Are there some times, places, and methods that are not proper for telling the Good News?

3. For further insight and discussion, two appropriate people from the audience may be asked to role-play the same situation to discover other possible outcomes.

Good News
A Dramatic Duet

SETTING: *Any room in a middle-class home.*

JOAN *(enters room, calling loudly):* Tommie! *(No answer.)* Hey, Tommie, where are you?

TOMMIE *(offstage; irritated):* Quit hollerin', will ya? I'm down here in the basement. What do you want?

JOAN *(taking off coat and putting down purse):* Can you come up here a minute? I've got some great news!

TOMMIE: Later, I'm busy.

JOAN: But it's important. Come on, please?

TOMMIE *(nearer):* OK, OK. But you'll have to make it short. I'm right in the middle of something. *(Now close to JOAN.)* So—what *is* it?

JOAN: It's just something that happened to me today while I was at Bible study class at Ethel's. Come on, sit down. I can't talk to you when you're standing up like that.

TOMMIE *(angrily sits):* Man, this had better be good, 'cause I just left a pile of work down there, and I haven't got all day to sit around and chat about your coffee klatches.

JOAN: Look, I'm trying to tell you something that's very important to me, and you're making it very hard.

TOMMIE: Well, I asked you to wait until later.

JOAN: But I told you this is important. You don't just wait until later when it's something important.

TOMMIE *(angrily):* All right; so I'm listening.

JOAN: No, you're not! It's not that easy to tell you right out what I have to tell you. *(Almost in tears.)* After all, I came in here all excited about some GOOD NEWS I wanted to share, and you don't even want to hear it.

TOMMIE: For Pete's sake, Joan, I came up here, didn't I?

JOAN: Yes, but look at your attitude. You take all the fun out of it for me.

TOMMIE *(standing):* That does it! I'm going back.

JOAN *(grabs him by the sleeve):* Look, I've got this GOOD NEWS to tell you, and you're going to listen whether you like it or not.

TOMMIE *(yelling):* Well, tell me already!!!!

JOAN *(looks up at him):* Oh, oh *(Gives up.)*, FORGET IT! *(As she says this, she hits him on the arm and stalks out.)*

Probes

1. Does modern family life basically consist of each individual doing as he or she pleases with little regard for the feelings or interests of others?

2. What implications does the problem in the first question have for evangelism? Are there some times, places, and methods that are not proper for telling the Good News?

3. For further insight and discussion, two appropriate people from the audience may be asked to role-play the same situation to discover other possible outcomes.

Good News
A Dramatic Duet

SETTING: *Any room in a middle-class home.*

JOAN *(enters room, calling loudly):* Tommie! *(No answer.)* Hey, Tommie, where are you?

TOMMIE *(offstage; irritated):* Quit hollerin', will ya? I'm down here in the basement. What do you want?

JOAN *(taking off coat and putting down purse):* Can you come up here a minute? I've got some great news!

TOMMIE: Later, I'm busy.

JOAN: But it's important. Come on, please?

TOMMIE *(nearer):* OK, OK. But you'll have to make it short. I'm right in the middle of something. *(Now close to JOAN.)* So—what *is* it?

JOAN: It's just something that happened to me today while I was at Bible study class at Ethel's. Come on, sit down. I can't talk to you when you're standing up like that.

TOMMIE *(angrily sits):* Man, this had better be good, 'cause I just left a pile of work down there, and I haven't got all day to sit around and chat about your coffee klatches.

JOAN: Look, I'm trying to tell you something that's very important to me, and you're making it very hard.

TOMMIE: Well, I asked you to wait until later.

JOAN: But I told you this is important. You don't just wait until later when it's something important.

TOMMIE *(angrily):* All right; so I'm listening.

JOAN: No, you're not! It's not that easy to tell you right out what I have to tell you. *(Almost in tears.)* After all, I came in here all excited about some GOOD NEWS I wanted to share, and you don't even want to hear it.

TOMMIE: For Pete's sake, Joan, I came up here, didn't I?

JOAN: Yes, but look at your attitude. You take all the fun out of it for me.

TOMMIE *(standing):* That does it! I'm going back.

JOAN *(grabs him by the sleeve):* Look, I've got this GOOD NEWS to tell you, and you're going to listen whether you like it or not.

TOMMIE *(yelling):* Well, tell me already!!!!

JOAN *(looks up at him):* Oh, oh *(Gives up.),* FORGET IT! *(As she says this, she hits him on the arm and stalks out.)*

Probes

1. Does modern family life basically consist of each individual doing as he or she pleases with little regard for the feelings or interests of others?

2. What implications does the problem in the first question have for evangelism? Are there some times, places, and methods that are not proper for telling the Good News?

3. For further insight and discussion, two appropriate people from the audience may be asked to role-play the same situation to discover other possible outcomes.

The Search

A Stinger in the Form of a Dramatic Duet

SETTING: *Complete darkness. Two figures stealthily enter the room. They are dressed completely in black so as to blend with the darkness. VOICE 1 is holding a flashlight. VOICE 2 stumbles.*

VOICE 1: Shhhh, don't make so much noise.

VOICE 2: I can't help it; I can't see. Hold that flashlight higher.

VOICE 1: I'm doing the best I can. If I hold it any higher, they'll see us from the outside.

VOICE 2: Then hold it more to the side. You're blocking all the light.

VOICE 1 *(moving light over):* Is this better?

VOICE 2: A little.

(The two move slowly toward downstage left.)

VOICE 2: Do you see anything yet?

VOICE 1: No, but I think I saw him put it over here this morning.

VOICE 2 *(startled):* What's that?

VOICE 1 *(moving light crazily):* What? Where?

VOICE 2: There—over to your right. I thought I saw something.

VOICE 1 *(moving light to right):* There's nothing there; just some empty boxes.

VOICE 2 *(disappointed):* Oh, dear, I thought we'd found it. *(Pause.)* Is this going to take much longer?

VOICE 1: I hope not. I thought we'd surely have found it by now.

VOICE 2 *(petulantly, sitting on floor):* I came along 'cause you said it would only take a few minutes.

VOICE 1: Since they're always showing it off, I thought finding it would be a cinch. I didn't expect them to hide it when they weren't using it.

VOICE 2: Shows you can't trust anyone these days.

VOICE 1: Maybe it's on the other side of the room. *(As he turns and moves across stage, he trips over VOICE 2 and falls to floor.)* OUCH! *(They tussle together in an effort to get up.)* What are you doing sitting in the middle of the floor? You could have killed me.

VOICE 2: You have the flashlight. Why don't you use it instead of kicking a person half to death?

VOICE 1: You were supposed to be behind me.

VOICE 2: I was.

VOICE 1: I meant standing up, not lying down.

VOICE 2 *(standing up ready to fight):* Just who do you think you are, bossing me around?

VOICE 1 *(moving to stage right):* We're wasting time arguing. Let's look on this side. *(Shines flashlight all over bare wall.)* Nothing!

VOICE 2: I told you it was useless; let's go home.

VOICE 1: I'm sure I saw it here. It's got to be here; there's nowhere else to look.

VOICE 2: What I don't understand is why you have to have this right now. Can't you go out and get some of your own?

VOICE 1: Impossible! You can't buy this at a store; you can only get it from someone else.

VOICE 2: That sounds crazy. How did the *first* guy get it?

VOICE 1: It was given to him.

VOICE 2: Then why don't you get someone to give *you* some? I don't understand why you have to come in the dead of night to steal something most people give away.

VOICE 1: But that's the problem. People just aren't sharing it anymore. I guess some of them are afraid that if they give too much away, they'll be left without any for themselves.

VOICE 2: So they hoard it?

VOICE 1: That's right. *Some* people keep it hidden for so long they forget where they put it. Then you have a real problem.

VOICE 2: Is it so important? Couldn't you get along without it?

VOICE 1: Well, I guess you could, but you wouldn't be very happy. I do so want to be happy. *(Moves flashlight so it picks up box with markings in big black letters—LOVE.)* I think I see it! *(VOICES 1 and 2 move to where the boxes are. VOICE 1 shines light so that audience can clearly see the word.)*

VOICE 2: Is this what you have been so anxious to get?

VOICE 1 *(brightly):* This is it!!

VOICE 2: Looks like you made a lot of fuss over nothing.

VOICE 1: It means an awful lot to those who need it. *(Loud footsteps are heard.)* Shhh, I think I hear someone coming.

VOICE 2: I'm getting out of here.

VOICE 1 (trying to lift box marked LOVE): Wait a minute. Help me with this, I can't carry it alone.

VOICE 2: Sorry, buddy; I'm not getting in trouble over a silly old box. (Runs out stage left. Sounds of footsteps get louder.)

VOICE 1 (shines flashlight on audience): Is there anyone here who can help me?

—blackout—

Probes

1. Discuss the statement "Love is not love when it is hidden; love becomes love only when given."

2. Can love be taken, even though it is not freely given?

3. Do many today really feel a strong need to give love? What kind of love? Is love a major value among many competing values in the modern day?

4. Discuss the Christian nature of love as found in the life and teachings of Jesus and in 1 Corinthians 13.

The Search

A Stinger in the Form of a Dramatic Duet

SETTING: *Complete darkness. Two figures stealthily enter the room. They are dressed completely in black so as to blend with the darkness. VOICE 1 is holding a flashlight. VOICE 2 stumbles.*

VOICE 1: Shhhh, don't make so much noise.

VOICE 2: I can't help it; I can't see. Hold that flashlight higher.

VOICE 1: I'm doing the best I can. If I hold it any higher, they'll see us from the outside.

VOICE 2: Then hold it more to the side. You're blocking all the light.

VOICE 1 *(moving light over):* Is this better?

VOICE 2: A little.

(The two move slowly toward downstage left.)

VOICE 2: Do you see anything yet?

VOICE 1: No, but I think I saw him put it over here this morning.

VOICE 2 *(startled):* What's that?

VOICE 1 *(moving light crazily):* What? Where?

VOICE 2: There—over to your right. I thought I saw something.

VOICE 1 *(moving light to right):* There's nothing there; just some empty boxes.

VOICE 2 *(disappointed):* Oh, dear, I thought we'd found it. *(Pause.)* Is this going to take much longer?

VOICE 1: I hope not. I thought we'd surely have found it by now.

VOICE 2 *(petulantly, sitting on floor):* I came along 'cause you said it would only take a few minutes.

VOICE 1: Since they're always showing it off, I thought finding it would be a cinch. I didn't expect them to hide it when they weren't using it.

VOICE 2: Shows you can't trust anyone these days.

VOICE 1: Maybe it's on the other side of the room. *(As he turns and moves across stage, he trips over VOICE 2 and falls to floor.)* OUCH! *(They tussle together in an effort to get up.)* What are you doing sitting in the middle of the floor? You could have killed me.

VOICE 2: You have the flashlight. Why don't you use it instead of kicking a person half to death?

VOICE 1: You were supposed to be behind me.

VOICE 2: I was.

VOICE 1: I meant standing up, not lying down.

VOICE 2 *(standing up ready to fight):* Just who do you think you are, bossing me around?

VOICE 1 *(moving to stage right):* We're wasting time arguing. Let's look on this side. *(Shines flashlight all over bare wall.)* Nothing!

VOICE 2: I told you it was useless; let's go home.

VOICE 1: I'm sure I saw it here. It's got to be here; there's nowhere else to look.

VOICE 2: What I don't understand is why you have to have this right now. Can't you go out and get some of your own?

VOICE 1: Impossible! You can't buy this at a store; you can only get it from someone else.

VOICE 2: That sounds crazy. How did the *first* guy get it?

VOICE 1: It was given to him.

VOICE 2: Then why don't you get someone to give *you* some? I don't understand why you have to come in the dead of night to steal something most people give away.

VOICE 1: But that's the problem. People just aren't sharing it anymore. I guess some of them are afraid that if they give too much away, they'll be left without any for themselves.

VOICE 2: So they hoard it?

VOICE 1: That's right. *Some* people keep it hidden for so long they forget where they put it. Then you have a real problem.

VOICE 2: Is it so important? Couldn't you get along without it?

VOICE 1: Well, I guess you could, but you wouldn't be very happy. I do so want to be happy. *(Moves flashlight so it picks up box with markings in big black letters—LOVE.)* I think I see it! *(VOICES 1 and 2 move to where the boxes are. VOICE 1 shines light so that audience can clearly see the word.)*

VOICE 2: Is this what you have been so anxious to get?

VOICE 1 *(brightly):* This is it!!

VOICE 2: Looks like you made a lot of fuss over nothing.

VOICE 1: It means an awful lot to those who need it. *(Loud footsteps are heard.)* Shhh, I think I hear someone coming.

119

VOICE 2: I'm getting out of here.

VOICE 1 (trying to lift box marked LOVE): Wait a minute. Help me with this, I can't carry it alone.

VOICE 2: Sorry, buddy; I'm not getting in trouble over a silly old box. (Runs out stage left.

Sounds of footsteps get louder.)

VOICE 1 (shines flashlight on audience): Is there anyone here who can help me?

—blackout—

Probes

1. Discuss the statement "Love is not love when it is hidden; love becomes love only when given."

2. Can love be taken, even though it is not freely given?

3. Do many today really feel a strong need to give love? What kind of love? Is love a major value among many competing values in the modern day?

4. Discuss the Christian nature of love as found in the life and teachings of Jesus and in 1 Corinthians 13.

The Search

A Stinger in the Form of a Dramatic Duet

SETTING: *Complete darkness. Two figures stealthily enter the room. They are dressed completely in black so as to blend with the darkness. VOICE 1 is holding a flashlight. VOICE 2 stumbles.*

VOICE 1: Shhhh, don't make so much noise.

VOICE 2: I can't help it; I can't see. Hold that flashlight higher.

VOICE 1: I'm doing the best I can. If I hold it any higher, they'll see us from the outside.

VOICE 2: Then hold it more to the side. You're blocking all the light.

VOICE 1 *(moving light over)*: Is this better?

VOICE 2: A little.

(The two move slowly toward downstage left.)

VOICE 2: Do you see anything yet?

VOICE 1: No, but I think I saw him put it over here this morning.

VOICE 2 *(startled)*: What's that?

VOICE 1 *(moving light crazily)*: What? Where?

VOICE 2: There—over to your right. I thought I saw something.

VOICE 1 *(moving light to right)*: There's nothing there; just some empty boxes.

VOICE 2 *(disappointed)*: Oh, dear, I thought we'd found it. *(Pause.)* Is this going to take much longer?

VOICE 1: I hope not. I thought we'd surely have found it by now.

VOICE 2 *(petulantly, sitting on floor)*: I came along 'cause you said it would only take a few minutes.

VOICE 1: Since they're always showing it off, I thought finding it would be a cinch. I didn't expect them to hide it when they weren't using it.

VOICE 2: Shows you can't trust anyone these days.

VOICE 1: Maybe it's on the other side of the room. *(As he turns and moves across stage, he trips over VOICE 2 and falls to floor.)* OUCH! *(They tussle together in an effort to get up.)* What are you doing sitting in the middle of the floor? You could have killed me.

VOICE 2: You have the flashlight. Why don't you use it instead of kicking a person half to death?

VOICE 1: You were supposed to be behind me.

VOICE 2: I was.

VOICE 1: I meant standing up, not lying down.

VOICE 2 *(standing up ready to fight)*: Just who do you think you are, bossing me around?

VOICE 1 *(moving to stage right)*: We're wasting time arguing. Let's look on this side. *(Shines flashlight all over bare wall.)* Nothing!

VOICE 2: I told you it was useless; let's go home.

VOICE 1: I'm sure I saw it here. It's got to be here; there's nowhere else to look.

VOICE 2: What I don't understand is why you have to have this right now. Can't you go out and get some of your own?

VOICE 1: Impossible! You can't buy this at a store; you can only get it from someone else.

VOICE 2: That sounds crazy. How did the *first* guy get it?

VOICE 1: It was given to him.

VOICE 2: Then why don't you get someone to give *you* some? I don't understand why you have to come in the dead of night to steal something most people give away.

VOICE 1: But that's the problem. People just aren't sharing it anymore. I guess some of them are afraid that if they give too much away, they'll be left without any for themselves.

VOICE 2: So they hoard it?

VOICE 1: That's right. *Some* people keep it hidden for so long they forget where they put it. Then you have a real problem.

VOICE 2: Is it so important? Couldn't you get along without it?

VOICE 1: Well, I guess you could, but you wouldn't be very happy. I do so want to be happy. *(Moves flashlight so it picks up box with markings in big black letters—LOVE.)* I think I see it! *(VOICES 1 and 2 move to where the boxes are. VOICE 1 shines light so that audience can clearly see the word.)*

VOICE 2: Is this what you have been so anxious to get?

VOICE 1 *(brightly)*: This is it!!

VOICE 2: Looks like you made a lot of fuss over nothing.

VOICE 1: It means an awful lot to those who need it. *(Loud footsteps are heard.)* Shhh, I think I hear someone coming.

VOICE 2: I'm getting out of here.

VOICE 1 (trying to lift box marked LOVE): Wait a minute. Help me with this, I can't carry it alone.

VOICE 2: Sorry, buddy; I'm not getting in trouble over a silly old box. (Runs out stage left. Sounds of footsteps get louder.)

VOICE 1 (shines flashlight on audience): Is there anyone here who can help me?

—blackout—

Probes

1. Discuss the statement "Love is not love when it is hidden; love becomes love only when given."

2. Can love be taken, even though it is not freely given?

3. Do many today really feel a strong need to give love? What kind of love? Is love a major value among many competing values in the modern day?

4. Discuss the Christian nature of love as found in the life and teachings of Jesus and in 1 Corinthians 13.

what are some characteristic of love 4-8
- when is it hard to love
   people we feel uncomfortable w/
   - aged, women, men, blacks, poor, rich Hispanic,
   Disable, conservative, liberal, senile,
   People who are or who think differently

The Ardent One

A Stinger in the Form of a Dramatic Duet

SETTING: *A man is seated at a table and is writing by candlelight. He does not notice his son, who is about twenty-five years old, quietly enter the room.*

SON *(softly):* Father, may I come in?

FATHER *(looking up):* What? Oh, yes, of course, come in. I'm almost finished.

SON: I'm sorry for interrupting you, but I have something I'd like to discuss with you.

FATHER: Certainly, son; I was just going over the accounts. If it's important, they can wait. Why don't you sit down by me? My eyes are not as sharp as they used to be. *(Rubs eyes.)* So, what is it?

SON *(sitting):* Remember when I told you last week that I had the feeling that soon I was going to meet the man who will solve all of Israel's problems?

FATHER: Yes, I do. But I also remember that I told you that one man alone couldn't do it.

SON: I agree. But the man I'm talking about will have helpers and counselors. He won't have to do it alone.

FATHER: That would be true of anyone. Even Caesar has counselors.

SON *(trying to contain his excitement):* Only this man is greater than Caesar.

FATHER: Greater than Caesar? Where would you find such a man?

SON: Last week Simon Bar-Jonas insisted that this man had made fish practically jump into the net, when only minutes before he himself had been unable to catch any at all. Naturally I didn't put much stock in his story, although his description of the man was intriguing. Then a few days later I heard the entire village of Cana telling how he had changed water into wine at Jonah's wedding feast. This *must* be the One we have been waiting for.

FATHER: When will you learn? *(Stands and walks away from SON.)* Are you so eager to have the Messiah come that you jump at conclusions on such flimsy evidence? *(Turns to face SON.)* You know that many prophets have come calling themselves the Mes-

siah and that they also work great wonders. What makes you think this one is different from all the others?

SON *(exploding):* Because I've met him, Father, and he *is* different. He heals the sick and helps the poor, and there is something very special about him. I don't know if I can put it into words, but he has a power that makes people listen to him. He seemed to know me long before I spoke to him. *(Walks up to FATHER, trying to make him understand.)* He never does any of the tricks all the others do. He works miracles only to help someone, and then he tells those he healed not to tell anyone about it. Does that sound like a false prophet to you?

FATHER: I don't know, son. So many have come, and we have waited so patiently. Something has to happen soon. Our people cannot live like this forever.

SON: Exactly! It's time we got together behind one man and brought the kingdom of Israel back to the glory God meant it to have.

FATHER *(kindly):* You're such a zealot. Always looking for a leader to follow. You remind me of myself when I was young. I envy you. I wish I still had the strength and faith to search for the Messiah.

SON: That's all I wanted to hear. You think I'm right, don't you?

FATHER: I don't know if you're right, but I do think you need to follow your own best instincts and find out.

SON: Good! I'm going to see if I can find him again. I'll tell him I want to be his disciple. John the Baptist's disciples are all going to him. He's a great teacher. Father, I know this is the start of the new kingdom.

FATHER: I hope you're right, son.

SON: Then will you give me your blessing?

FATHER: Kneel down in front of me. *(SON kneels.)* May the blessing of the Lord Jehovah be with you, now and forever more. Receive my blessing, dear son, *Judas.*

—curtain—

Probes

1. Does the characterization of Judas fit your thought of what he might have been like in his first attraction to the gospel?

2. Judas's motives sound pure, but do you detect an underlying impulse that will predictably lead him to trouble?

3. How is this Judas related to modern church members who flock to leaders whom they think can solve all problems, and then fall away when the leaders do not meet their specific expectations?

4. Do we, like Judas, still misunderstand the true mission and message of Christ?

The Ardent One

A Stinger in the Form of a Dramatic Duet

SETTING: *A man is seated at a table and is writing by candlelight. He does not notice his son, who is about twenty-five years old, quietly enter the room.*

SON *(softly):* Father, may I come in?

FATHER *(looking up):* What? Oh, yes, of course, come in. I'm almost finished.

SON: I'm sorry for interrupting you, but I have something I'd like to discuss with you.

FATHER: Certainly, son; I was just going over the accounts. If it's important, they can wait. Why don't you sit down by me? My eyes are not as sharp as they used to be. *(Rubs eyes.)* So, what is it?

SON *(sitting):* Remember when I told you last week that I had the feeling that soon I was going to meet the man who will solve all of Israel's problems?

FATHER: Yes, I do. But I also remember that I told you that one man alone couldn't do it.

SON: I agree. But the man I'm talking about will have helpers and counselors. He won't have to do it alone.

FATHER: That would be true of anyone. Even Caesar has counselors.

SON *(trying to contain his excitement):* Only this man is greater than Caesar.

FATHER: Greater than Caesar? Where would you find such a man?

SON: Last week Simon Bar-Jonas insisted that this man had made fish practically jump into the net, when only minutes before he himself had been unable to catch any at all. Naturally I didn't put much stock in his story, although his description of the man was intriguing. Then a few days later I heard the entire village of Cana telling how he had changed water into wine at Jonah's wedding feast. This *must* be the One we have been waiting for.

FATHER: When will you learn? *(Stands and walks away from SON.)* Are you so eager to have the Messiah come that you jump at conclusions on such flimsy evidence? *(Turns to face SON.)* You know that many prophets have come calling themselves the Mes-

siah and that they also work great wonders. What makes you think this one is different from all the others?

SON *(exploding):* Because I've met him, Father, and he *is* different. He heals the sick and helps the poor, and there is something very special about him. I don't know if I can put it into words, but he has a power that makes people listen to him. He seemed to know me long before I spoke to him. *(Walks up to FATHER, trying to make him understand.)* He never does any of the tricks all the others do. He works miracles only to help someone, and then he tells those he healed not to tell anyone about it. Does that sound like a false prophet to you?

FATHER: I don't know, son. So many have come, and we have waited so patiently. Something has to happen soon. Our people cannot live like this forever.

SON: Exactly! It's time we got together behind one man and brought the kingdom of Israel back to the glory God meant it to have.

FATHER *(kindly):* You're such a zealot. Always looking for a leader to follow. You remind me of myself when I was young. I envy you. I wish I still had the strength and faith to search for the Messiah.

SON: That's all I wanted to hear. You think I'm right, don't you?

FATHER: I don't know if you're right, but I do think you need to follow your own best instincts and find out.

SON: Good! I'm going to see if I can find him again. I'll tell him I want to be his disciple. John the Baptist's disciples are all going to him. He's a great teacher. Father, I know this is the start of the new kingdom.

FATHER: I hope you're right, son.

SON: Then will you give me your blessing?

FATHER: Kneel down in front of me. *(SON kneels.)* May the blessing of the Lord Jehovah be with you, now and forever more. Receive my blessing, dear son, *Judas.*

—curtain—

Probes

1. Does the characterization of Judas fit your thought of what he might have been like in his first attraction to the gospel?

2. Judas's motives sound pure, but do you detect an underlying impulse that will predictably lead him to trouble?

3. How is this Judas related to modern church members who flock to leaders whom they think can solve all problems, and then fall away when the leaders do not meet their specific expectations?

4. Do we, like Judas, still misunderstand the true mission and message of Christ?

The Ardent One

A Stinger in the Form of a Dramatic Duet

SETTING: *A man is seated at a table and is writing by candlelight. He does not notice his son, who is about twenty-five years old, quietly enter the room.*

SON *(softly):* Father, may I come in?

FATHER *(looking up):* What? Oh, yes, of course, come in. I'm almost finished.

SON: I'm sorry for interrupting you, but I have something I'd like to discuss with you.

FATHER: Certainly, son; I was just going over the accounts. If it's important, they can wait. Why don't you sit down by me? My eyes are not as sharp as they used to be. *(Rubs eyes.)* So, what is it?

SON *(sitting):* Remember when I told you last week that I had the feeling that soon I was going to meet the man who will solve all of Israel's problems?

FATHER: Yes, I do. But I also remember that I told you that one man alone couldn't do it.

SON: I agree. But the man I'm talking about will have helpers and counselors. He won't have to do it alone.

FATHER: That would be true of anyone. Even Caesar has counselors.

SON *(trying to contain his excitement):* Only this man is greater than Caesar.

FATHER: Greater than Caesar? Where would you find such a man?

SON: Last week Simon Bar-Jonas insisted that this man had made fish practically jump into the net, when only minutes before he himself had been unable to catch any at all. Naturally I didn't put much stock in his story, although his description of the man was intriguing. Then a few days later I heard the entire village of Cana telling how he had changed water into wine at Jonah's wedding feast. This *must* be the One we have been waiting for.

FATHER: When will you learn? *(Stands and walks away from SON.)* Are you so eager to have the Messiah come that you jump at conclusions on such flimsy evidence? *(Turns to face SON.)* You know that many prophets have come calling themselves the Messiah and that they also work great wonders. What makes you think this one is different from all the others?

SON *(exploding):* Because I've met him, Father, and he *is* different. He heals the sick and helps the poor, and there is something very special about him. I don't know if I can put it into words, but he has a power that makes people listen to him. He seemed to know me long before I spoke to him. *(Walks up to FATHER, trying to make him understand.)* He never does any of the tricks all the others do. He works miracles only to help someone, and then he tells those he healed not to tell anyone about it. Does that sound like a false prophet to you?

FATHER: I don't know, son. So many have come, and we have waited so patiently. Something has to happen soon. Our people cannot live like this forever.

SON: Exactly! It's time we got together behind one man and brought the kingdom of Israel back to the glory God meant it to have.

FATHER *(kindly):* You're such a zealot. Always looking for a leader to follow. You remind me of myself when I was young. I envy you. I wish I still had the strength and faith to search for the Messiah.

SON: That's all I wanted to hear. You think I'm right, don't you?

FATHER: I don't know if you're right, but I do think you need to follow your own best instincts and find out.

SON: Good! I'm going to see if I can find him again. I'll tell him I want to be his disciple. John the Baptist's disciples are all going to him. He's a great teacher. Father, I know this is the start of the new kingdom.

FATHER: I hope you're right, son.

SON: Then will you give me your blessing?

FATHER: Kneel down in front of me. *(SON kneels.)* May the blessing of the Lord Jehovah be with you, now and forever more. Receive my blessing, dear son, *Judas.*

—curtain—

Probes

1. Does the characterization of Judas fit your thought of what he might have been like in his first attraction to the gospel?

2. Judas's motives sound pure, but do you detect an underlying impulse that will predictably lead him to trouble?

3. How is this Judas related to modern church members who flock to leaders whom they think can solve all problems, and then fall away when the leaders do not meet their specific expectations?

4. Do we, like Judas, still misunderstand the true mission and message of Christ?

Room Arrest

A Dramatic Trio

Room Arrest is based on the true-life experiences of Louise Giffin, missionary for the American Baptist Churches, U.S.A. Born into a Baptist missionary family in South China, Louise came to the U.S. to acquire her professional training and after a few years returned to South China to teach. She endured the Japanese occupation during World War II, but her career there was ended by twenty-one months of solitary confinement when the Communists took over South China in 1949.

While the scene recreated here actually took place throughout her entire confinement, freedom has been exercised in telescoping the events into one day. Liberty has also been taken in selecting hymns and Scripture that relate the feeling Miss Giffin expressed in a personal interview. Incarcerated at the same time as Miss Giffin were Loren Noren, Abby Sanderson, Dr. Emanuel Giedt (pronounced Geet), all American Baptist missionaries, and a Catholic priest.

STAGING: This confinement took place in a Catholic convent, and it is assumed that Miss Giffin's room was a nun's cell. Loren's cell, which is never seen, is understood to be catercornered so that he is able to see all the other rooms, while Louise can see only his. In her room she has a table, a chair, a cot (fold-up type would be appropriate), and a lamp. It is not necessary to have an actual door on the set. An exit downstage right is all that is needed. When Louise speaks to Loren, she will actually face the *audience* downstage right.

CHARACTERIZATION AND MOOD: While Loren is never seen by the audience, his role is pivotal to the movement of the scene. He memorized a total of 180 hymns during his imprisonment. The directions indicate that it is not important for him to "sing especially well"; however, it is important for him to be able to carry a tune. One of the ways in which Loren kept up his physical fitness was by pacing back and forth (ten steps in each direction) in his cell. His pacing must be heard clearly, as it not only highlights a vital aspect of his personality, but also the rhythm of his pacing and the meaning of the words of the hymns have been

---

The facts for this play came from a taped interview with Louise Giffin.

combined to create a specific mood; timelessness and the presence of God must be felt throughout the drama.

SETTING: *A woman about thirty-five years of age is sitting on a straight-backed chair, knitting a sweater. She is using parts of a bamboo clothes hanger for knitting needles. LOREN's voice is always heard offstage. If his voice is not strong enough, it is suggested that a microphone be used with the sound set at a medium level. It does not matter if LOREN does not sing especially well. The words and the mood are what is most important.*

LOREN *(singing):* What a friend we have in Jesus,
All our sins and griefs to bear.
What a privilege to carry
Everything to God in prayer.
Oh, what peace. . . .

LOUISE *(looking up from her knitting and whispering):* Why have you stopped singing? *(No answer. She puts her knitting down and goes to the cell door.)* Loren, are you OK? Why have you stopped singing? *(Still no answer. Sounds of keys in lock next door. Footsteps are heard moving away, and a door slams.)* Oh, poor Loren. Not again!

LOREN *(half whisper):* No, Louise, I'm all right. I think they took Dr. Giedt, though.

LOUISE *(returns to her knitting):* Poor Dr. Geidt. I hope he's strong enough to withstand another interrogation. I wonder what they're accusing him of now.

LOREN: He's strong enough. *(Begins pacing. Audience hears ten steps in one direction, then ten steps back. He continues pacing in this fashion throughout LOUISE's next speech. The pacing must be deliberate and steady.)*

LOUISE *(speaking to herself—stream of consciousness):* I guess we all have to be strong. I thought I knew what fear was during the war. I remember when I first saw those Japanese gun boats come sailing into Swatow [Swah-toe] Harbor. I thought my heart would stop beating. It was 10 A.M. exactly when the first group of soldiers came swarming over the hills surrounding the

missionary compound. I didn't want to show it, but I was afraid! I knew God was taking care of us; nevertheless, I was terrified! *(She pauses—sounds of pacing become louder.)* It sent shivers up and down my spine to see those guards stationed all over the city. I think *they* frightened me more than the bombs had. Until then, the *they* who bombed us were anonymous. But now *they* had faces and *they* stood by my door at night and watched my every move during the day.

(LOREN continues pacing—starts to sing quietly "Sweet Hour of Prayer." He sings it hesitantly, stopping frequently to go over the same words.)

LOUISE: Hasn't he finished memorizing that one yet? *(Goes to door; in half whisper.)* Loren, Loren?

LOREN *(stops singing and pacing):* Yes?

LOUISE: How many hymns have you memorized so far?

LOREN: One hundred fifty-three. Thank God for this English language hymnal. It's the only thing keeping my mind alert.

LOUISE: That and your pacing ten steps forward, ten steps back. Sometimes I walk them with you for the exercise.

LOREN: Why don't you try memorizing hymns, too?

LOUISE: I did, but I have only a Chinese hymnal, and it's just not the same.

LOREN: That's true. Well, at least you have your knitting. How many times have you knitted that sweater?

LOUISE *(laughing softly):* I think this makes four, or is it five? I don't know. I do remember that last time I knit two left front sides.

LOREN: Your yarn holding out OK?

LOUISE: Pretty good *(holding up knitting)*, but it looks like it's getting curlier and curlier. *(Both laugh.)* Not much you can do with a pair of knitting needles whittled from a bamboo coat hanger with the top of a tin can.

LOREN: Shh—I think I hear the guards coming back. Better not talk anymore.

LOUISE *(moves to the opposite wall, speaking to herself again):* How nice. Our Communist buddies are back. I wish God would send us an angel to open these doors the way he

did for Peter. Wouldn't that be a shock for dear old Mao? *(Returns to her knitting. The pacing backstage resumes. LOUISE continues her reverie as though she had never stopped.)* Going inland on vacation in the summer of '41 was certainly a blessing. Who could guess that the harbor would be blockaded and that we'd not be able to get back to Swatow? At least that was one time the Lord delivered me from a concentration camp. The other missionaries were not as fortunate. Did God feel I'd not be able to survive imprisonment twice? He knew this imprisonment was coming. I wonder.

LOREN *(quietly reciting the words of "In the Hour of Trial." LOUISE sits and listens as LOREN's voice gets louder):*

In the hour of trial, Jesus, plead for me,
Lest, by base denial, I depart from Thee.
When Thou seest me waver, with a look recall,
Nor for fear or favor suffer me to fall.
(She joins him with great conviction.)

LOREN AND
LOUISE: Should Thy mercy send me sorrow, toil, and woe;
Or should pain attend me on my path below;
Grant that I may never fail Thy hand to see;
Grant that I may ever cast my care on Thee.

LOUISE *(quietly to herself):* Thank you, Loren! How did you know I needed that just now? My thoughts are bringing me a lot of pain today.... *(Angrily.)* The Communists! Oh, in '49 they didn't come swarming over the hills the way the Japanese did. *(Sighing.)* No, they came in quietly; they didn't even get much resistance from the common people. They had done a good job of intimidating anyone who disagreed with them. They held political meetings on Sunday morning so no one would dare come to services. Thank God for the faithful few who resisted. That reminds me: it's time to write my monthly letter to the government. Who knows—maybe this time they'll pay some attention to me. *(Starts rummaging through a few papers and items on her table. She*

finds a stub of a pencil, goes to the door and calls out.) Guards . . . guards . . . may I please have a piece of paper? . . . Yes, I'm sure it's time for my next letter. It's the end of the month, isn't it? . . . But why must I wait until tomorrow? Surely one day can't make any difference. . . . *(Backing away from door.)* Very well, whatever you say. . . . Silly old man, what could it possible hurt to let me write it today? *(Violently throws pencil on table. She begins pacing floor.)* I still can't believe they think I'm a spy. Imagine—*me!* The most political thing I ever did is meet Harry Truman along with a group of missionaries on furlough. "Spy for the Inner Circle"—indeed! The biggest secret he ever told us was that he was a Baptist, too! *(Sounds of key in her door. A young Chinese woman enters carrying a tray with a bowl and a cup.)* Oh, Ah-Sim, is it dinner time already?

AH-SIM: Yes, ma'am. And I have a little surprise for you. Look! I was able to get an egg from my sister, Goo Ma. *(Puts tray on table.)*

LOUISE: An egg! How lovely! But can she spare it? *(Sits at table.)*

AH-SIM: Oh, yes, her chicken is laying a little better these days. Besides, she remembers you with much affection. *(Checks to make sure no one is listening by the door.)* She asked me to tell you that no one believes the accusations that have been brought against you. Most of your accusers felt they *had* to make something up or be imprisoned themselves. She asked you to try to understand.

LOUISE: Please assure her that I understand and, what's more important, that I forgive her.

AH-SIM: Bad as accusing you may be, the situation is even more serious than that, ma'am. Everyone is being taught to watch others and find fault. The children at school are required to take part in oral criticism sessions in which they accuse each other of real and imaginary faults in front of the entire class. If they refuse to participate, they are accused of poor citizenship, and it's recorded in the student's personal file.

LOUISE: Is that so? I didn't realize things had gotten so bad. I really am sorry, Ah-Sim.

AH-SIM: I didn't mean to worry you, but I wanted to be sure you understood what is really happening to us. Now, eat your dinner while it's still hot. I'll wait here until you have finished. *(Sits on edge of cot.)*

LOUISE *(bows head and prays):* Thank you, Father, for your constant care and blessings. Thank you for Goo Ma who has shared this beautiful egg with me. Help us to be loving to those who revile us and persecute us for your sake. Help us to be constant in our faith. Bless all who are imprisoned this evening, and give them courage and strength. In Jesus' name. Amen.

AH-SIM: How was it last night? Have they stopped trying to scare you with all that yelling and stomping about?

LOUISE: Not really, though it's not nearly as bad here as it was when I was confined in my house. There I thought I would go mad with all the banging on the walls and the noise at night. It was the things they screamed at me that were the most frightening: "Now we've got her! Now we've got her!" Somehow that scared me more than anything else they did. *(Stops to eat a bit of food.)* What I really wish I could have now is some peaceful darkness at night. They keep the light on all through the night, and I find it difficult to sleep. *(Wiping mouth with napkin.)* Ummm, that egg tasted wonderful. Please thank Goo Ma for me. There, I've finished. That was such a lovely treat. *(Puts napkin on tray and gets up.)*

AH-SIM *(standing and picking up tray):* I'd better leave now. It's getting late.

LOUISE: Yes, of course. Ah-Sim, will you do me a favor on your way out? Please stop by Loren Noren's door and signal him that I want to speak to him?

AH-SIM *(alarmed):* But, ma'am, you're not allowed. If you were caught . . .

LOUISE: Don't worry, dear; I didn't mean that we would speak out loud. We have our own sign language, and when the guards are not paying close attention, we talk that way. Very rarely are we able to talk out loud. Usually that only happens when one of us is being taken out for interrogation. Feel better?

AH-SIM: I should have known you wouldn't do anything foolish. Of course I'll tell him. Good night. (*AH-SIM exits, sound of keys turning in the lock.*)

(*LOUISE walks to door, or exit, smiles, and makes the motions of forming letters on the window. She spells out her message and speaks out loud the words she is forming. She will also relate for the audience what LOREN answers.*)

LOUISE: A-m stop (*points finger as signal for stop or next word*) f-e-a-r-f-u-l stop. N-e-e-d stop t-o stop d-o stop m-o-r-e stop t-o-w-a-r-d-s stop r-e-l-e-a-s-e stop.

(*Begins to read LOREN's message in the same manner.*) P-s-a-l-m stop 3-7 stop 7. Psalm 37:7. What is that? Oh, how I wish I still had my Bible with me. Let me see; oh, yes, I remember: "Rest in the Lord; wait patiently for him." Oh, Loren. I'm tired of waiting. (*Begins to spell for LOREN.*) P-h-i-l-i-p-p-i-a-n-s stop 2 stop 1-2-b stop. There, he ought to remember that quotation easily: "Work out your own salvation with fear and trembling."

(*Reads again.*) S-a-m-e stop 2 stop 1-4 stop. D-o stop a-l-l stop t-h-i-n-g-s stop w-i-t-h-o-u-t stop g-r-u-m-b-l-i-n-g stop o-r stop q-u-e-s-t-i-o-n-i-n-g. (*Leaves window and sits on cot with head in hands.*) "Do all things without grumbling or questioning." Dear God, I know you're watching over us. It just seems to me that you want us to *do* more. How can all this sitting be useful? (*Pause.*) The truth is that I'm scared, just plain scared. I trust you in *all* things, Lord, especially the important things. It's the little things that upset me most. I feel so helpless. I'm used to *doing* things—planning, organizing, leading. Dear Lord, speak to me in this cell. Tell me what you want me to do, how you want me to feel. (*LOREN's voice is heard singing clearly. The words to the following hymn are very important.*)

He leadeth me: O blessed thought!
O words with heavenly comfort fraught!
Whate'er I do, where'er I be,
Still 'tis God's hand that leadeth me.

(*Two other voices, a man's and a woman's, join in the chorus.*)

He leadeth me, He leadeth me,

By His own hand He leadeth me:
(*Singers continue with hymn while LOUISE speaks the following words.*)
Dr. Giedt, Abby, Loren, how wonderful of you to sing directly to my need! I hear you, Lord, and I'm ready to listen.

His faithful follower I would be,
For by His hand He leadeth me.
Sometimes 'mid scenes of deepest gloom,
Sometimes where Eden's bowers bloom,
By waters calm, o'er troubled sea,
Still 'tis His hand that leadeth me.
He leadeth me, He leadeth me,
By His own hand He leadeth me:
His faithful follower I would be,
For by His hand He leadeth me.

(*LOUISE stands facing audience. Her face is radiant. She begins to sing with the other captives—triumphantly.*)

Lord, I would clasp Thy hand in mine,
Nor ever murmur nor repine;
Content, whatever lot I see,
Since 'tis my God that leadeth me.
He leadeth me, He leadeth me,
By His own hand He leadeth me:
His faithful follower I would be,
For by His hand He leadeth me.

—curtain—

Epilogue

(*This should be read to the audience while the room is still in darkness.*)

Twenty-one months after their "room arrest" began, the missionaries were suddenly and unceremoniously released. Christmas night of the second Christmas they had been captives, they were told to get out! "It was as if we'd been wanting to stay there," relates Miss Giffin. She and Miss Sanderson were released together. The guards escorted both Miss Giffin and Miss Sanderson home. "So after twenty-one months I was suddenly just perfectly free. It seemed impossible to me."

Miss Giffin indicated that the greatest lesson she learned during this experience was to rely completely on God. She says, "I can remember so clearly the day that the thought came to me: 'Well, the Lord knows all about this; whether you live or die, you are still a witness; you are a testimony to your faith, and you don't need to fear.' After that, life was much easier."

Probes

1. Do you feel sympathy for imprisoned missionaries, or do you consider that this is just a risk of their profession?

2. How do you think you would react if you found yourself in a situation similar to that of Louise Giffin?

3. Are modern missionaries still facing dangers and threats of imprisonment or death, or are they simply pastors and other specialists serving in other countries?

4. Review the experiences of Paul as a missionary. Were his imprisonments and hardships different from or similar to difficulties suffered by modern missionaries? The experiences of Adoniram Judson and Ann Judson would be revealing.

Room Arrest

A Dramatic Trio

Room Arrest is based on the true-life experiences of Louise Giffin, missionary for the American Baptist Churches, U.S.A. Born into a Baptist missionary family in South China, Louise came to the U.S. to acquire her professional training and after a few years returned to South China to teach. She endured the Japanese occupation during World War II, but her career there was ended by twenty-one months of solitary confinement when the Communists took over South China in 1949.

While the scene recreated here actually took place throughout her entire confinement, freedom has been exercised in telescoping the events into one day. Liberty has also been taken in selecting hymns and Scripture that relate the feeling Miss Giffin expressed in a personal interview. Incarcerated at the same time as Miss Giffin were Loren Noren, Abby Sanderson, Dr. Emanuel Giedt (pronounced Geet), all American Baptist missionaries, and a Catholic priest.

STAGING: This confinement took place in a Catholic convent, and it is assumed that Miss Giffin's room was a nun's cell. Loren's cell, which is never seen, is understood to be catercornered so that he is able to see all the other rooms, while Louise can see only his. In her room she has a table, a chair, a cot (fold-up type would be appropriate), and a lamp. It is not necessary to have an actual door on the set. An exit downstage right is all that is needed. When Louise speaks to Loren, she will actually face the *audience* downstage right.

CHARACTERIZATION AND MOOD: While Loren is never seen by the audience, his role is pivotal to the movement of the scene. He memorized a total of 180 hymns during his imprisonment. The directions indicate that it is not important for him to "sing especially well"; however, it is important for him to be able to carry a tune. One of the ways in which Loren kept up his physical fitness was by pacing back and forth (ten steps in each direction) in his cell. His pacing must be heard clearly, as it not only highlights a vital aspect of his personality, but also the rhythm of his pacing and the meaning of the words of the hymns have been

---

The facts for this play came from a taped interview with Louise Giffin.

combined to create a specific mood; timelessness and the presence of God must be felt throughout the drama.

SETTING: *A woman about thirty-five years of age is sitting on a straight-backed chair, knitting a sweater. She is using parts of a bamboo clothes hanger for knitting needles. LOREN's voice is always heard offstage. If his voice is not strong enough, it is suggested that a microphone be used with the sound set at a medium level. It does not matter if LOREN does not sing especially well. The words and the mood are what is most important.*

LOREN *(singing):* What a friend we have in Jesus,
All our sins and griefs to bear.
What a privilege to carry
Everything to God in prayer.
Oh, what peace. . . .

LOUISE *(looking up from her knitting and whispering):* Why have you stopped singing? *(No answer. She puts her knitting down and goes to the cell door.)* Loren, are you OK? Why have you stopped singing? *(Still no answer. Sounds of keys in lock next door. Footsteps are heard moving away, and a door slams.)* Oh, poor Loren. Not again!

LOREN *(half whisper):* No, Louise, I'm all right. I think they took Dr. Giedt, though.

LOUISE *(returns to her knitting):* Poor Dr. Geidt. I hope he's strong enough to withstand another interrogation. I wonder what they're accusing him of now.

LOREN: He's strong enough. *(Begins pacing. Audience hears ten steps in one direction, then ten steps back. He continues pacing in this fashion throughout LOUISE's next speech. The pacing must be deliberate and steady.)*

LOUISE *(speaking to herself—stream of consciousness):* I guess we all have to be strong. I thought I knew what fear was during the war. I remember when I first saw those Japanese gun boats come sailing into Swatow [Swah-toe] Harbor. I thought my heart would stop beating. It was 10 A.M. exactly when the first group of soldiers came swarming over the hills surrounding the

missionary compound. I didn't want to show it, but I was afraid! I knew God was taking care of us; nevertheless, I was terrified! (She pauses—sounds of pacing become louder.) It sent shivers up and down my spine to see those guards stationed all over the city. I think *they* frightened me more than the bombs had. Until then, the *they* who bombed us were anonymous. But now *they* had faces and *they* stood by my door at night and watched my every move during the day.

(LOREN continues pacing—starts to sing quietly "Sweet Hour of Prayer." He sings it hesitantly, stopping frequently to go over the same words.)

LOUISE: Hasn't he finished memorizing that one yet? (Goes to door; in half whisper.) Loren, Loren?

LOREN (stops singing and pacing): Yes?

LOUISE: How many hymns have you memorized so far?

LOREN: One hundred fifty-three. Thank God for this English language hymnal. It's the only thing keeping my mind alert.

LOUISE: That and your pacing ten steps forward, ten steps back. Sometimes I walk them with you for the exercise.

LOREN: Why don't you try memorizing hymns, too?

LOUISE: I did, but I have only a Chinese hymnal, and it's just not the same.

LOREN: That's true. Well, at least you have your knitting. How many times have you knitted that sweater?

LOUISE (laughing softly): I think this makes four, or is it five? I don't know. I do remember that last time I knit two left front sides.

LOREN: Your yarn holding out OK?

LOUISE: Pretty good (holding up knitting), but it looks like it's getting curlier and curlier. (Both laugh.) Not much you can do with a pair of knitting needles whittled from a bamboo coat hanger with the top of a tin can.

LOREN: Shh—I think I hear the guards coming back. Better not talk anymore.

LOUISE (moves to the opposite wall, speaking to herself again): How nice. Our Communist buddies are back. I wish God would send us an angel to open these doors the way he did for Peter. Wouldn't that be a shock for dear old Mao? (Returns to her knitting. The pacing backstage resumes. LOUISE continues her reverie as though she had never stopped.) Going inland on vacation in the summer of '41 was certainly a blessing. Who could guess that the harbor would be blockaded and that we'd not be able to get back to Swatow? At least that was one time the Lord delivered me from a concentration camp. The other missionaries were not as fortunate. Did God feel I'd not be able to survive imprisonment twice? He knew this imprisonment was coming. I wonder.

LOREN (quietly reciting the words of "In the Hour of Trial." LOUISE sits and listens as LOREN's voice gets louder):

In the hour of trial, Jesus, plead for me,
Lest, by base denial, I depart from Thee.
When Thou seest me waver, with a look recall,
Nor for fear or favor suffer me to fall.
(She joins him with great conviction.)

LOREN AND
LOUISE: Should Thy mercy send me sorrow, toil, and woe;
Or should pain attend me on my path below;
Grant that I may never fail Thy hand to see;
Grant that I may ever cast my care on Thee.

LOUISE (quietly to herself): Thank you, Loren! How did you know I needed that just now? My thoughts are bringing me a lot of pain today. . . . (Angrily.) The Communists! Oh, in '49 they didn't come swarming over the hills the way the Japanese did. (Sighing.) No, they came in quietly; they didn't even get much resistance from the common people. They had done a good job of intimidating anyone who disagreed with them. They held political meetings on Sunday morning so no one would dare come to services. Thank God for the faithful few who resisted. That reminds me: it's time to write my monthly letter to the government. Who knows—maybe this time they'll pay some attention to me. (Starts rummaging through a few papers and items on her table. She

finds a stub of a pencil, goes to the door and calls out.) Guards . . . guards . . . may I please have a piece of paper? . . . Yes, I'm sure it's time for my next letter. It's the end of the month, isn't it? . . . But why must I wait until tomorrow? Surely one day can't make any difference. . . . *(Backing away from door.)* Very well, whatever you say. . . . Silly old man, what could it possible hurt to let me write it today? *(Violently throws pencil on table. She begins pacing floor.)* I still can't believe they think I'm a spy. Imagine—*me!* The most political thing I ever did is meet Harry Truman along with a group of missionaries on furlough. "Spy for the Inner Circle"—indeed! The biggest secret he ever told us was that he was a Baptist, too! *(Sounds of key in her door. A young Chinese woman enters carrying a tray with a bowl and a cup.)* Oh, Ah-Sim, is it dinner time already?

AH-SIM: Yes, ma'am. And I have a little surprise for you. Look! I was able to get an egg from my sister, Goo Ma. *(Puts tray on table.)*

LOUISE: An egg! How lovely! But can she spare it? *(Sits at table.)*

AH-SIM: Oh, yes, her chicken is laying a little better these days. Besides, she remembers you with much affection. *(Checks to make sure no one is listening by the door.)* She asked me to tell you that no one believes the accusations that have been brought against you. Most of your accusers felt they *had* to make something up or be imprisoned themselves. She asked you to try to understand.

LOUISE: Please assure her that I understand and, what's more important, that I forgive her.

AH-SIM: Bad as accusing you may be, the situation is even more serious than that, ma'am. Everyone is being taught to watch others and find fault. The children at school are required to take part in oral criticism sessions in which they accuse each other of real and imaginary faults in front of the entire class. If they refuse to participate, they are accused of poor citizenship, and it's recorded in the student's personal file.

LOUISE: Is that so? I didn't realize things had gotten so bad. I really am sorry, Ah-Sim.

AH-SIM: I didn't mean to worry you, but I wanted to be sure you understood what is really happening to us. Now, eat your dinner while it's still hot. I'll wait here until you have finished. *(Sits on edge of cot.)*

LOUISE *(bows head and prays):* Thank you, Father, for your constant care and blessings. Thank you for Goo Ma who has shared this beautiful egg with me. Help us to be loving to those who revile us and persecute us for your sake. Help us to be constant in our faith. Bless all who are imprisoned this evening, and give them courage and strength. In Jesus' name. Amen.

AH-SIM: How was it last night? Have they stopped trying to scare you with all that yelling and stomping about?

LOUISE: Not really, though it's not nearly as bad here as it was when I was confined in my house. There I thought I would go mad with all the banging on the walls and the noise at night. It was the things they screamed at me that were the most frightening: "Now we've got her! Now we've got her!" Somehow that scared me more than anything else they did. *(Stops to eat a bit of food.)* What I really wish I could have now is some peaceful darkness at night. They keep the light on all through the night, and I find it difficult to sleep. *(Wiping mouth with napkin.)* Ummm, that egg tasted wonderful. Please thank Goo Ma for me. There, I've finished. That was such a lovely treat. *(Puts napkin on tray and gets up.)*

AH-SIM *(standing and picking up tray):* I'd better leave now. It's getting late.

LOUISE: Yes, of course. Ah-Sim, will you do me a favor on your way out? Please stop by Loren Noren's door and signal him that I want to speak to him?

AH-SIM *(alarmed):* But, ma'am, you're not allowed. If you were caught . . .

LOUISE: Don't worry, dear; I didn't mean that we would speak out loud. We have our own sign language, and when the guards are not paying close attention, we talk that way. Very rarely are we able to talk out loud. Usually that only happens when one of us is being taken out for interrogation. Feel better?

AH-SIM: I should have known you wouldn't do anything foolish. Of course I'll tell him. Good night. *(AH-SIM exits, sound of keys turning in the lock.)*

(LOUISE walks to door, or exit, smiles, and makes the motions of forming letters on the window. She spells out her message and speaks out loud the words she is forming. She will also relate for the audience what LOREN answers.)

LOUISE: A-m stop *(points finger as signal for stop or next word)* f-e-a-r-f-u-l stop. N-e-e-d stop t-o stop d-o stop m-o-r-e stop t-o-w-a-r-d-s stop r-e-l-e-a-s-e stop.

(Begins to read LOREN's message in the same manner.) P-s-a-l-m stop 3-7 stop 7. Psalm 37:7. What is that? Oh, how I wish I still had my Bible with me. Let me see; oh, yes, I remember: "Rest in the Lord; wait patiently for him." Oh, Loren. I'm tired of waiting. *(Begins to spell for LOREN.)* P-h-i-l-i-p-p-i-a-n-s stop 2 stop 1-2-b stop. There, he ought to remember that quotation easily: "Work out your own salvation with fear and trembling."

(Reads again.) S-a-m-e stop 2 stop 1-4 stop. D-o stop a-l-l stop t-h-i-n-g-s stop w-i-t-h-o-u-t stop g-r-u-m-b-l-i-n-g stop o-r stop q-u-e-s-t-i-o-n-i-n-g. *(Leaves window and sits on cot with head in hands.)* "Do all things without grumbling or questioning." Dear God, I know you're watching over us. It just seems to me that you want us to *do* more. How can all this sitting be useful? *(Pause.)* The truth is that I'm scared, just plain scared. I trust you in *all* things, Lord, especially the important things. It's the little things that upset me most. I feel so helpless. I'm used to *doing* things—planning, organizing, leading. Dear Lord, speak to me in this cell. Tell me what you want me to do, how you want me to feel. *(LOREN's voice is heard singing clearly. The words to the following hymn are very important.)*

He leadeth me: O blessed thought!
O words with heavenly comfort fraught!
Whate'er I do, where'er I be,
Still 'tis God's hand that leadeth me.
(Two other voices, a man's and a woman's, join in the chorus.)
He leadeth me, He leadeth me,

By His own hand He leadeth me:
(Singers continue with hymn while LOUISE speaks the following words.)
Dr. Giedt, Abby, Loren, how wonderful of you to sing directly to my need! I hear you, Lord, and I'm ready to listen.
His faithful follower I would be,
For by His hand He leadeth me.
Sometimes 'mid scenes of deepest gloom,
Sometimes where Eden's bowers bloom,
By waters calm, o'er troubled sea,
Still 'tis His hand that leadeth me.
He leadeth me, He leadeth me,
By His own hand He leadeth me:
His faithful follower I would be,
For by His hand He leadeth me.
(LOUISE stands facing audience. Her face is radiant. She begins to sing with the other captives—triumphantly.)
Lord, I would clasp Thy hand in mine,
Nor ever murmur nor repine;
Content, whatever lot I see,
Since 'tis my God that leadeth me.
He leadeth me, He leadeth me,
By His own hand He leadeth me:
His faithful follower I would be,
For by His hand He leadeth me.

—curtain—

Epilogue

(This should be read to the audience while the room is still in darkness.)

Twenty-one months after their "room arrest" began, the missionaries were suddenly and unceremoniously released. Christmas night of the second Christmas they had been captives, they were told to get out! "It was as if we'd been wanting to stay there," relates Miss Giffin. She and Miss Sanderson were released together. The guards escorted both Miss Giffin and Miss Sanderson home. "So after twenty-one months I was suddenly just perfectly free. It seemed impossible to me."

Miss Giffin indicated that the greatest lesson she learned during this experience was to rely completely on God. She says, "I can remember so clearly the day that the thought came to me: 'Well, the Lord knows all about this; whether you live or die, you are still a witness; you are a testimony to your faith, and you don't need to fear.' After that, life was much easier."

Probes

1. Do you feel sympathy for imprisoned missionaries, or do you consider that this is just a risk of their profession?

2. How do you think you would react if you found yourself in a situation similar to that of Louise Giffin?

3. Are modern missionaries still facing dangers and threats of imprisonment or death, or are they simply pastors and other specialists serving in other countries?

4. Review the experiences of Paul as a missionary. Were his imprisonments and hardships different from or similar to difficulties suffered by modern missionaries? The experiences of Adoniram Judson and Ann Judson would be revealing.

Room Arrest
A Dramatic Trio

Room Arrest is based on the true-life experiences of Louise Giffin, missionary for the American Baptist Churches, U.S.A. Born into a Baptist missionary family in South China, Louise came to the U.S. to acquire her professional training and after a few years returned to South China to teach. She endured the Japanese occupation during World War II, but her career there was ended by twenty-one months of solitary confinement when the Communists took over South China in 1949.

While the scene recreated here actually took place throughout her entire confinement, freedom has been exercised in telescoping the events into one day. Liberty has also been taken in selecting hymns and Scripture that relate the feeling Miss Giffin expressed in a personal interview. Incarcerated at the same time as Miss Giffin were Loren Noren, Abby Sanderson, Dr. Emanuel Giedt (pronounced Geet), all American Baptist missionaries, and a Catholic priest.

STAGING: This confinement took place in a Catholic convent, and it is assumed that Miss Giffin's room was a nun's cell. Loren's cell, which is never seen, is understood to be catercornered so that he is able to see all the other rooms, while Louise can see only his. In her room she has a table, a chair, a cot (fold-up type would be appropriate), and a lamp. It is not necessary to have an actual door on the set. An exit downstage right is all that is needed. When Louise speaks to Loren, she will actually face the *audience* downstage right.

CHARACTERIZATION AND MOOD: While Loren is never seen by the audience, his role is pivotal to the movement of the scene. He memorized a total of 180 hymns during his imprisonment. The directions indicate that it is not important for him to "sing especially well"; however, it is important for him to be able to carry a tune. One of the ways in which Loren kept up his physical fitness was by pacing back and forth (ten steps in each direction) in his cell. His pacing must be heard clearly, as it not only highlights a vital aspect of his personality, but also the rhythm of his pacing and the meaning of the words of the hymns have been

---

The facts for this play came from a taped interview with Louise Giffin.

combined to create a specific mood; timelessness and the presence of God must be felt throughout the drama.

SETTING: *A woman about thirty-five years of age is sitting on a straight-backed chair, knitting a sweater. She is using parts of a bamboo clothes hanger for knitting needles. LOREN's voice is always heard offstage. If his voice is not strong enough, it is suggested that a microphone be used with the sound set at a medium level. It does not matter if LOREN does not sing especially well. The words and the mood are what is most important.*

LOREN *(singing):* What a friend we have in Jesus,
All our sins and griefs to bear.
What a privilege to carry
Everything to God in prayer.
Oh, what peace. . . .

LOUISE *(looking up from her knitting and whispering):* Why have you stopped singing? *(No answer. She puts her knitting down and goes to the cell door.)* Loren, are you OK? Why have you stopped singing? *(Still no answer. Sounds of keys in lock next door. Footsteps are heard moving away, and a door slams.)* Oh, poor Loren. Not again!

LOREN *(half whisper):* No, Louise, I'm all right. I think they took Dr. Giedt, though.

LOUISE *(returns to her knitting):* Poor Dr. Geidt. I hope he's strong enough to withstand another interrogation. I wonder what they're accusing him of now.

LOREN: He's strong enough. *(Begins pacing. Audience hears ten steps in one direction, then ten steps back. He continues pacing in this fashion throughout LOUISE's next speech. The pacing must be deliberate and steady.)*

LOUISE *(speaking to herself—stream of consciousness):* I guess we all have to be strong. I thought I knew what fear was during the war. I remember when I first saw those Japanese gun boats come sailing into Swatow [Swah-toe] Harbor. I thought my heart would stop beating. It was 10 A.M. exactly when the first group of soldiers came swarming over the hills surrounding the

missionary compound. I didn't want to show it, but I was afraid! I knew God was taking care of us; nevertheless, I was terrified! *(She pauses—sounds of pacing become louder.)* It sent shivers up and down my spine to see those guards stationed all over the city. I think *they* frightened me more than the bombs had. Until then, the *they* who bombed us were anonymous. But now *they* had faces and *they* stood by my door at night and watched my every move during the day.

(LOREN continues pacing—starts to sing quietly "Sweet Hour of Prayer." He sings it hesitantly, stopping frequently to go over the same words.)

LOUISE: Hasn't he finished memorizing that one yet? *(Goes to door; in half whisper.)* Loren, Loren?

LOREN *(stops singing and pacing)*: Yes?

LOUISE: How many hymns have you memorized so far?

LOREN: One hundred fifty-three. Thank God for this English language hymnal. It's the only thing keeping my mind alert.

LOUISE: That and your pacing ten steps forward, ten steps back. Sometimes I walk them with you for the exercise.

LOREN: Why don't you try memorizing hymns, too?

LOUISE: I did, but I have only a Chinese hymnal, and it's just not the same.

LOREN: That's true. Well, at least you have your knitting. How many times have you knitted that sweater?

LOUISE *(laughing softly)*: I think this makes four, or is it five? I don't know. I do remember that last time I knit two left front sides.

LOREN: Your yarn holding out OK?

LOUISE: Pretty good *(holding up knitting)*, but it looks like it's getting curlier and curlier. *(Both laugh.)* Not much you can do with a pair of knitting needles whittled from a bamboo coat hanger with the top of a tin can.

LOREN: Shh—I think I hear the guards coming back. Better not talk anymore.

LOUISE *(moves to the opposite wall, speaking to herself again)*: How nice. Our Communist buddies are back. I wish God would send us an angel to open these doors the way he

did for Peter. Wouldn't that be a shock for dear old Mao? *(Returns to her knitting. The pacing backstage resumes. LOUISE continues her reverie as though she had never stopped.)* Going inland on vacation in the summer of '41 was certainly a blessing. Who could guess that the harbor would be blockaded and that we'd not be able to get back to Swatow? At least that was one time the Lord delivered me from a concentration camp. The other missionaries were not as fortunate. Did God feel I'd not be able to survive imprisonment twice? He knew this imprisonment was coming. I wonder.

LOREN *(quietly reciting the words of "In the Hour of Trial." LOUISE sits and listens as LOREN's voice gets louder)*:

In the hour of trial, Jesus, plead for me,
Lest, by base denial, I depart from Thee.
When Thou seest me waver, with a look recall,
Nor for fear or favor suffer me to fall.
(She joins him with great conviction.)

LOREN AND
LOUISE: Should Thy mercy send me sorrow, toil, and woe;
Or should pain attend me on my path below;
Grant that I may never fail Thy hand to see;
Grant that I may ever cast my care on Thee.

LOUISE *(quietly to herself)*: Thank you, Loren! How did you know I needed that just now? My thoughts are bringing me a lot of pain today.... *(Angrily.)* The Communists! Oh, in '49 they didn't come swarming over the hills the way the Japanese did. *(Sighing.)* No, they came in quietly; they didn't even get much resistance from the common people. They had done a good job of intimidating anyone who disagreed with them. They held political meetings on Sunday morning so no one would dare come to services. Thank God for the faithful few who resisted. That reminds me: it's time to write my monthly letter to the government. Who knows—maybe this time they'll pay some attention to me. *(Starts rummaging through a few papers and items on her table. She finds a stub of a pencil, goes to the door and calls out.)* Guards ... guards ... may I please have a piece of paper? ... Yes, I'm sure it's time for my next letter. It's the end of the month, isn't it? ... But why must I wait until tomorrow? Surely one day can't make any difference. ... *(Backing away from door.)* Very well, whatever you say. ... Silly old man, what could it possible hurt to let me write it today? *(Violently throws pencil on table. She begins pacing floor.)* I still can't believe they think I'm a spy. Imagine—*me!* The most political thing I ever did is meet Harry Truman along with a group of missionaries on furlough. "Spy for the Inner Circle"—indeed! The biggest secret he ever told us was that he was a Baptist, too! *(Sounds of key in her door. A young Chinese woman enters carrying a tray with a bowl and a cup.)* Oh, Ah-Sim, is it dinner time already?

AH-SIM: Yes, ma'am. And I have a little surprise for you. Look! I was able to get an egg from my sister, Goo Ma. *(Puts tray on table.)*

LOUISE: An egg! How lovely! But can she spare it? *(Sits at table.)*

AH-SIM: Oh, yes, her chicken is laying a little better these days. Besides, she remembers you with much affection. *(Checks to make sure no one is listening by the door.)* She asked me to tell you that no one believes the accusations that have been brought against you. Most of your accusers felt they *had* to make something up or be imprisoned themselves. She asked you to try to understand.

LOUISE: Please assure her that I understand and, what's more important, that I forgive her.

AH-SIM: Bad as accusing you may be, the situation is even more serious than that, ma'am. Everyone is being taught to watch others and find fault. The children at school are required to take part in oral criticism sessions in which they accuse each other of real and imaginary faults in front of the entire class. If they refuse to participate, they are accused of poor citizenship, and it's recorded in the student's personal file.

LOUISE: Is that so? I didn't realize things had gotten so bad. I really am sorry, Ah-Sim.

AH-SIM: I didn't mean to worry you, but I wanted to be sure you understood what is really happening to us. Now, eat your dinner while it's still hot. I'll wait here until you have finished. *(Sits on edge of cot.)*

LOUISE *(bows head and prays):* Thank you, Father, for your constant care and blessings. Thank you for Goo Ma who has shared this beautiful egg with me. Help us to be loving to those who revile us and persecute us for your sake. Help us to be constant in our faith. Bless all who are imprisoned this evening, and give them courage and strength. In Jesus' name. Amen.

AH-SIM: How was it last night? Have they stopped trying to scare you with all that yelling and stomping about?

LOUISE: Not really, though it's not nearly as bad here as it was when I was confined in my house. There I thought I would go mad with all the banging on the walls and the noise at night. It was the things they screamed at me that were the most frightening: "Now we've got her! Now we've got her!" Somehow that scared me more than anything else they did. *(Stops to eat a bit of food.)* What I really wish I could have now is some peaceful darkness at night. They keep the light on all through the night, and I find it difficult to sleep. *(Wiping mouth with napkin.)* Ummm, that egg tasted wonderful. Please thank Goo Ma for me. There, I've finished. That was such a lovely treat. *(Puts napkin on tray and gets up.)*

AH-SIM *(standing and picking up tray):* I'd better leave now. It's getting late.

LOUISE: Yes, of course. Ah-Sim, will you do me a favor on your way out? Please stop by Loren Noren's door and signal him that I want to speak to him?

AH-SIM *(alarmed):* But, ma'am, you're not allowed. If you were caught ...

LOUISE: Don't worry, dear; I didn't mean that we would speak out loud. We have our own sign language, and when the guards are not paying close attention, we talk that way. Very rarely are we able to talk out loud. Usually that only happens when one of us is being taken out for interrogation. Feel better?

AH-SIM: I should have known you wouldn't do anything foolish. Of course I'll tell him. Good night. (*AH-SIM exits, sound of keys turning in the lock.*)

(*LOUISE walks to door, or exit, smiles, and makes the motions of forming letters on the window. She spells out her message and speaks out loud the words she is forming. She will also relate for the audience what LOREN answers.*)

LOUISE: A-m stop (*points finger as signal for stop or next word*) f-e-a-r-f-u-l stop. N-e-e-d stop t-o stop d-o stop m-o-r-e stop t-o-w-a-r-d-s stop r-e-l-e-a-s-e stop.

(*Begins to read LOREN's message in the same manner.*) P-s-a-l-m stop 3-7 stop 7. Psalm 37:7. What is that? Oh, how I wish I still had my Bible with me. Let me see; oh, yes, I remember: "Rest in the Lord; wait patiently for him." Oh, Loren. I'm tired of waiting. (*Begins to spell for LOREN.*) P-h-i-l-l-i-p-p-i-a-n-s stop 2 stop 1-2-b stop. There, he ought to remember that quotation easily: "Work out your own salvation with fear and trembling."

(*Reads again.*) S-a-m-e stop 2 stop 1-4 stop. D-o stop a-l-l stop t-h-i-n-g-s stop w-i-t-h-o-u-t stop g-r-u-m-b-l-i-n-g stop o-r stop q-u-e-s-t-i-o-n-i-n-g. (*Leaves window and sits on cot with head in hands.*) "Do all things without grumbling or questioning." Dear God, I know you're watching over us. It just seems to me that you want us to *do* more. How can all this sitting be useful? (*Pause.*) The truth is that I'm scared, just plain scared. I trust you in *all* things, Lord, especially the important things. It's the little things that upset me most. I feel so helpless. I'm used to *doing* things—planning, organizing, leading. Dear Lord, speak to me in this cell. Tell me what you want me to do, how you want me to feel. (*LOREN's voice is heard singing clearly. The words to the following hymn are very important.*)

He leadeth me: O blessed thought!
O words with heavenly comfort fraught!
Whate'er I do, where'er I be,
Still 'tis God's hand that leadeth me.
(*Two other voices, a man's and a woman's, join in the chorus.*)
He leadeth me, He leadeth me,

By His own hand He leadeth me:
(*Singers continue with hymn while LOUISE speaks the following words.*)
Dr. Giedt, Abby, Loren, how wonderful of you to sing directly to my need! I hear you, Lord, and I'm ready to listen.

His faithful follower I would be,
For by His hand He leadeth me.
Sometimes 'mid scenes of deepest gloom,
Sometimes where Eden's bowers bloom,
By waters calm, o'er troubled sea,
Still 'tis His hand that leadeth me.
He leadeth me, He leadeth me,
By His own hand He leadeth me:
His faithful follower I would be,
For by His hand He leadeth me.
(*LOUISE stands facing audience. Her face is radiant. She begins to sing with the other captives—triumphantly.*)
Lord, I would clasp Thy hand in mine,
Nor ever murmur nor repine;
Content, whatever lot I see,
Since 'tis my God that leadeth me.
He leadeth me, He leadeth me,
By His own hand He leadeth me:
His faithful follower I would be,
For by His hand He leadeth me.

—curtain—

Epilogue

(*This should be read to the audience while the room is still in darkness.*)

Twenty-one months after their "room arrest" began, the missionaries were suddenly and unceremoniously released. Christmas night of the second Christmas they had been captives, they were told to get out! "It was as if we'd been wanting to stay there," relates Miss Giffin. She and Miss Sanderson were released together. The guards escorted both Miss Giffin and Miss Sanderson home. "So after twenty-one months I was suddenly just perfectly free. It seemed impossible to me."

Miss Giffin indicated that the greatest lesson she learned during this experience was to rely completely on God. She says, "I can remember so clearly the day that the thought came to me: 'Well, the Lord knows all about this; whether you live or die, you are still a witness; you are a testimony to your faith, and you don't need to fear.' After that, life was much easier."

Probes

1. Do you feel sympathy for imprisoned missionaries, or do you consider that this is just a risk of their profession?

2. How do you think you would react if you found yourself in a situation similar to that of Louise Giffin?

3. Are modern missionaries still facing dangers and threats of imprisonment or death, or are they simply pastors and other specialists serving in other countries?

4. Review the experiences of Paul as a missionary. Were his imprisonments and hardships different from or similar to difficulties suffered by modern missionaries? The experiences of Adoniram Judson and Ann Judson would be revealing.

Room Arrest
A Dramatic Trio

Room Arrest is based on the true-life experiences of Louise Giffin, missionary for the American Baptist Churches, U.S.A. Born into a Baptist missionary family in South China, Louise came to the U.S. to acquire her professional training and after a few years returned to South China to teach. She endured the Japanese occupation during World War II, but her career there was ended by twenty-one months of solitary confinement when the Communists took over South China in 1949.

While the scene recreated here actually took place throughout her entire confinement, freedom has been exercised in telescoping the events into one day. Liberty has also been taken in selecting hymns and Scripture that relate the feeling Miss Giffin expressed in a personal interview. Incarcerated at the same time as Miss Giffin were Loren Noren, Abby Sanderson, Dr. Emanuel Giedt (pronounced Geet), all American Baptist missionaries, and a Catholic priest.

STAGING: This confinement took place in a Catholic convent, and it is assumed that Miss Giffin's room was a nun's cell. Loren's cell, which is never seen, is understood to be catercornered so that he is able to see all the other rooms, while Louise can see only his. In her room she has a table, a chair, a cot (fold-up type would be appropriate), and a lamp. It is not necessary to have an actual door on the set. An exit downstage right is all that is needed. When Louise speaks to Loren, she will actually face the *audience* downstage right.

CHARACTERIZATION AND MOOD: While Loren is never seen by the audience, his role is pivotal to the movement of the scene. He memorized a total of 180 hymns during his imprisonment. The directions indicate that it is not important for him to "sing especially well"; however, it is important for him to be able to carry a tune. One of the ways in which Loren kept up his physical fitness was by pacing back and forth (ten steps in each direction) in his cell. His pacing must be heard clearly, as it not only highlights a vital aspect of his personality, but also the rhythm of his pacing and the meaning of the words of the hymns have been

---

The facts for this play came from a taped interview with Louise Giffin.

combined to create a specific mood; timelessness and the presence of God must be felt throughout the drama.

SETTING: *A woman about thirty-five years of age is sitting on a straight-backed chair, knitting a sweater. She is using parts of a bamboo clothes hanger for knitting needles. LOREN's voice is always heard offstage. If his voice is not strong enough, it is suggested that a microphone be used with the sound set at a medium level. It does not matter if LOREN does not sing especially well. The words and the mood are what is most important.*

LOREN *(singing):* What a friend we have in Jesus,
All our sins and griefs to bear.
What a privilege to carry
Everything to God in prayer.
Oh, what peace. . . .

LOUISE *(looking up from her knitting and whispering):* Why have you stopped singing? *(No answer. She puts her knitting down and goes to the cell door.)* Loren, are you OK? Why have you stopped singing? *(Still no answer. Sounds of keys in lock next door. Footsteps are heard moving away, and a door slams.)* Oh, poor Loren. Not again!

LOREN *(half whisper):* No, Louise, I'm all right. I think they took Dr. Giedt, though.

LOUISE *(returns to her knitting):* Poor Dr. Geidt. I hope he's strong enough to withstand another interrogation. I wonder what they're accusing him of now.

LOREN: He's strong enough. *(Begins pacing. Audience hears ten steps in one direction, then ten steps back. He continues pacing in this fashion throughout LOUISE's next speech. The pacing must be deliberate and steady.)*

LOUISE *(speaking to herself—stream of consciousness):* I guess we all have to be strong. I thought I knew what fear was during the war. I remember when I first saw those Japanese gun boats come sailing into Swatow [Swah-toe] Harbor. I thought my heart would stop beating. It was 10 A.M. exactly when the first group of soldiers came swarming over the hills surrounding the

147

missionary compound. I didn't want to show it, but I was afraid! I knew God was taking care of us; nevertheless, I was terrified! *(She pauses—sounds of pacing become louder.)* It sent shivers up and down my spine to see those guards stationed all over the city. I think *they* frightened me more than the bombs had. Until then, the *they* who bombed us were anonymous. But now *they* had faces and *they* stood by my door at night and watched my every move during the day.

(LOREN continues pacing—starts to sing quietly "Sweet Hour of Prayer." He sings it hesitantly, stopping frequently to go over the same words.)

LOUISE: Hasn't he finished memorizing that one yet? *(Goes to door; in half whisper.)* Loren, Loren?

LOREN *(stops singing and pacing)*: Yes?

LOUISE: How many hymns have you memorized so far?

LOREN: One hundred fifty-three. Thank God for this English language hymnal. It's the only thing keeping my mind alert.

LOUISE: That and your pacing ten steps forward, ten steps back. Sometimes I walk them with you for the exercise.

LOREN: Why don't you try memorizing hymns, too?

LOUISE: I did, but I have only a Chinese hymnal, and it's just not the same.

LOREN: That's true. Well, at least you have your knitting. How many times have you knitted that sweater?

LOUISE *(laughing softly)*: I think this makes four, or is it five? I don't know. I do remember that last time I knit two left front sides.

LOREN: Your yarn holding out OK?

LOUISE: Pretty good *(holding up knitting)*, but it looks like it's getting curlier and curlier. *(Both laugh.)* Not much you can do with a pair of knitting needles whittled from a bamboo coat hanger with the top of a tin can.

LOREN: Shh—I think I hear the guards coming back. Better not talk anymore.

LOUISE *(moves to the opposite wall, speaking to herself again)*: How nice. Our Communist buddies are back. I wish God would send us an angel to open these doors the way he did for Peter. Wouldn't that be a shock for dear old Mao? *(Returns to her knitting. The pacing backstage resumes. LOUISE continues her reverie as though she had never stopped.)* Going inland on vacation in the summer of '41 was certainly a blessing. Who could guess that the harbor would be blockaded and that we'd not be able to get back to Swatow? At least that was one time the Lord delivered me from a concentration camp. The other missionaries were not as fortunate. Did God feel I'd not be able to survive imprisonment twice? He knew this imprisonment was coming. I wonder.

LOREN *(quietly reciting the words of "In the Hour of Trial." LOUISE sits and listens as LOREN's voice gets louder)*:

In the hour of trial, Jesus, plead for me,
Lest, by base denial, I depart from Thee.
When Thou seest me waver, with a look recall,
Nor for fear or favor suffer me to fall.
(She joins him with great conviction.)

LOREN AND
LOUISE: Should Thy mercy send me sorrow, toil, and woe;
Or should pain attend me on my path below;
Grant that I may never fail Thy hand to see;
Grant that I may ever cast my care on Thee.

LOUISE *(quietly to herself)*: Thank you, Loren! How did you know I needed that just now? My thoughts are bringing me a lot of pain today.... *(Angrily.)* The Communists! Oh, in '49 they didn't come swarming over the hills the way the Japanese did. *(Sighing.)* No, they came in quietly; they didn't even get much resistance from the common people. They had done a good job of intimidating anyone who disagreed with them. They held political meetings on Sunday morning so no one would dare come to services. Thank God for the faithful few who resisted. That reminds me: it's time to write my monthly letter to the government. Who knows—maybe this time they'll pay some attention to me. *(Starts rummaging through a few papers and items on her table. She*

finds a stub of a pencil, goes to the door and calls out.) Guards . . . guards . . . may I please have a piece of paper? . . . Yes, I'm sure it's time for my next letter. It's the end of the month, isn't it? . . . But why must I wait until tomorrow? Surely one day can't make any difference. . . . *(Backing away from door.)* Very well, whatever you say. . . . Silly old man, what could it possible hurt to let me write it today? *(Violently throws pencil on table. She begins pacing floor.)* I still can't believe they think I'm a spy. Imagine—*me!* The most political thing I ever did is meet Harry Truman along with a group of missionaries on furlough. "Spy for the Inner Circle"—indeed! The biggest secret he ever told us was that he was a Baptist, too! *(Sounds of key in her door. A young Chinese woman enters carrying a tray with a bowl and a cup.)* Oh, Ah-Sim, is it dinner time already?

AH-SIM: Yes, ma'am. And I have a little surprise for you. Look! I was able to get an egg from my sister, Goo Ma. *(Puts tray on table.)*

LOUISE: An egg! How lovely! But can she spare it? *(Sits at table.)*

AH-SIM: Oh, yes, her chicken is laying a little better these days. Besides, she remembers you with much affection. *(Checks to make sure no one is listening by the door.)* She asked me to tell you that no one believes the accusations that have been brought against you. Most of your accusers felt they *had* to make something up or be imprisoned themselves. She asked you to try to understand.

LOUISE: Please assure her that I understand and, what's more important, that I forgive her.

AH-SIM: Bad as accusing you may be, the situation is even more serious than that, ma'am. Everyone is being taught to watch others and find fault. The children at school are required to take part in oral criticism sessions in which they accuse each other of real and imaginary faults in front of the entire class. If they refuse to participate, they are accused of poor citizenship, and it's recorded in the student's personal file.

LOUISE: Is that so? I didn't realize things had gotten so bad. I really am sorry, Ah-Sim.

AH-SIM: I didn't mean to worry you, but I wanted to be sure you understood what is really happening to us. Now, eat your dinner while it's still hot. I'll wait here until you have finished. *(Sits on edge of cot.)*

LOUISE *(bows head and prays):* Thank you, Father, for your constant care and blessings. Thank you for Goo Ma who has shared this beautiful egg with me. Help us to be loving to those who revile us and persecute us for your sake. Help us to be constant in our faith. Bless all who are imprisoned this evening, and give them courage and strength. In Jesus' name. Amen.

AH-SIM: How was it last night? Have they stopped trying to scare you with all that yelling and stomping about?

LOUISE: Not really, though it's not nearly as bad here as it was when I was confined in my house. There I thought I would go mad with all the banging on the walls and the noise at night. It was the things they screamed at me that were the most frightening: "Now we've got her! Now we've got her!" Somehow that scared me more than anything else they did. *(Stops to eat a bit of food.)* What I really wish I could have now is some peaceful darkness at night. They keep the light on all through the night, and I find it difficult to sleep. *(Wiping mouth with napkin.)* Ummm, that egg tasted wonderful. Please thank Goo Ma for me. There, I've finished. That was such a lovely treat. *(Puts napkin on tray and gets up.)*

AH-SIM *(standing and picking up tray):* I'd better leave now. It's getting late.

LOUISE: Yes, of course. Ah-Sim, will you do me a favor on your way out? Please stop by Loren Noren's door and signal him that I want to speak to him?

AH-SIM *(alarmed):* But, ma'am, you're not allowed. If you were caught . . .

LOUISE: Don't worry, dear; I didn't mean that we would speak out loud. We have our own sign language, and when the guards are not paying close attention, we talk that way. Very rarely are we able to talk out loud. Usually that only happens when one of us is being taken out for interrogation. Feel better?

149

AH-SIM: I should have known you wouldn't do anything foolish. Of course I'll tell him. Good night. *(AH-SIM exits, sound of keys turning in the lock.)*

(LOUISE walks to door, or exit, smiles, and makes the motions of forming letters on the window. She spells out her message and speaks out loud the words she is forming. She will also relate for the audience what LOREN answers.)

LOUISE: A-m stop *(points finger as signal for stop or next word)* f-e-a-r-f-u-l stop. N-e-e-d stop t-o stop d-o stop m-o-r-e stop t-o-w-a-r-d-s stop r-e-l-e-a-s-e stop.

(Begins to read LOREN's message in the same manner.) P-s-a-l-m stop 3-7 stop 7. Psalm 37:7. What is that? Oh, how I wish I still had my Bible with me. Let me see; oh, yes, I remember: "Rest in the Lord; wait patiently for him." Oh, Loren. I'm tired of waiting. *(Begins to spell for LOREN.)* P-h-i-l-i-p-p-i-a-n-s stop 2 stop 1-2-b stop. There, he ought to remember that quotation easily: "Work out your own salvation with fear and trembling."

(Reads again.) S-a-m-e stop 2 stop 1-4 stop. D-o stop a-l-l stop t-h-i-n-g-s stop w-i-t-h-o-u-t stop g-r-u-m-b-l-i-n-g stop o-r stop q-u-e-s-t-i-o-n-i-n-g. *(Leaves window and sits on cot with head in hands.)* "Do all things without grumbling or questioning." Dear God, I know you're watching over us. It just seems to me that you want us to *do* more. How can all this sitting be useful? *(Pause.)* The truth is that I'm scared, just plain scared. I trust you in *all* things, Lord, especially the important things. It's the little things that upset me most. I feel so helpless. I'm used to *doing* things—planning, organizing, leading. Dear Lord, speak to me in this cell. Tell me what you want me to do, how you want me to feel. *(LOREN's voice is heard singing clearly. The words to the following hymn are very important.)*

He leadeth me: O blessed thought!
O words with heavenly comfort fraught!
Whate'er I do, where'er I be,
Still 'tis God's hand that leadeth me.
(Two other voices, a man's and a woman's, join in the chorus.)
He leadeth me, He leadeth me,
By His own hand He leadeth me:
(Singers continue with hymn while LOUISE speaks the following words.)
Dr. Giedt, Abby, Loren, how wonderful of you to sing directly to my need! I hear you, Lord, and I'm ready to listen.
His faithful follower I would be,
For by His hand He leadeth me.
Sometimes 'mid scenes of deepest gloom,
Sometimes where Eden's bowers bloom,
By waters calm, o'er troubled sea,
Still 'tis His hand that leadeth me.
He leadeth me, He leadeth me,
By His own hand He leadeth me:
His faithful follower I would be,
For by His hand He leadeth me.
(LOUISE stands facing audience. Her face is radiant. She begins to sing with the other captives—triumphantly.)
Lord, I would clasp Thy hand in mine,
Nor ever murmur nor repine;
Content, whatever lot I see,
Since 'tis my God that leadeth me.
He leadeth me, He leadeth me,
By His own hand He leadeth me:
His faithful follower I would be,
For by His hand He leadeth me.

—curtain—

Epilogue

(This should be read to the audience while the room is still in darkness.)

Twenty-one months after their "room arrest " began, the missionaries were suddenly and unceremoniously released. Christmas night of the second Christmas they had been captives, they were told to get out! "It was as if we'd been wanting to stay there," relates Miss Giffin. She and Miss Sanderson were released together. The guards escorted both Miss Giffin and Miss Sanderson home. "So after twenty-one months I was suddenly just perfectly free. It seemed impossible to me."

Miss Giffin indicated that the greatest lesson she learned during this experience was to rely completely on God. She says, "I can remember so clearly the day that the thought came to me: 'Well, the Lord knows all about this; whether you live or die, you are still a witness; you are a testimony to your faith, and you don't need to fear.' After that, life was much easier."

Probes

1. Do you feel sympathy for imprisoned missionaries, or do you consider that this is just a risk of their profession?

2. How do you think you would react if you found yourself in a situation similar to that of Louise Giffin?

3. Are modern missionaries still facing dangers and threats of imprisonment or death, or are they simply pastors and other specialists serving in other countries?

4. Review the experiences of Paul as a missionary. Were his imprisonments and hardships different from or similar to difficulties suffered by modern missionaries? The experiences of Adoniram Judson and Ann Judson would be revealing.

Cheap Grace
Three Satirical Stingers

Part I

SETTING: *A bare room with an empty counter (or table). A young person is busy working when another walks in. Over the counter is a sign which reads:*

> G
> I
> N
> O

WAITER *(wiping counter):* Yeah, what can I get ya?

CUSTOMER *(self-consciously):* Ah—I heard you could get a full course—ah—inexpensively here.

WAITER: Yeah, that's right. So, what do ya want?

CUSTOMER: I don't know; what do you have?

WAITER: Are ya serious?

CUSTOMER: Of course. I haven't seen your menu.

WAITER *(exasperated):* Look, this is a fast-service place. We don't have no menus. We just sell one thing. If you want menus, you'll have to go to . . .

CUSTOMER *(interrupting):* No, no, this is the place I want. It's just that I don't understand your sign.

WAITER *(turning around):* Wha . . . Oh, yeah, sorry, thought I had put it up this morning. Just a minute. *(WAITER gets out cards from under counter and completes the sign.)*

> *G* race
> *I* n a hurry
> *N* o
> *O* bligation

There you are, mister. How much cheap grace can I give ya?

CUSTOMER: Well, I'm in a hurry; so why don't you just give me the large bucket size? That way I won't have to worry about it for a while.

—blackout—

Part II

SETTING: *The same counter remains, but now sign reads BARGAIN BASEMENT.*

Two women walk in and start rummaging through sundry articles on the counter. An elderly person comes to wait on them.

SALESPERSON: May I help you?

WOMAN #1: No, we're just looking. *(Picks up a garment and puts it up against herself as if measuring it for size.)*

WOMAN #2: Find something good?

WOMAN #1: I don't know—maybe.

SALESPERSON: Oh, that's a nice number, and at a good price, too.

WOMAN #1 *(looks at price tag):* Oh, no, this is no bargain. I could get this cheaper at Simpson's.

SALESPERSON: Yes, but the quality here is much finer.

WOMAN #2: We're not interested in paying a lot of money. We came here looking for something cheap—a bargain. *(Searches a bit more among articles on counter; comes upon a book.)* What's this?

SALESPERSON: Oh, that's nothing; just a book.

WOMAN #2: Yeah? *(Flips through pages.)* Look. *(Shows book to friend.)* This is just what I need.

WOMAN #1: What does it say?

WOMAN #2: THE GOOD NEWS. Hey, that sounds OK.

WOMAN #1: Yeah, I could use some good news. *(Taking out purse.)* What's it cost, Miss?

SALESPERSON: Oh, not much. Some even think it comes free.

WOMEN #1 AND #2: SOLD!

—blackout—

Part III

SETTING: *The same counter remains, but now the sign reads GARAGE SALE. Two persons walk in.*

PERSON #1: Whew! It stinks in here.

PERSON #2: It's a musty garage, so what? We're looking for a bargain, and you don't get nice decor with a bargain.

PERSON #1: I guess not.

PERSON #2: Hey, look at some of this stuff. Makes you wonder who would buy this kind of junk.

PERSON #1: Speak kindly of the customers, dear. Remember, you are one of them.

PERSON #2: I guess so, but I wish the owner would get here.

OWNER *(entering stage left):* Someone call for me?

PERSON #2: Yes; we were told that this would be a fine place to pick up a good bargain.

OWNER: *I* think so. Some of these things have been in the family for years. Some of them are really quite nice.

PERSON #2: Yes. As a matter of fact, we saw your ad in the paper and were attracted by the wooden cross.

PERSON #1: We think it might make a good conversation piece in our home. All the best families have one. What did you pay for it originally?

OWNER: To be honest with you, we didn't pay anything for it. Someone else did.

PERSON #2: So, how much do *you* want for it.

OWNER: Me? Nothing. I don't want to own it anymore.

PERSON #1: Fine. We'll take it.

—blackout—

Probes

1. Discuss the statement "Cheap grace means grace sold on the market like cheapjack's wares. The sacraments, the forgiveness of sin, and the consolations of religion are thrown away at cut prices."[1]

2. Compare the following statement with the statement in the first probe: "Costly grace is the treasure hidden in the field; for the sake of it a man will gladly go and sell all that he has. . . . it is the call of Jesus Christ at which the disciple leaves his nets and follows him."[2]

3. Discuss the place of faith and works in the Christian life, referring to the biblical ideas of "justification by faith" and "faith without works is dead."

4. We are saved by grace through faith without works (Ephesians 2:8-9). The Good News and the cross assuredly are freely given to us. What other biblical references point to our responsibility? See, for example, Romans 10:17 and Matthew 10:38.

[1]Dietrich Bonhoeffer, *The Cost of Discipleship* (New York: The Macmillan Company, 1959), p. 35.
[2]*Ibid.,* p. 36.

154

Cheap Grace
Three Satirical Stingers

Part I

SETTING: *A bare room with an empty counter (or table). A young person is busy working when another walks in. Over the counter is a sign which reads:*

G
I
N
O

WAITER *(wiping counter):* Yeah, what can I get ya?

CUSTOMER *(self-consciously):* Ah—I heard you could get a full course—ah—inexpensively here.

WAITER: Yeah, that's right. So, what do ya want?

CUSTOMER: I don't know; what do you have?

WAITER: Are ya serious?

CUSTOMER: Of course. I haven't seen your menu.

WAITER *(exasperated):* Look, this is a fast-service place. We don't have no menus. We just sell one thing. If you want menus, you'll have to go to . . .

CUSTOMER *(interrupting):* No, no, this is the place I want. It's just that I don't understand your sign.

WAITER *(turning around):* Wha . . . Oh, yeah, sorry, thought I had put it up this morning. Just a minute. *(WAITER gets out cards from under counter and completes the sign.)*

G race
I n a hurry
N o
O bligation

There you are, mister. How much cheap grace can I give ya?

CUSTOMER: Well, I'm in a hurry; so why don't you just give me the large bucket size? That way I won't have to worry about it for a while.

—*blackout*—

Part II

SETTING: *The same counter remains, but now sign reads BARGAIN BASEMENT.*

Two women walk in and start rummaging through sundry articles on the counter. An elderly person comes to wait on them.

SALESPERSON: May I help you?

WOMAN #1: No, we're just looking. *(Picks up a garment and puts it up against herself as if measuring it for size.)*

WOMAN #2: Find something good?

WOMAN #1: I don't know—maybe.

SALESPERSON: Oh, that's a nice number, and at a good price, too.

WOMAN #1 *(looks at price tag):* Oh, no, this is no bargain. I could get this cheaper at Simpson's.

SALESPERSON: Yes, but the quality here is much finer.

WOMAN #2: We're not interested in paying a lot of money. We came here looking for something cheap—a bargain. *(Searches a bit more among articles on counter; comes upon a book.)* What's this?

SALESPERSON: Oh, that's nothing; just a book.

WOMAN #2: Yeah? *(Flips through pages.)* Look. *(Shows book to friend.)* This is just what I need.

WOMAN #1: What does it say?

WOMAN #2: THE GOOD NEWS. Hey, that sounds OK.

WOMAN #1: Yeah, I could use some good news. *(Taking out purse.)* What's it cost, Miss?

SALESPERSON: Oh, not much. Some even think it comes free.

WOMEN #1 AND #2: SOLD!

—*blackout*—

Part III

SETTING: *The same counter remains, but now the sign reads GARAGE SALE. Two persons walk in.*

PERSON #1: Whew! It stinks in here.

PERSON #2: It's a musty garage, so what? We're looking for a bargain, and you don't get nice decor with a bargain.

PERSON #1: I guess not.

PERSON #2: Hey, look at some of this stuff. Makes you wonder who would buy this kind of junk.

PERSON #1: Speak kindly of the customers, dear. Remember, you are one of them.

PERSON #2: I guess so, but I wish the owner would get here.

OWNER (entering stage left): Someone call for me?

PERSON #2: Yes; we were told that this would be a fine place to pick up a good bargain.

OWNER: I think so. Some of these things have been in the family for years. Some of them are really quite nice.

PERSON #2: Yes. As a matter of fact, we saw your ad in the paper and were attracted by the wooden cross.

PERSON #1: We think it might make a good conversation piece in our home. All the best families have one. What did you pay for it originally?

OWNER: To be honest with you, we didn't pay anything for it. Someone else did.

PERSON #2: So, how much do *you* want for it.

OWNER: Me? Nothing. I don't want to own it anymore.

PERSON #1: Fine. We'll take it.

—blackout—

Probes

1. Discuss the statement "Cheap grace means grace sold on the market like cheapjack's wares. The sacraments, the forgiveness of sin, and the consolations of religion are thrown away at cut prices." [1]

2. Compare the following statement with the statement in the first probe: "Costly grace is the treasure hidden in the field; for the sake of it a man will gladly go and sell all that he has. . . . it is the call of Jesus Christ at which the disciple leaves his nets and follows him." [2]

3. Discuss the place of faith and works in the Christian life, referring to the biblical ideas of "justification by faith" and "faith without works is dead."

4. We are saved by grace through faith without works (Ephesians 2:8-9). The Good News and the cross assuredly are freely given to us. What other biblical references point to our responsibility? See, for example, Romans 10:17 and Matthew 10:38.

[1]Dietrich Bonhoeffer, *The Cost of Discipleship* (New York: The Macmillan Company, 1959), p. 35.
[2]*Ibid.*, p. 36.

Cheap Grace
Three Satirical Stingers

Part I

SETTING: *A bare room with an empty counter (or table). A young person is busy working when another walks in. Over the counter is a sign which reads:*

G
I
N
O

WAITER *(wiping counter):* Yeah, what can I get ya?

CUSTOMER *(self-consciously):* Ah—I heard you could get a full course—ah—inexpensively here.

WAITER: Yeah, that's right. So, what do ya want?

CUSTOMER: I don't know; what do you have?

WAITER: Are ya serious?

CUSTOMER: Of course. I haven't seen your menu.

WAITER *(exasperated):* Look, this is a fast-service place. We don't have no menus. We just sell one thing. If you want menus, you'll have to go to . . .

CUSTOMER *(interrupting):* No, no, this is the place I want. It's just that I don't understand your sign.

WAITER *(turning around):* Wha . . . Oh, yeah, sorry, thought I had put it up this morning. Just a minute. *(WAITER gets out cards from under counter and completes the sign.)*

G race
I n a hurry
N o
O bligation

There you are, mister. How much cheap grace can I give ya?

CUSTOMER: Well, I'm in a hurry; so why don't you just give me the large bucket size? That way I won't have to worry about it for a while.

—*blackout*—

Part II

SETTING: *The same counter remains, but now sign reads BARGAIN BASEMENT.*

Two women walk in and start rummaging through sundry articles on the counter. An elderly person comes to wait on them.

SALESPERSON: May I help you?

WOMAN #1: No, we're just looking. *(Picks up a garment and puts it up against herself as if measuring it for size.)*

WOMAN #2: Find something good?

WOMAN #1: I don't know—maybe.

SALESPERSON: Oh, that's a nice number, and at a good price, too.

WOMAN #1 *(looks at price tag):* Oh, no, this is no bargain. I could get this cheaper at Simpson's.

SALESPERSON: Yes, but the quality here is much finer.

WOMAN #2: We're not interested in paying a lot of money. We came here looking for something cheap—a bargain. *(Searches a bit more among articles on counter; comes upon a book.)* What's this?

SALESPERSON: Oh, that's nothing; just a book.

WOMAN #2: Yeah? *(Flips through pages.)* Look. *(Shows book to friend.)* This is just what I need.

WOMAN #1: What does it say?

WOMAN #2: THE GOOD NEWS. Hey, that sounds OK.

WOMAN #1: Yeah, I could use some good news. *(Taking out purse.)* What's it cost, Miss?

SALESPERSON: Oh, not much. Some even think it comes free.

WOMEN #1 AND #2: SOLD!

—*blackout*—

Part III

SETTING: *The same counter remains, but now the sign reads GARAGE SALE. Two persons walk in.*

PERSON #1: Whew! It stinks in here.

PERSON #2: It's a musty garage, so what? We're looking for a bargain, and you don't get nice decor with a bargain.

PERSON #1: I guess not.

PERSON #2: Hey, look at some of this stuff. Makes you wonder who would buy this kind of junk.

PERSON #1: Speak kindly of the customers, dear. Remember, you are one of them.

PERSON #2: I guess so, but I wish the owner would get here.

OWNER *(entering stage left)*: Someone call for me?

PERSON #2: Yes; we were told that this would be a fine place to pick up a good bargain.

OWNER: *I* think so. Some of these things have been in the family for years. Some of them are really quite nice.

PERSON #2: Yes. As a matter of fact, we saw your ad in the paper and were attracted by the wooden cross.

PERSON #1: We think it might make a good conversation piece in our home. All the best families have one. What did you pay for it originally?

OWNER: To be honest with you, we didn't pay anything for it. Someone else did.

PERSON #2: So, how much do *you* want for it.

OWNER: Me? Nothing. I don't want to own it anymore.

PERSON #1: Fine. We'll take it.

—blackout—

Probes

1. Discuss the statement "Cheap grace means grace sold on the market like cheapjack's wares. The sacraments, the forgiveness of sin, and the consolations of religion are thrown away at cut prices."[1]

2. Compare the following statement with the statement in the first probe: "Costly grace is the treasure hidden in the field; for the sake of it a man will gladly go and sell all that he has. . . . it is the call of Jesus Christ at which the disciple leaves his nets and follows him."[2]

3. Discuss the place of faith and works in the Christian life, referring to the biblical ideas of "justification by faith" and "faith without works is dead."

4. We are saved by grace through faith without works (Ephesians 2:8-9). The Good News and the cross assuredly are freely given to us. What other biblical references point to our responsibility? See, for example, Romans 10:17 and Matthew 10:38.

[1] Dietrich Bonhoeffer, *The Cost of Discipleship* (New York: The Macmillan Company, 1959), p. 35.

[2] *Ibid.*, p. 36.

Cheap Grace
Three Satirical Stingers

Part I

SETTING: *A bare room with an empty counter (or table). A young person is busy working when another walks in. Over the counter is a sign which reads:*

> G
> I
> N
> O

WAITER *(wiping counter):* Yeah, what can I get ya?

CUSTOMER *(self-consciously):* Ah—I heard you could get a full course—ah—inexpensively here.

WAITER: Yeah, that's right. So, what do ya want?

CUSTOMER: I don't know; what do you have?

WAITER: Are ya serious?

CUSTOMER: Of course. I haven't seen your menu.

WAITER *(exasperated):* Look, this is a fast-service place. We don't have no menus. We just sell one thing. If you want menus, you'll have to go to . . .

CUSTOMER *(interrupting):* No, no, this is the place I want. It's just that I don't understand your sign.

WAITER *(turning around):* Wha . . . Oh, yeah, sorry, thought I had put it up this morning. Just a minute. *(WAITER gets out cards from under counter and completes the sign.)*

> G race
> I n a hurry
> N o
> O bligation

There you are, mister. How much cheap grace can I give ya?

CUSTOMER: Well, I'm in a hurry; so why don't you just give me the large bucket size? That way I won't have to worry about it for a while.

—blackout—

Part II

SETTING: *The same counter remains, but now sign reads BARGAIN BASEMENT.*

Two women walk in and start rummaging through sundry articles on the counter. An elderly person comes to wait on them.

SALESPERSON: May I help you?

WOMAN #1: No, we're just looking. *(Picks up a garment and puts it up against herself as if measuring it for size.)*

WOMAN #2: Find something good?

WOMAN #1: I don't know—maybe.

SALESPERSON: Oh, that's a nice number, and at a good price, too.

WOMAN #1 *(looks at price tag):* Oh, no, this is no bargain. I could get this cheaper at Simpson's.

SALESPERSON: Yes, but the quality here is much finer.

WOMAN #2: We're not interested in paying a lot of money. We came here looking for something cheap—a bargain. *(Searches a bit more among articles on counter; comes upon a book.)* What's this?

SALESPERSON: Oh, that's nothing; just a book.

WOMAN #2: Yeah? *(Flips through pages.)* Look. *(Shows book to friend.)* This is just what I need.

WOMAN #1: What does it say?

WOMAN #2: THE GOOD NEWS. Hey, that sounds OK.

WOMAN #1: Yeah, I could use some good news. *(Taking out purse.)* What's it cost, Miss?

SALESPERSON: Oh, not much. Some even think it comes free.

WOMEN #1 AND #2: SOLD!

—blackout—

Part III

SETTING: *The same counter remains, but now the sign reads GARAGE SALE. Two persons walk in.*

PERSON #1: Whew! It stinks in here.

PERSON #2: It's a musty garage, so what? We're looking for a bargain, and you don't get nice decor with a bargain.

PERSON #1: I guess not.

PERSON #2: Hey, look at some of this stuff. Makes you wonder who would buy this kind of junk.

PERSON #1: Speak kindly of the customers, dear. Remember, you are one of them.

PERSON #2: I guess so, but I wish the owner would get here.

OWNER (entering stage left): Someone call for me?

PERSON #2: Yes; we were told that this would be a fine place to pick up a good bargain.

OWNER: I think so. Some of these things have been in the family for years. Some of them are really quite nice.

PERSON #2: Yes. As a matter of fact, we saw your ad in the paper and were attracted by the wooden cross.

PERSON #1: We think it might make a good conversation piece in our home. All the best families have one. What did you pay for it originally?

OWNER: To be honest with you, we didn't pay anything for it. Someone else did.

PERSON #2: So, how much do you want for it.

OWNER: Me? Nothing. I don't want to own it anymore.

PERSON #1: Fine. We'll take it.

—blackout—

Probes

1. Discuss the statement "Cheap grace means grace sold on the market like cheapjack's wares. The sacraments, the forgiveness of sin, and the consolations of religion are thrown away at cut prices."[1]

2. Compare the following statement with the statement in the first probe: "Costly grace is the treasure hidden in the field; for the sake of it a man will gladly go and sell all that he has. . . . it is the call of Jesus Christ at which the disciple leaves his nets and follows him."[2]

3. Discuss the place of faith and works in the Christian life, referring to the biblical ideas of "justification by faith" and "faith without works is dead."

4. We are saved by grace through faith without works (Ephesians 2:8-9). The Good News and the cross assuredly are freely given to us. What other biblical references point to our responsibility? See, for example, Romans 10:17 and Matthew 10:38.

[1]Dietrich Bonhoeffer, *The Cost of Discipleship* (New York: The Macmillan Company, 1959), p. 35.
[2]*Ibid.*, p. 36.

Cheap Grace
Three Satirical Stingers

Part I

SETTING: *A bare room with an empty counter (or table). A young person is busy working when another walks in. Over the counter is a sign which reads:*
> G
> I
> N
> O

WAITER *(wiping counter):* Yeah, what can I get ya?

CUSTOMER *(self-consciously):* Ah—I heard you could get a full course—ah—inexpensively here.

WAITER: Yeah, that's right. So, what do ya want?

CUSTOMER: I don't know; what do you have?

WAITER: Are ya serious?

CUSTOMER: Of course. I haven't seen your menu.

WAITER *(exasperated):* Look, this is a fast-service place. We don't have no menus. We just sell one thing. If you want menus, you'll have to go to . . .

CUSTOMER *(interrupting):* No, no, this is the place I want. It's just that I don't understand your sign.

WAITER *(turning around):* Wha . . . Oh, yeah, sorry, thought I had put it up this morning. Just a minute. *(WAITER gets out cards from under counter and completes the sign.)*
> *G* race
> *I* n a hurry
> *N* o
> *O* bligation

There you are, mister. How much cheap grace can I give ya?

CUSTOMER: Well, I'm in a hurry; so why don't you just give me the large bucket size? That way I won't have to worry about it for a while.

—blackout—

Part II

SETTING: *The same counter remains, but now sign reads BARGAIN BASEMENT.*

Two women walk in and start rummaging through sundry articles on the counter. An elderly person comes to wait on them.

SALESPERSON: May I help you?

WOMAN #1: No, we're just looking. *(Picks up a garment and puts it up against herself as if measuring it for size.)*

WOMAN #2: Find something good?

WOMAN #1: I don't know—maybe.

SALESPERSON: Oh, that's a nice number, and at a good price, too.

WOMAN #1 *(looks at price tag):* Oh, no, this is no bargain. I could get this cheaper at Simpson's.

SALESPERSON: Yes, but the quality here is much finer.

WOMAN #2: We're not interested in paying a lot of money. We came here looking for something cheap—a bargain. *(Searches a bit more among articles on counter; comes upon a book.)* What's this?

SALESPERSON: Oh, that's nothing; just a book.

WOMAN #2: Yeah? *(Flips through pages.)* Look. *(Shows book to friend.)* This is just what I need.

WOMAN #1: What does it say?

WOMAN #2: THE GOOD NEWS. Hey, that sounds OK.

WOMAN #1: Yeah, I could use some good news. *(Taking out purse.)* What's it cost, Miss?

SALESPERSON: Oh, not much. Some even think it comes free.

WOMEN #1 AND #2: SOLD!

—blackout—

Part III

SETTING: *The same counter remains, but now the sign reads GARAGE SALE. Two persons walk in.*

PERSON #1: Whew! It stinks in here.

PERSON #2: It's a musty garage, so what? We're looking for a bargain, and you don't get nice decor with a bargain.

PERSON #1: I guess not.

PERSON #2: Hey, look at some of this stuff. Makes you wonder who would buy this kind of junk.

PERSON #1: Speak kindly of the customers, dear. Remember, you are one of them.

PERSON #2: I guess so, but I wish the owner would get here.

OWNER (entering stage left): Someone call for me?

PERSON #2: Yes; we were told that this would be a fine place to pick up a good bargain.

OWNER: I think so. Some of these things have been in the family for years. Some of them are really quite nice.

PERSON #2: Yes. As a matter of fact, we saw your ad in the paper and were attracted by the wooden cross.

PERSON #1: We think it might make a good conversation piece in our home. All the best families have one. What did you pay for it originally?

OWNER: To be honest with you, we didn't pay anything for it. Someone else did.

PERSON #2: So, how much do *you* want for it.

OWNER: Me? Nothing. I don't want to own it anymore.

PERSON #1: Fine. We'll take it.

—blackout—

Probes

1. Discuss the statement "Cheap grace means grace sold on the market like cheapjack's wares. The sacraments, the forgiveness of sin, and the consolations of religion are thrown away at cut prices."[1]

2. Compare the following statement with the statement in the first probe: "Costly grace is the treasure hidden in the field; for the sake of it a man will gladly go and sell all that he has. . . . it is the call of Jesus Christ at which the disciple leaves his nets and follows him."[2]

3. Discuss the place of faith and works in the Christian life, referring to the biblical ideas of "justification by faith" and "faith without works is dead."

4. We are saved by grace through faith without works (Ephesians 2:8-9). The Good News and the cross assuredly are freely given to us. What other biblical references point to our responsibility? See, for example, Romans 10:17 and Matthew 10:38.

[1]Dietrich Bonhoeffer, *The Cost of Discipleship* (New York: The Macmillan Company, 1959), p. 35.

[2]*Ibid.*, p. 36.

Cheap Grace
Three Satirical Stingers

Part I

SETTING: *A bare room with an empty counter (or table). A young person is busy working when another walks in. Over the counter is a sign which reads:*

G
I
N
O

WAITER *(wiping counter):* Yeah, what can I get ya?

CUSTOMER *(self-consciously):* Ah—I heard you could get a full course—ah—inexpensively here.

WAITER: Yeah, that's right. So, what do ya want?

CUSTOMER: I don't know; what do you have?

WAITER: Are ya serious?

CUSTOMER: Of course. I haven't seen your menu.

WAITER *(exasperated):* Look, this is a fast-service place. We don't have no menus. We just sell one thing. If you want menus, you'll have to go to . . .

CUSTOMER *(interrupting):* No, no, this is the place I want. It's just that I don't understand your sign.

WAITER *(turning around):* Wha . . . Oh, yeah, sorry, thought I had put it up this morning. Just a minute. *(WAITER gets out cards from under counter and completes the sign.)*

G race
I n a hurry
N o
O bligation

There you are, mister. How much cheap grace can I give ya?

CUSTOMER: Well, I'm in a hurry; so why don't you just give me the large bucket size? That way I won't have to worry about it for a while.

—*blackout*—

Part II

SETTING: *The same counter remains, but now sign reads BARGAIN BASEMENT.*

Two women walk in and start rummaging through sundry articles on the counter. An elderly person comes to wait on them.

SALESPERSON: May I help you?

WOMAN #1: No, we're just looking. *(Picks up a garment and puts it up against herself as if measuring it for size.)*

WOMAN #2: Find something good?

WOMAN #1: I don't know—maybe.

SALESPERSON: Oh, that's a nice number, and at a good price, too.

WOMAN #1 *(looks at price tag):* Oh, no, this is no bargain. I could get this cheaper at Simpson's.

SALESPERSON: Yes, but the quality here is much finer.

WOMAN #2: We're not interested in paying a lot of money. We came here looking for something cheap—a bargain. *(Searches a bit more among articles on counter; comes upon a book.)* What's this?

SALESPERSON: Oh, that's nothing; just a book.

WOMAN #2: Yeah? *(Flips through pages.)* Look. *(Shows book to friend.)* This is just what I need.

WOMAN #1: What does it say?

WOMAN #2: THE GOOD NEWS. Hey, that sounds OK.

WOMAN #1: Yeah, I could use some good news. *(Taking out purse.)* What's it cost, Miss?

SALESPERSON: Oh, not much. Some even think it comes free.

WOMEN #1 AND #2: SOLD!

—*blackout*—

Part III

SETTING: *The same counter remains, but now the sign reads GARAGE SALE. Two persons walk in.*

PERSON #1: Whew! It stinks in here.

PERSON #2: It's a musty garage, so what? We're looking for a bargain, and you don't get nice decor with a bargain.

PERSON #1: I guess not.

PERSON #2: Hey, look at some of this stuff. Makes you wonder who would buy this kind of junk.

PERSON #1: Speak kindly of the customers, dear. Remember, you are one of them.

PERSON #2: I guess so, but I wish the owner would get here.

OWNER *(entering stage left):* Someone call for me?

PERSON #2: Yes; we were told that this would be a fine place to pick up a good bargain.

OWNER: *I* think so. Some of these things have been in the family for years. Some of them are really quite nice.

PERSON #2: Yes. As a matter of fact, we saw your ad in the paper and were attracted by the wooden cross.

PERSON #1: We think it might make a good conversation piece in our home. All the best families have one. What did you pay for it originally?

OWNER: To be honest with you, we didn't pay anything for it. Someone else did.

PERSON #2: So, how much do *you* want for it.

OWNER: Me? Nothing. I don't want to own it anymore.

PERSON #1: Fine. We'll take it.

—blackout—

Probes

1. Discuss the statement "Cheap grace means grace sold on the market like cheapjack's wares. The sacraments, the forgiveness of sin, and the consolations of religion are thrown away at cut prices."[1]

2. Compare the following statement with the statement in the first probe: "Costly grace is the treasure hidden in the field; for the sake of it a man will gladly go and sell all that he has. . . . it is the call of Jesus Christ at which the disciple leaves his nets and follows him."[2]

3. Discuss the place of faith and works in the Christian life, referring to the biblical ideas of "justification by faith" and "faith without works is dead."

4. We are saved by grace through faith without works (Ephesians 2:8-9). The Good News and the cross assuredly are freely given to us. What other biblical references point to our responsibility? See, for example, Romans 10:17 and Matthew 10:38.

[1]Dietrich Bonhoeffer, *The Cost of Discipleship* (New York: The Macmillan Company, 1959), p. 35.
[2]*Ibid.,* p. 36.

Cheap Grace
Three Satirical Stingers

Part I

SETTING: *A bare room with an empty counter (or table). A young person is busy working when another walks in. Over the counter is a sign which reads:*

G
I
N
O

WAITER *(wiping counter):* Yeah, what can I get ya?

CUSTOMER *(self-consciously):* Ah—I heard you could get a full course—ah—inexpensively here.

WAITER: Yeah, that's right. So, what do ya want?

CUSTOMER: I don't know; what do you have?

WAITER: Are ya serious?

CUSTOMER: Of course. I haven't seen your menu.

WAITER *(exasperated):* Look, this is a fast-service place. We don't have no menus. We just sell one thing. If you want menus, you'll have to go to . . .

CUSTOMER *(interrupting):* No, no, this is the place I want. It's just that I don't understand your sign.

WAITER *(turning around):* Wha . . . Oh, yeah, sorry, thought I had put it up this morning. Just a minute. *(WAITER gets out cards from under counter and completes the sign.)*

G race
I n a hurry
N o
O bligation

There you are, mister. How much cheap grace can I give ya?

CUSTOMER: Well, I'm in a hurry; so why don't you just give me the large bucket size? That way I won't have to worry about it for a while.

—blackout—

Part II

SETTING: *The same counter remains, but now sign reads BARGAIN BASEMENT.*

Two women walk in and start rummaging through sundry articles on the counter. An elderly person comes to wait on them.

SALESPERSON: May I help you?

WOMAN #1: No, we're just looking. *(Picks up a garment and puts it up against herself as if measuring it for size.)*

WOMAN #2: Find something good?

WOMAN #1: I don't know—maybe.

SALESPERSON: Oh, that's a nice number, and at a good price, too.

WOMAN #1 *(looks at price tag):* Oh, no, this is no bargain. I could get this cheaper at Simpson's.

SALESPERSON: Yes, but the quality here is much finer.

WOMAN #2: We're not interested in paying a lot of money. We came here looking for something cheap—a bargain. *(Searches a bit more among articles on counter; comes upon a book.)* What's this?

SALESPERSON: Oh, that's nothing; just a book.

WOMAN #2: Yeah? *(Flips through pages.)* Look. *(Shows book to friend.)* This is just what I need.

WOMAN #1: What does it say?

WOMAN #2: THE GOOD NEWS. Hey, that sounds OK.

WOMAN #1: Yeah, I could use some good news. *(Taking out purse.)* What's it cost, Miss?

SALESPERSON: Oh, not much. Some even think it comes free.

WOMEN #1 AND #2: SOLD!

—blackout—

Part III

SETTING: *The same counter remains, but now the sign reads GARAGE SALE. Two persons walk in.*

PERSON #1: Whew! It stinks in here.

PERSON #2: It's a musty garage, so what? We're looking for a bargain, and you don't get nice decor with a bargain.

PERSON #1: I guess not.

PERSON #2: Hey, look at some of this stuff. Makes you wonder who would buy this kind of junk.

PERSON #1: Speak kindly of the customers, dear. Remember, you are one of them.

PERSON #2: I guess so, but I wish the owner would get here.

OWNER (entering stage left): Someone call for me?

PERSON #2: Yes; we were told that this would be a fine place to pick up a good bargain.

OWNER: I think so. Some of these things have been in the family for years. Some of them are really quite nice.

PERSON #2: Yes. As a matter of fact, we saw your ad in the paper and were attracted by the wooden cross.

PERSON #1: We think it might make a good conversation piece in our home. All the best families have one. What did you pay for it originally?

OWNER: To be honest with you, we didn't pay anything for it. Someone else did.

PERSON #2: So, how much do you want for it.

OWNER: Me? Nothing. I don't want to own it anymore.

PERSON #1: Fine. We'll take it.

—blackout—

Probes

1. Discuss the statement "Cheap grace means grace sold on the market like cheapjack's wares. The sacraments, the forgiveness of sin, and the consolations of religion are thrown away at cut prices."[1]

2. Compare the following statement with the statement in the first probe: "Costly grace is the treasure hidden in the field; for the sake of it a man will gladly go and sell all that he has. . . . it is the call of Jesus Christ at which the disciple leaves his nets and follows him."[2]

3. Discuss the place of faith and works in the Christian life, referring to the biblical ideas of "justification by faith" and "faith without works is dead."

4. We are saved by grace through faith without works (Ephesians 2:8-9). The Good News and the cross assuredly are freely given to us. What other biblical references point to our responsibility? See, for example, Romans 10:17 and Matthew 10:38.

[1]Dietrich Bonhoeffer, *The Cost of Discipleship* (New York: The Macmillan Company, 1959), p. 35.
[2]*Ibid.*, p. 36.

Cheap Grace
Three Satirical Stingers

Part I

SETTING: *A bare room with an empty counter (or table). A young person is busy working when another walks in. Over the counter is a sign which reads:*

G
I
N
O

WAITER *(wiping counter):* Yeah, what can I get ya?

CUSTOMER *(self-consciously):* Ah—I heard you could get a full course—ah—inexpensively here.

WAITER: Yeah, that's right. So, what do ya want?

CUSTOMER: I don't know; what do you have?

WAITER: Are ya serious?

CUSTOMER: Of course. I haven't seen your menu.

WAITER *(exasperated):* Look, this is a fast-service place. We don't have no menus. We just sell one thing. If you want menus, you'll have to go to . . .

CUSTOMER *(interrupting):* No, no, this is the place I want. It's just that I don't understand your sign.

WAITER *(turning around):* Wha . . . Oh, yeah, sorry, thought I had put it up this morning. Just a minute. *(WAITER gets out cards from under counter and completes the sign.)*

G race
I n a hurry
N o
O bligation

There you are, mister. How much cheap grace can I give ya?

CUSTOMER: Well, I'm in a hurry; so why don't you just give me the large bucket size? That way I won't have to worry about it for a while.

—blackout—

Part II

SETTING: *The same counter remains, but now sign reads BARGAIN BASEMENT.*

Two women walk in and start rummaging through sundry articles on the counter. An elderly person comes to wait on them.

SALESPERSON: May I help you?

WOMAN #1: No, we're just looking. *(Picks up a garment and puts it up against herself as if measuring it for size.)*

WOMAN #2: Find something good?

WOMAN #1: I don't know—maybe.

SALESPERSON: Oh, that's a nice number, and at a good price, too.

WOMAN #1 *(looks at price tag):* Oh, no, this is no bargain. I could get this cheaper at Simpson's.

SALESPERSON: Yes, but the quality here is much finer.

WOMAN #2: We're not interested in paying a lot of money. We came here looking for something cheap—a bargain. *(Searches a bit more among articles on counter; comes upon a book.)* What's this?

SALESPERSON: Oh, that's nothing; just a book.

WOMAN #2: Yeah? *(Flips through pages.)* Look. *(Shows book to friend.)* This is just what I need.

WOMAN #1: What does it say?

WOMAN #2: THE GOOD NEWS. Hey, that sounds OK.

WOMAN #1: Yeah, I could use some good news. *(Taking out purse.)* What's it cost, Miss?

SALESPERSON: Oh, not much. Some even think it comes free.

WOMEN #1 AND #2: SOLD!

—blackout—

Part III

SETTING: *The same counter remains, but now the sign reads GARAGE SALE. Two persons walk in.*

PERSON #1: Whew! It stinks in here.

PERSON #2: It's a musty garage, so what? We're looking for a bargain, and you don't get nice decor with a bargain.

PERSON #1: I guess not.

PERSON #2: Hey, look at some of this stuff. Makes you wonder who would buy this kind of junk.

PERSON #1: Speak kindly of the customers, dear. Remember, you are one of them.

PERSON #2: I guess so, but I wish the owner would get here.

OWNER (entering stage left): Someone call for me?

PERSON #2: Yes; we were told that this would be a fine place to pick up a good bargain.

OWNER: *I* think so. Some of these things have been in the family for years. Some of them are really quite nice.

PERSON #2: Yes. As a matter of fact, we saw your ad in the paper and were attracted by the wooden cross.

PERSON #1: We think it might make a good conversation piece in our home. All the best families have one. What did you pay for it originally?

OWNER: To be honest with you, we didn't pay anything for it. Someone else did.

PERSON #2: So, how much do *you* want for it.

OWNER: Me? Nothing. I don't want to own it anymore.

PERSON #1: Fine. We'll take it.

—blackout—

Probes

1. Discuss the statement "Cheap grace means grace sold on the market like cheapjack's wares. The sacraments, the forgiveness of sin, and the consolations of religion are thrown away at cut prices."[1]

2. Compare the following statement with the statement in the first probe: "Costly grace is the treasure hidden in the field; for the sake of it a man will gladly go and sell all that he has. . . . it is the call of Jesus Christ at which the disciple leaves his nets and follows him."[2]

3. Discuss the place of faith and works in the Christian life, referring to the biblical ideas of "justification by faith" and "faith without works is dead."

4. We are saved by grace through faith without works (Ephesians 2:8-9). The Good News and the cross assuredly are freely given to us. What other biblical references point to our responsibility? See, for example, Romans 10:17 and Matthew 10:38.

[1] Dietrich Bonhoeffer, *The Cost of Discipleship* (New York: The Macmillan Company, 1959), p. 35.

[2] *Ibid.*, p. 36.

Cheap Grace
Three Satirical Stingers

Part I

SETTING: *A bare room with an empty counter (or table). A young person is busy working when another walks in. Over the counter is a sign which reads:*

G
I
N
O

WAITER *(wiping counter):* Yeah, what can I get ya?

CUSTOMER *(self-consciously):* Ah—I heard you could get a full course—ah—inexpensively here.

WAITER: Yeah, that's right. So, what do ya want?

CUSTOMER: I don't know; what do you have?

WAITER: Are ya serious?

CUSTOMER: Of course. I haven't seen your menu.

WAITER *(exasperated):* Look, this is a fast-service place. We don't have no menus. We just sell one thing. If you want menus, you'll have to go to . . .

CUSTOMER *(interrupting):* No, no, this is the place I want. It's just that I don't understand your sign.

WAITER *(turning around):* Wha . . . Oh, yeah, sorry, thought I had put it up this morning. Just a minute. *(WAITER gets out cards from under counter and completes the sign.)*

G race
I n a hurry
N o
O bligation

There you are, mister. How much cheap grace can I give ya?

CUSTOMER: Well, I'm in a hurry; so why don't you just give me the large bucket size? That way I won't have to worry about it for a while.

—blackout—

Part II

SETTING: *The same counter remains, but now sign reads BARGAIN BASEMENT.*

Two women walk in and start rummaging through sundry articles on the counter. An elderly person comes to wait on them.

SALESPERSON: May I help you?

WOMAN #1: No, we're just looking. *(Picks up a garment and puts it up against herself as if measuring it for size.)*

WOMAN #2: Find something good?

WOMAN #1: I don't know—maybe.

SALESPERSON: Oh, that's a nice number, and at a good price, too.

WOMAN #1 *(looks at price tag):* Oh, no, this is no bargain. I could get this cheaper at Simpson's.

SALESPERSON: Yes, but the quality here is much finer.

WOMAN #2: We're not interested in paying a lot of money. We came here looking for something cheap—a bargain. *(Searches a bit more among articles on counter; comes upon a book.)* What's this?

SALESPERSON: Oh, that's nothing; just a book.

WOMAN #2: Yeah? *(Flips through pages.)* Look. *(Shows book to friend.)* This is just what I need.

WOMAN #1: What does it say?

WOMAN #2: THE GOOD NEWS. Hey, that sounds OK.

WOMAN #1: Yeah, I could use some good news. *(Taking out purse.)* What's it cost, Miss?

SALESPERSON: Oh, not much. Some even think it comes free.

WOMEN #1 AND #2: SOLD!

—blackout—

Part III

SETTING: *The same counter remains, but now the sign reads GARAGE SALE. Two persons walk in.*

PERSON #1: Whew! It stinks in here.

PERSON #2: It's a musty garage, so what? We're looking for a bargain, and you don't get nice decor with a bargain.

PERSON #1: I guess not.

169

PERSON #2: Hey, look at some of this stuff. Makes you wonder who would buy this kind of junk.

PERSON #1: Speak kindly of the customers, dear. Remember, you are one of them.

PERSON #2: I guess so, but I wish the owner would get here.

OWNER (entering stage left): Someone call for me?

PERSON #2: Yes; we were told that this would be a fine place to pick up a good bargain.

OWNER: *I* think so. Some of these things have been in the family for years. Some of them are really quite nice.

PERSON #2: Yes. As a matter of fact, we saw your ad in the paper and were attracted by the wooden cross.

PERSON #1: We think it might make a good conversation piece in our home. All the best families have one. What did you pay for it originally?

OWNER: To be honest with you, we didn't pay anything for it. Someone else did.

PERSON #2: So, how much do *you* want for it.

OWNER: Me? Nothing. I don't want to own it anymore.

PERSON #1: Fine. We'll take it.

—blackout—

Probes

1. Discuss the statement "Cheap grace means grace sold on the market like cheapjack's wares. The sacraments, the forgiveness of sin, and the consolations of religion are thrown away at cut prices."[1]

2. Compare the following statement with the statement in the first probe: "Costly grace is the treasure hidden in the field; for the sake of it a man will gladly go and sell all that he has. . . . it is the call of Jesus Christ at which the disciple leaves his nets and follows him."[2]

3. Discuss the place of faith and works in the Christian life, referring to the biblical ideas of "justification by faith" and "faith without works is dead."

4. We are saved by grace through faith without works (Ephesians 2:8-9). The Good News and the cross assuredly are freely given to us. What other biblical references point to our responsibility? See, for example, Romans 10:17 and Matthew 10:38.

[1]Dietrich Bonhoeffer, *The Cost of Discipleship* (New York: The Macmillan Company, 1959), p. 35.
[2]*Ibid.*, p. 36.

Truth
Audience Participation Drama

SETTING: *The stage is in complete darkness except for a spotlight on a lectern placed on the extreme downstage right of the MODERATOR. He/she is dressed in modern clothing, as are the VOICES which will come from the audience. The other major characters, CAIAPHAS, PILATE, WOMAN, and DISMAS are dressed in biblical garb. Basically, the introductory speeches of the four major characters are dramatic monologues. The rest is a audience particiption drama.*

MODERATOR *(enters to polite applause)*: Thank you, ladies and gentlemen. It gives me great pleasure to welcome all of you to our annual conference of Truth and Justice. Today we are honored to have with us four well-known persons who have consented to address this question: "Does the truth really make you free?" Joseph Caiaphas will be our first speaker.

(Spotlight comes up center stage right on CAIA- PHAS who is seated in an arrogant pose. Pompously he pushes his chair back and stands up. In a condescending voice.)

CAIAPHAS: "Does the truth really make you free?" That is a *good* question. In my many years as high priest I have had numerous opportunities to deal with this problem. I have concluded that truth is that which is found in the *law* and cannot be altered by men. *(Begins to pace back and forth.)* Now—what things are in the law? *(Clears throat.)* I contend that the law is very clear. The rules of behavior on the sabbath, for instance, leave no room for discussion *or* exemption. One does not labor on the sabbath, *ever,* no matter what the circumstances. *(Pointing to audience.)* Oh, I know what you're thinking: What if a man is starving and needs food? What can he do? Can we let him suffer? The answer is *yes!* It's too bad that he's hungry, but we all know that the poor will always be with us. It is God's will. The law is clear and cannot be altered. If we allow every little person who has a complaint to voice it and then *act* on it, what would become of order and tradition? No, truth lies in the *law! (Sits.)*

MODERATOR: Thank you, Joseph Caiaphas; we appreciate your words of introduction. Now, then, for our next speaker we will hear from the Woman. *(Lights go up on stage left on WOMAN who is standing. She makes no move to speak.)* Please, ma'am, you have the floor.

WOMAN *(after a few moments of silence, timidly begins to speak)*: I feel a bit out of place among all of you learned people . . . and perhaps it is a bit presumptuous of me to speak directly after the eminent high priest Caiaphas. . . .

CAIAPHAS *(interrupting, but always keeping his back to WOMAN)*: It is indeed. Every morning when I wake, I thank God that I am not a woman.

MODERATOR: Please, Mr. Caiaphas, we must have order.

CAIAPHAS *(insincerely)*: Of course, let the chattle speak.

(MODERATOR makes move to reprimand CAIA- PHAS, but WOMAN stops him.)

WOMAN: Please, sir, it is all right; really it is. I am quite used to it. *(Facing audience.)* The truth is a very hard thing to understand, never mind discuss. Yet it seems to me that the truth must lie somewhere *beyond* the law. I'm not sure how far beyond, but I do know that it was something beyond the law which saved me from the temper of the crowd. I know I sinned, and badly, but when I was about to be stoned by the people, I was rescued by the Teacher. I have always wondered why the man I sinned with was not condemned to the same sentence as I. I certainly didn't sin alone; yet I was expected to carry the weight of guilt alone. Is it true that only *I* was guilty? If not, then why was I the only one punished? Can the truth be one thing for some and another for others? May the rich, for example, call it "truth" when they find ways to pay fewer taxes and "evasion" when the poor do the same? The Teacher seemed to feel that we are all guilty, and yet I did not feel condemnation from him—just cleansing, and an admonition not to sin again.

CAIAPHAS: Young woman, you are misguided. I

have spent my life debunking so-called prophets and self-proclaimed messiahs. Cleansing, indeed ... *(WOMAN meekly bows her head.)*

MODERATOR *(kindly):* Ma'am, is your statement finished?

WOMAN: Yes, sir, that was all I wanted to say.

MODERATOR: Very well then. *(Announcing in a louder voice.)* Our third speaker, His Excellency, Pontius Pilate.

(A young boy rushes in carrying a chair, places it center stage, then rushes out. PILATE enters and sits regally.)

PILATE: Mr.(Ms.) Moderator, ladies and gentlemen. I cannot in good conscience agree with either of the previous speakers. I once asked this same Teacher, "What is truth?" He didn't answer me; he only said that he had come to bear witness to the truth. Can anyone here *really* answer the question? I doubt it. If truth were known, I didn't want to condemn Jesus. I was *forced* to by circumstances. The *circumstances* were the truth in that case, not the guilt or innocence of one man. The "truth" for me was that Caesar had his eye on my work and I could not fail him. That man posed a threat to my career. What else could I do? There is no such thing as "truth," only relative "circumstances."

DISMAS *(calling while he strides in from the rear of auditorium):* I can no longer sit here and listen to this nonsense. *(Continues walking until up on stage. Stage lights are on full now.)*

MODERATOR: Mr. Dismas, you are out of order.

PILATE: Oh, why not allow him to speak, Mr. (Ms.) Moderator? I would like to know what a peasant-thief, whose only claim to fame was death by execution, has to say to learned men about "the truth."

MODERATOR: Very well. Mr. Dismas, you may continue.

DISMAS *(to PILATE):* I may be a thief, an unschooled peasant, and I may even be unwashed, but I have much to say about the truth and salvation. *(Both CAIAPHAS and PILATE begin shouting at him at once, and the MODERATOR has to rap on the table for order.)*

MODERATOR: Gentlemen, please!

DISMAS: It is my turn, sirs, and I mean to have my say. *(To audience.)* I never felt any peace in my life. Growing up in Jerusalem was hard. We were not slaves, but neither were we free. We were taxed beyond endurance. It seemed to me that thieving was the only recourse a man had aside from begging, and that I would *not* do! What can I say to you other than that I always believed that I could waste away and no one would care one way or the other. Truth for me meant living, eating, drinking, and trying to have some fun in my dismal life. Hope was gone, fear was constant, and the future was irrelevant. What about those from whom I stole? What about their freedom from fear? Well, it was every man for himself. I knew what my end was to be, and I wasn't afraid of it. What could be worse than a life full of disease and want? I knew I had earned the cross and was glad of it. Since that was the way I was born to die, I decided to live as I chose. But when Jesus was nailed on the cross next to mine, I knew that there was something wrong. He had done no one any harm. He had loved and healed the afflicted. Jonah, a friend of mine, had heard him speak and had returned to our gang a changed man. He tried to make me change, too, but I wouldn't listen. On the cross I had no choice. I heard his voice and I suddenly understood everything Jonah had been trying to tell me. What this man represented—*that* was the truth. Not *my* way of life *(turning to other characters),* not yours *(turning to audience),* and not even *yours!*

CAIAPHAS *(standing, outraged):* Do you, a miserable worm, presume to tell me, a scholar, about the truth?

PILATE *(also angry):* Even your great Teacher didn't presume to answer that question when I, an official of Rome, asked him.

VOICE 1 *(from audience, raises hand and calls out as he or she stands):* Mr.(Ms.) Moderator, may I speak?

MODERATOR: Yes, you may. *(CAIAPHAS sits angrily.)*

VOICE 1: Pontius Pilate, you are wrong. Jesus

did answer that question.

PILATE: When? I certainly don't remember.

VOICE 1: You wouldn't. It was when he was speaking to his disciples that he said, "If you continue in my word, you are truly my disciples, and you will know the truth, and the truth will make you free" (John 8:31-32).

PILATE: So what? Am I a slave that I should seek to be set free?

VOICE 2 (from another part of the auditorium): Jesus said, "You are slaves of sin. . . . And slaves don't have rights, but the Son has every right there is! So if the Son sets you free, you will indeed be free" (John 8:34-36, The Living Bible).

WOMAN: Of course. That is what he did for me. He set me free from sin.

DISMAS (walking over to WOMAN): He did more than that. (Puts arm around her.) He set us free from sin and death.

PILATE: I have a hundred witnesses who saw you die on the cross that afternoon.

DISMAS: My body died, but my soul lives on with Him. Didn't you hear him when he promised me, "Today you will be with me in Paradise"? (Luke 23:43).

CAIAPHAS (stands): Mr.(Ms.) Moderator, this is a disgusting display of heresy and sentimentalism. I will not remain here and listen to this. . . . (Stomps out in disgust.)

VOICES (all at once from different parts of the auditorium): Moderator . . . May I please have the floor? . . . Come back, Mr. Caiaphas. . . . I agree with him. . . . Who does he think he is? . . . Please, I'd like to speak. . . . You don't deserve . . . Is this supposed to be a democratic . . . ? (Improvise some more noisy statements.)

MODERATOR (throughout the confusion, raps on the lectern, looks beseechingly toward CAIAPHAS as he leaves, and finally manages to achieve some semblance of attention): Ladies and gentlemen, . . . please, your attention. We cannot continue this discussion if we do not remain calm.

PILATE: Mr.(Ms.) Moderator, it is pretty evident that we have not been dealt with in good faith. I, too, must take my departure. It is beyond the dignity of my office to remain under these conditions. (Stands, nods to audience, and exits. Some boos and jeers are heard from the audience, though it is not as angry as when CAIAPHAS exited.)

MODERATOR: Order . . . please, ladies and gentlemen, order. (The audience quiets down.)

VOICE 3: Mr.(Ms.) Moderator, may I have the floor?

MODERATOR: Yes, but please be brief.

VOICE 3: I don't think this question "Does the truth really make you free?" can be answered properly in this hostile atmosphere. I propose that we divide into smaller groups and discuss this question in a more rational manner. That will give many more an opportunity to air their views, and perhaps later we can all come together in fellowship and share what we have learned.

MODERATOR: That is a fine idea. We will recess for a few minutes. When we reconvene, I will give you instructions and indicate where each group will meet. The meeting is adjourned for five minutes.

—curtain—

Probes

1. Although Jewish practice allowed medical help on the sabbath if life was endangered, Caiaphas seems to be thinking of the law in terms of the debate between Jesus and the authorities in Mark 2:23–3:6. What is the truth that Jesus discloses here?

2. Do you think that the crowd would have actually stoned the woman taken in adultery? Can humiliating words and actions hurt as much as sticks and stones? Discuss the truth in the healing words of Jesus to the woman.

3. Discuss the kind of expediency demonstrated by Pilate that is found in contemporary life. Is truth that which brings success and approval or that which brings ultimate fulfillment?

4. In what ways does falsehood enslave one to sin? In what ways does truth free one for life?

Truth
Audience Participation Drama

SETTING: *The stage is in complete darkness except for a spotlight on a lectern placed on the extreme downstage right of the MODERATOR. He/she is dressed in modern clothing, as are the VOICES which will come from the audience. The other major characters, CAIAPHAS, PILATE, WOMAN, and DISMAS are dressed in biblical garb. Basically, the introductory speeches of the four major characters are dramatic monologues. The rest is a audience participation drama.*

MODERATOR *(enters to polite applause):* Thank you, ladies and gentlemen. It gives me great pleasure to welcome all of you to our annual conference of Truth and Justice. Today we are honored to have with us four well-known persons who have consented to address this question: "Does the truth really make you free?" Joseph Caiaphas will be our first speaker.

(Spotlight comes up center stage right on CAIAPHAS who is seated in an arrogant pose. Pompously he pushes his chair back and stands up. In a condescending voice.)

CAIAPHAS: "Does the truth really make you free?" That is a *good* question. In my many years as high priest I have had numerous opportunities to deal with this problem. I have concluded that truth is that which is found in the *law* and cannot be altered by men. *(Begins to pace back and forth.)* Now—what things are in the law? *(Clears throat.)* I contend that the law is very clear. The rules of behavior on the sabbath, for instance, leave no room for discussion *or* exemption. One does not labor on the sabbath, *ever*, no matter what the circumstances. *(Pointing to audience.)* Oh, I know what you're thinking: What if a man is starving and needs food? What can he do? Can we let him suffer? The answer is *yes!* It's too bad that he's hungry, but we all know that the poor will always be with us. It is God's will. The law is clear and cannot be altered. If we allow every little person who has a complaint to voice it and then *act* on it, what would become of order and tradition? No, truth

lies in the *law! (Sits.)*

MODERATOR: Thank you, Joseph Caiaphas; we appreciate your words of introduction. Now, then, for our next speaker we will hear from the Woman. *(Lights go up on stage left on WOMAN who is standing. She makes no move to speak.)* Please, ma'am, you have the floor.

WOMAN *(after a few moments of silence, timidly begins to speak):* I feel a bit out of place among all of you learned people . . . and perhaps it is a bit presumptuous of me to speak directly after the eminent high priest Caiaphas. . . .

CAIAPHAS *(interrupting, but always keeping his back to WOMAN):* It is indeed. Every morning when I wake, I thank God that I am not a woman.

MODERATOR: Please, Mr. Caiaphas, we must have order.

CAIAPHAS *(insincerely):* Of course, let the chattle speak.

(MODERATOR makes move to reprimand CAIAPHAS, but WOMAN stops him.)

WOMAN: Please, sir, it is all right; really it is. I am quite used to it. *(Facing audience.)* The truth is a very hard thing to understand, never mind discuss. Yet it seems to me that the truth must lie somewhere *beyond* the law. I'm not sure how far beyond, but I do know that it was something beyond the law which saved me from the temper of the crowd. I know I sinned, and badly, but when I was about to be stoned by the people, I was rescued by the Teacher. I have always wondered why the man I sinned with was not condemned to the same sentence as I. I certainly didn't sin alone; yet I was expected to carry the weight of guilt alone. Is it true that only *I* was guilty? If not, then why was I the only one punished? Can the truth be one thing for some and another for others? May the rich, for example, call it "truth" when they find ways to pay fewer taxes and "evasion" when the poor do the same? The Teacher seemed to feel that we are all guilty, and yet I did not feel condemnation from him—just cleansing, and an admonition not to sin again.

CAIAPHAS: Young woman, you are misguided. I

175

have spent my life debunking so-called prophets and self-proclaimed messiahs. Cleansing, indeed ... *(WOMAN meekly bows her head.)*

MODERATOR *(kindly):* Ma'am, is your statement finished?

WOMAN: Yes, sir, that was all I wanted to say.

MODERATOR: Very well then. *(Announcing in a louder voice.)* Our third speaker, His Excellency, Pontius Pilate.

(A young boy rushes in carrying a chair, places it center stage, then rushes out. PILATE enters and sits regally.)

PILATE: Mr.(Ms.) Moderator, ladies and gentlemen. I cannot in good conscience agree with either of the previous speakers. I once asked this same Teacher, "What is truth?" He didn't answer me; he only said that he had come to bear witness to the truth. Can anyone here *really* answer the question? I doubt it. If truth were known, I didn't want to condemn Jesus. I was *forced* to by circumstances. The *circumstances* were the truth in that case, not the guilt or innocence of one man. The "truth" for me was that Caesar had his eye on my work and I could not fail him. That man posed a threat to my career. What else could I do? There is no such thing as "truth," only relative "circumstances."

DISMAS *(calling while he strides in from the rear of auditorium):* I can no longer sit here and listen to this nonsense. *(Continues walking until up on stage. Stage lights are on full now.)*

MODERATOR: Mr. Dismas, you are out of order.

PILATE: Oh, why not allow him to speak, Mr. (Ms.) Moderator? I would like to know what a peasant-thief, whose only claim to fame was death by execution, has to say to learned men about "the truth."

MODERATOR: Very well. Mr. Dismas, you may continue.

DISMAS *(to PILATE):* I may be a thief, an unschooled peasant, and I may even be unwashed, but I have much to say about the truth and salvation. *(Both CAIAPHAS and PILATE begin shouting at him at once, and the MODERATOR has to rap on the table for order.)*

MODERATOR: Gentlemen, please!

DISMAS: It is my turn, sirs, and I mean to have my say. *(To audience.)* I never felt any peace in my life. Growing up in Jerusalem was hard. We were not slaves, but neither were we free. We were taxed beyond endurance. It seemed to me that thieving was the only recourse a man had aside from begging, and that I would *not* do! What can I say to you other than that I always believed that I could waste away and no one would care one way or the other. Truth for me meant living, eating, drinking, and trying to have some fun in my dismal life. Hope was gone, fear was constant, and the future was irrelevant. What about those from whom I stole? What about their freedom from fear? Well, it was every man for himself. I knew what my end was to be, and I wasn't afraid of it. What could be worse than a life full of disease and want? I knew I had earned the cross and was glad of it. Since that was the way I was born to die, I decided to live as I chose. But when Jesus was nailed on the cross next to mine, I knew that there was something wrong. He had done no one any harm. He had loved and healed the afflicted. Jonah, a friend of mine, had heard him speak and had returned to our gang a changed man. He tried to make me change, too, but I wouldn't listen. On the cross I had no choice. I heard his voice and I suddenly understood everything Jonah had been trying to tell me. What this man represented—*that* was the truth. Not *my* way of life *(turning to other characters),* not yours *(turning to audience),* and not even *yours!*

CAIAPHAS *(standing, outraged):* Do you, a miserable worm, presume to tell me, a scholar, about the truth?

PILATE *(also angry):* Even your great Teacher didn't presume to answer that question when I, an official of Rome, asked him.

VOICE 1 *(from audience, raises hand and calls out as he or she stands):* Mr.(Ms.) Moderator, may I speak?

MODERATOR: Yes, you may. *(CAIAPHAS sits angrily.)*

VOICE 1: Pontius Pilate, you are wrong. Jesus

did answer that question.

PILATE: When? I certainly don't remember.

VOICE 1: You wouldn't. It was when he was speaking to his disciples that he said, "If you continue in my word, you are truly my disciples, and you will know the truth, and the truth will make you free" (John 8:31-32).

PILATE: So what? Am I a slave that I should seek to be set free?

VOICE 2 *(from another part of the auditorium):* Jesus said, "You are slaves of sin. . . . And slaves don't have rights, but the Son has every right there is! So if the Son sets you free, you will indeed be free" (John 8:34-36, *The Living Bible*).

WOMAN: Of course. *That* is what he did for me. He set me free from sin.

DISMAS *(walking over to WOMAN):* He did more than that. *(Puts arm around her.)* He set us free from sin and *death.*

PILATE: I have a hundred witnesses who saw you die on the cross that afternoon.

DISMAS: My body died, but my soul lives on with Him. Didn't you hear him when he promised me, "Today you will be with me in Paradise"? (Luke 23:43).

CAIAPHAS *(stands):* Mr.(Ms.) Moderator, this is a disgusting display of heresy and sentimentalism. I will not remain here and listen to this. . . . *(Stomps out in disgust.)*

VOICES *(all at once from different parts of the auditorium):* Moderator . . . May I please have the floor? . . . Come back, Mr. Caiaphas. . . . I agree with him. . . . Who does he think he is? . . . Please, I'd like to speak. . . . You don't deserve . . . Is this supposed to be a democratic . . . ? *(Improvise some more noisy statements.)*

MODERATOR *(throughout the confusion, raps on the lectern, looks beseechingly toward CAIAPHAS as he leaves, and finally manages to achieve some semblance of attention):* Ladies and gentlemen, . . . please, your attention. We cannot continue this discussion if we do not remain calm.

PILATE: Mr.(Ms.) Moderator, it is pretty evident that we have not been dealt with in good faith. I, too, must take my departure. It is beyond the dignity of my office to remain under these conditions. *(Stands, nods to audience, and exits. Some boos and jeers are heard from the audience, though it is not as angry as when CAIAPHAS exited.)*

MODERATOR: Order . . . please, ladies and gentlemen, order. *(The audience quiets down.)*

VOICE 3: Mr.(Ms.) Moderator, may I have the floor?

MODERATOR: Yes, but please be brief.

VOICE 3: I don't think this question "Does the truth really make you free?" can be answered properly in this hostile atmosphere. I propose that we divide into smaller groups and discuss this question in a more rational manner. That will give many more an opportunity to air their views, and perhaps later we can all come together in fellowship and share what we have learned.

MODERATOR: That is a fine idea. We will recess for a few minutes. When we reconvene, I will give you instructions and indicate where each group will meet. The meeting is adjourned for five minutes.

—*curtain*—

Probes

1. Although Jewish practice allowed medical help on the sabbath if life was endangered, Caiaphas seems to be thinking of the law in terms of the debate between Jesus and the authorities in Mark 2:23–3:6. What is the truth that Jesus discloses here?

2. Do you think that the crowd would have actually stoned the woman taken in adultery? Can humiliating words and actions hurt as much as sticks and stones? Discuss the truth in the healing words of Jesus to the woman.

3. Discuss the kind of expediency demonstrated by Pilate that is found in contemporary life. Is truth that which brings success and approval or that which brings ultimate fulfillment?

4. In what ways does falsehood enslave one to sin? In what ways does truth free one for life?

Truth
Audience Participation Drama

SETTING: *The stage is in complete darkness except for a spotlight on a lectern placed on the extreme downstage right of the MODERATOR. He/she is dressed in modern clothing, as are the VOICES which will come from the audience. The other major characters, CAIAPHAS, PILATE, WOMAN, and DISMAS are dressed in biblical garb. Basically, the introductory speeches of the four major characters are dramatic monologues. The rest is a audience particiption drama.*

MODERATOR *(enters to polite applause):* Thank you, ladies and gentlemen. It gives me great pleasure to welcome all of you to our annual conference of Truth and Justice. Today we are honored to have with us four well-known persons who have consented to address this question: "Does the truth really make you free?" Joseph Caiaphas will be our first speaker.

(Spotlight comes up center stage right on CAIAPHAS who is seated in an arrogant pose. Pompously he pushes his chair back and stands up. In a condescending voice.)

CAIAPHAS: "Does the truth really make you free?" That is a *good* question. In my many years as high priest I have had numerous opportunities to deal with this problem. I have concluded that truth is that which is found in the *law* and cannot be altered by men. *(Begins to pace back and forth.)* Now—what things are in the law? *(Clears throat.)* I contend that the law is very clear. The rules of behavior on the sabbath, for instance, leave no room for discussion *or* exemption. One does not labor on the sabbath, *ever*, no matter what the circumstances. *(Pointing to audience.)* Oh, I know what you're thinking: What if a man is starving and needs food? What can he do? Can we let him suffer? The answer is *yes!* It's too bad that he's hungry, but we all know that the poor will always be with us. It is God's will. The law is clear and cannot be altered. If we allow every little person who has a complaint to voice it and then *act* on it, what would become of order and tradition? No, truth

lies in the *law! (Sits.)*

MODERATOR: Thank you, Joseph Caiaphas; we appreciate your words of introduction. Now, then, for our next speaker we will hear from the Woman. *(Lights go up on stage left on WOMAN who is standing. She makes no move to speak.)* Please, ma'am, you have the floor.

WOMAN *(after a few moments of silence, timidly begins to speak):* I feel a bit out of place among all of you learned people . . . and perhaps it is a bit presumptuous of me to speak directly after the eminent high priest Caiaphas. . . .

CAIAPHAS *(interrupting, but always keeping his back to WOMAN):* It is indeed. Every morning when I wake, I thank God that I am not a woman.

MODERATOR: Please, Mr. Caiaphas, we must have order.

CAIAPHAS *(insincerely):* Of course, let the chattle speak.

(MODERATOR makes move to reprimand CAIAPHAS, but WOMAN stops him.)

WOMAN: Please, sir, it is all right; really it is. I am quite used to it. *(Facing audience.)* The truth is a very hard thing to understand, never mind discuss. Yet it seems to me that the truth must lie somewhere *beyond* the law. I'm not sure how far beyond, but I do know that it was something beyond the law which saved me from the temper of the crowd. I know I sinned, and badly, but when I was about to be stoned by the people, I was rescued by the Teacher. I have always wondered why the man I sinned with was not condemned to the same sentence as I. I certainly didn't sin alone; yet I was expected to carry the weight of guilt alone. Is it true that only *I* was guilty? If not, then why was I the only one punished? Can the truth be one thing for some and another for others? May the rich, for example, call it "truth" when they find ways to pay fewer taxes and "evasion" when the poor do the same? The Teacher seemed to feel that we are all guilty, and yet I did not feel condemnation from him—just cleansing, and an admonition not to sin again.

CAIAPHAS: Young woman, you are misguided. I

have spent my life debunking so-called prophets and self-proclaimed messiahs. Cleansing, indeed ... *(WOMAN meekly bows her head.)*

MODERATOR *(kindly):* Ma'am, is your statement finished?

WOMAN: Yes, sir, that was all I wanted to say.

MODERATOR: Very well then. *(Announcing in a louder voice.)* Our third speaker, His Excellency, Pontius Pilate.

(A young boy rushes in carrying a chair, places it center stage, then rushes out. PILATE enters and sits regally.)

PILATE: Mr.(Ms.) Moderator, ladies and gentlemen. I cannot in good conscience agree with either of the previous speakers. I once asked this same Teacher, "What is truth?" He didn't answer me; he only said that he had come to bear witness to the truth. Can anyone here *really* answer the question? I doubt it. If truth were known, I didn't want to condemn Jesus. I was *forced* to by circumstances. The *circumstances* were the truth in that case, not the guilt or innocence of one man. The "truth" for me was that Caesar had his eye on my work and I could not fail him. That man posed a threat to my career. What else could I do? There is no such thing as "truth," only relative "circumstances."

DISMAS *(calling while he strides in from the rear of auditorium):* I can no longer sit here and listen to this nonsense. *(Continues walking until up on stage. Stage lights are on full now.)*

MODERATOR: Mr. Dismas, you are out of order.

PILATE: Oh, why not allow him to speak, Mr.(Ms.) Moderator? I would like to know what a peasant-thief, whose only claim to fame was death by execution, has to say to learned men about "the truth."

MODERATOR: Very well. Mr. Dismas, you may continue.

DISMAS *(to PILATE):* I may be a thief, an unschooled peasant, and I may even be unwashed, but I have much to say about the truth and salvation. *(Both CAIAPHAS and PILATE begin shouting at him at once, and the MODERATOR has to rap on the table for order.)*

MODERATOR: Gentlemen, please!

DISMAS: It is my turn, sirs, and I mean to have my say. *(To audience.)* I never felt any peace in my life. Growing up in Jerusalem was hard. We were not slaves, but neither were we free. We were taxed beyond endurance. It seemed to me that thieving was the only recourse a man had aside from begging, and that I would *not* do! What can I say to you other than that I always believed that I could waste away and no one would care one way or the other. Truth for me meant living, eating, drinking, and trying to have some fun in my dismal life. Hope was gone, fear was constant, and the future was irrelevant. What about those from whom I stole? What about their freedom from fear? Well, it was every man for himself. I knew what my end was to be, and I wasn't afraid of it. What could be worse than a life full of disease and want? I knew I had earned the cross and was glad of it. Since that was the way I was born to die, I decided to live as I chose. But when Jesus was nailed on the cross next to mine, I knew that there was something wrong. He had done no one any harm. He had loved and healed the afflicted. Jonah, a friend of mine, had heard him speak and had returned to our gang a changed man. He tried to make me change, too, but I wouldn't listen. On the cross I had no choice. I heard his voice and I suddenly understood everything Jonah had been trying to tell me. What this man represented—*that* was the truth. Not *my* way of life *(turning to other characters)*, not yours *(turning to audience)*, and not even *yours!*

CAIAPHAS *(standing, outraged):* Do you, a miserable worm, presume to tell me, a scholar, about the truth?

PILATE *(also angry):* Even your great Teacher didn't presume to answer that question when I, an official of Rome, asked him.

VOICE 1 *(from audience, raises hand and calls out as he or she stands):* Mr.(Ms.) Moderator, may I speak?

MODERATOR: Yes, you may. *(CAIAPHAS sits angrily.)*

VOICE 1: Pontius Pilate, you are wrong. Jesus

did answer that question.

PILATE: When? I certainly don't remember.

VOICE 1: You wouldn't. It was when he was speaking to his disciples that he said, "If you continue in my word, you are truly my disciples, and you will know the truth, and the truth will make you free" (John 8:31-32).

PILATE: So what? Am I a slave that I should seek to be set free?

VOICE 2 (from another part of the auditorium): Jesus said, "You are slaves of sin. . . . And slaves don't have rights, but the Son has every right there is! So if the Son sets you free, you will indeed be free" (John 8:34-36, The Living Bible).

WOMAN: Of course. That is what he did for me. He set me free from sin.

DISMAS (walking over to WOMAN): He did more than that. (Puts arm around her.) He set us free from sin and death.

PILATE: I have a hundred witnesses who saw you die on the cross that afternoon.

DISMAS: My body died, but my soul lives on with Him. Didn't you hear him when he promised me, "Today you will be with me in Paradise"? (Luke 23:43).

CAIAPHAS (stands): Mr.(Ms.) Moderator, this is a disgusting display of heresy and sentimentalism. I will not remain here and listen to this. . . . (Stomps out in disgust.)

VOICES (all at once from different parts of the auditorium): Moderator . . . May I please have the floor? . . . Come back, Mr. Caiaphas. . . . I agree with him. . . . Who does he think he is? . . . Please, I'd like to speak. . . . You don't deserve . . . Is this supposed to be a democratic . . . ? (Improvise some more noisy statements.)

MODERATOR (throughout the confusion, raps on the lectern, looks beseechingly toward CAIAPHAS as he leaves, and finally manages to achieve some semblance of attention): Ladies and gentlemen, . . . please, your attention. We cannot continue this discussion if we do not remain calm.

PILATE: Mr.(Ms.) Moderator, it is pretty evident that we have not been dealt with in good faith. I, too, must take my departure. It is beyond the dignity of my office to remain under these conditions. (Stands, nods to audience, and exits. Some boos and jeers are heard from the audience, though it is not as angry as when CAIAPHAS exited.)

MODERATOR: Order . . . please, ladies and gentlemen, order. (The audience quiets down.)

VOICE 3: Mr.(Ms.) Moderator, may I have the floor?

MODERATOR: Yes, but please be brief.

VOICE 3: I don't think this question "Does the truth really make you free?" can be answered properly in this hostile atmosphere. I propose that we divide into smaller groups and discuss this question in a more rational manner. That will give many more an opportunity to air their views, and perhaps later we can all come together in fellowship and share what we have learned.

MODERATOR: That is a fine idea. We will recess for a few minutes. When we reconvene, I will give you instructions and indicate where each group will meet. The meeting is adjourned for five minutes.

—curtain—

Probes

1. Although Jewish practice allowed medical help on the sabbath if life was endangered, Caiaphas seems to be thinking of the law in terms of the debate between Jesus and the authorities in Mark 2:23–3:6. What is the truth that Jesus discloses here?

2. Do you think that the crowd would have actually stoned the woman taken in adultery? Can humiliating words and actions hurt as much as sticks and stones? Discuss the truth in the healing words of Jesus to the woman.

3. Discuss the kind of expediency demonstrated by Pilate that is found in contemporary life. Is truth that which brings success and approval or that which brings ultimate fulfillment?

4. In what ways does falsehood enslave one to sin? In what ways does truth free one for life?

Truth

Audience Participation Drama

SETTING: *The stage is in complete darkness except for a spotlight on a lectern placed on the extreme downstage right of the MODERATOR. He/she is dressed in modern clothing, as are the VOICES which will come from the audience. The other major characters, CAIAPHAS, PILATE, WOMAN, and DISMAS are dressed in biblical garb. Basically, the introductory speeches of the four major characters are dramatic monologues. The rest is a audience participation drama.*

MODERATOR *(enters to polite applause):* Thank you, ladies and gentlemen. It gives me great pleasure to welcome all of you to our annual conference of Truth and Justice. Today we are honored to have with us four well-known persons who have consented to address this question: "Does the truth really make you free?" Joseph Caiaphas will be our first speaker.

(Spotlight comes up center stage right on CAIAPHAS who is seated in an arrogant pose. Pompously he pushes his chair back and stands up. In a condescending voice.)

CAIAPHAS: "Does the truth really make you free?" That is a *good* question. In my many years as high priest I have had numerous opportunities to deal with this problem. I have concluded that truth is that which is found in the *law* and cannot be altered by men. *(Begins to pace back and forth.)* Now—what things are in the law? *(Clears throat.)* I contend that the law is very clear. The rules of behavior on the sabbath, for instance, leave no room for discussion *or* exemption. One does not labor on the sabbath, *ever,* no matter what the circumstances. *(Pointing to audience.)* Oh, I know what you're thinking: What if a man is starving and needs food? What can he do? Can we let him suffer? The answer is *yes!* It's too bad that he's hungry, but we all know that the poor will always be with us. It is God's will. The law is clear and cannot be altered. If we allow every little person who has a complaint to voice it and then *act* on it, what would become of order and tradition? No, truth lies in the *law! (Sits.)*

MODERATOR: Thank you, Joseph Caiaphas; we appreciate your words of introduction. Now, then, for our next speaker we will hear from the Woman. *(Lights go up on stage left on WOMAN who is standing. She makes no move to speak.)* Please, ma'am, you have the floor.

WOMAN *(after a few moments of silence, timidly begins to speak):* I feel a bit out of place among all of you learned people . . . and perhaps it is a bit presumptuous of me to speak directly after the eminent high priest Caiaphas. . . .

CAIAPHAS *(interrupting, but always keeping his back to WOMAN):* It is indeed. Every morning when I wake, I thank God that I am not a woman.

MODERATOR: Please, Mr. Caiaphas, we must have order.

CAIAPHAS *(insincerely):* Of course, let the chattle speak.

(MODERATOR makes move to reprimand CAIAPHAS, but WOMAN stops him.)

WOMAN: Please, sir, it is all right; really it is. I am quite used to it. *(Facing audience.)* The truth is a very hard thing to understand, never mind discuss. Yet it seems to me that the truth must lie somewhere *beyond* the law. I'm not sure how far beyond, but I do know that it was something beyond the law which saved me from the temper of the crowd. I know I sinned, and badly, but when I was about to be stoned by the people, I was rescued by the Teacher. I have always wondered why the man I sinned with was not condemned to the same sentence as I. I certainly didn't sin alone; yet I was expected to carry the weight of guilt alone. Is it true that only *I* was guilty? If not, then why was I the only one punished? Can the truth be one thing for some and another for others? May the rich, for example, call it "truth" when they find ways to pay fewer taxes and "evasion" when the poor do the same? The Teacher seemed to feel that we are all guilty, and yet I did not feel condemnation from him—just cleansing, and an admonition not to sin again.

CAIAPHAS: Young woman, you are misguided. I

have spent my life debunking so-called prophets and self-proclaimed messiahs. Cleansing, indeed ... (WOMAN meekly bows her head.)

MODERATOR (kindly): Ma'am, is your statement finished?

WOMAN: Yes, sir, that was all I wanted to say.

MODERATOR: Very well then. (Announcing in a louder voice.) Our third speaker, His Excellency, Pontius Pilate.

(A young boy rushes in carrying a chair, places it center stage, then rushes out. PILATE enters and sits regally.)

PILATE: Mr.(Ms.) Moderator, ladies and gentlemen. I cannot in good conscience agree with either of the previous speakers. I once asked this same Teacher, "What is truth?" He didn't answer me; he only said that he had come to bear witness to the truth. Can anyone here *really* answer the question? I doubt it. If truth were known, I didn't want to condemn Jesus. I was *forced* to by circumstances. The *circumstances* were the truth in that case, not the guilt or innocence of one man. The "truth" for me was that Caesar had his eye on my work and I could not fail him. That man posed a threat to my career. What else could I do? There is no such thing as "truth," only relative "circumstances."

DISMAS (calling while he strides in from the rear of auditorium): I can no longer sit here and listen to this nonsense. (Continues walking until up on stage. Stage lights are on full now.)

MODERATOR: Mr. Dismas, you are out of order.

PILATE: Oh, why not allow him to speak, Mr. (Ms.) Moderator? I would like to know what a peasant-thief, whose only claim to fame was death by execution, has to say to learned men about "the truth."

MODERATOR: Very well. Mr. Dismas, you may continue.

DISMAS (to PILATE): I may be a thief, an unschooled peasant, and I may even be unwashed, but I have much to say about the truth and salvation. (Both CAIAPHAS and PILATE begin shouting at him at once, and the MODERATOR has to rap on the table for order.)

MODERATOR: Gentlemen, please!

DISMAS: It is my turn, sirs, and I mean to have my say. (To audience.) I never felt any peace in my life. Growing up in Jerusalem was hard. We were not slaves, but neither were we free. We were taxed beyond endurance. It seemed to me that thieving was the only recourse a man had aside from begging, and that I would *not* do! What can I say to you other than that I always believed that I could waste away and no one would care one way or the other. Truth for me meant living, eating, drinking, and trying to have some fun in my dismal life. Hope was gone, fear was constant, and the future was irrelevant. What about those from whom I stole? What about their freedom from fear? Well, it was every man for himself. I knew what my end was to be, and I wasn't afraid of it. What could be worse than a life full of disease and want? I knew I had earned the cross and was glad of it. Since that was the way I was born to die, I decided to live as I chose. But when Jesus was nailed on the cross next to mine, I knew that there was something wrong. He had done no one any harm. He had loved and healed the afflicted. Jonah, a friend of mine, had heard him speak and had returned to our gang a changed man. He tried to make me change, too, but I wouldn't listen. On the cross I had no choice. I heard his voice and I suddenly understood everything Jonah had been trying to tell me. What this man represented—*that* was the truth. Not *my* way of life (turning to other characters), not yours (turning to audience), and not even *yours*!

CAIAPHAS (standing, outraged): Do you, a miserable worm, presume to tell me, a scholar, about the truth?

PILATE (also angry): Even your great Teacher didn't presume to answer that question when I, an official of Rome, asked him.

VOICE 1 (from audience, raises hand and calls out as he or she stands): Mr.(Ms.) Moderator, may I speak?

MODERATOR: Yes, you may. (CAIAPHAS sits angrily.)

VOICE 1: Pontius Pilate, you are wrong. Jesus

did answer that question.

PILATE: When? I certainly don't remember.

VOICE 1: You wouldn't. It was when he was speaking to his disciples that he said, "If you continue in my word, you are truly my disciples, and you will know the truth, and the truth will make you free" (John 8:31-32).

PILATE: So what? Am I a slave that I should seek to be set free?

VOICE 2 *(from another part of the auditorium)*: Jesus said, "You are slaves of sin. . . . And slaves don't have rights, but the Son has every right there is! So if the Son sets you free, you will indeed be free" (John 8:34-36, *The Living Bible*).

WOMAN: Of course. *That* is what he did for me. He set me free from sin.

DISMAS *(walking over to WOMAN)*: He did more than that. *(Puts arm around her.)* He set us free from sin and *death*.

PILATE: I have a hundred witnesses who saw you die on the cross that afternoon.

DISMAS: My body died, but my soul lives on with Him. Didn't you hear him when he promised me, "Today you will be with me in Paradise"? (Luke 23:43).

CAIAPHAS *(stands)*: Mr.(Ms.) Moderator, this is a disgusting display of heresy and sentimentalism. I will not remain here and listen to this. . . . *(Stomps out in disgust.)*

VOICES *(all at once from different parts of the auditorium)*: Moderator . . . May I please have the floor? . . . Come back, Mr. Caiaphas. . . . I agree with him. . . . Who does he think he is? . . . Please, I'd like to speak. . . . You don't deserve . . . Is this supposed to be a democratic . . . ? *(Improvise some more noisy statements.)*

MODERATOR *(throughout the confusion, raps on the lectern, looks beseechingly toward CAIAPHAS as he leaves, and finally manages to achieve some semblance of attention)*: Ladies and gentlemen, . . . please, your attention. We cannot continue this discussion if we do not remain calm.

PILATE: Mr.(Ms.) Moderator, it is pretty evident that we have not been dealt with in good faith. I, too, must take my departure. It is beyond the dignity of my office to remain under these conditions. *(Stands, nods to audience, and exits. Some boos and jeers are heard from the audience, though it is not as angry as when CAIAPHAS exited.)*

MODERATOR: Order . . . please, ladies and gentlemen, order. *(The audience quiets down.)*

VOICE 3: Mr.(Ms.) Moderator, may I have the floor?

MODERATOR: Yes, but please be brief.

VOICE 3: I don't think this question "Does the truth really make you free?" can be answered properly in this hostile atmosphere. I propose that we divide into smaller groups and discuss this question in a more rational manner. That will give many more an opportunity to air their views, and perhaps later we can all come together in fellowship and share what we have learned.

MODERATOR: That is a fine idea. We will recess for a few minutes. When we reconvene, I will give you instructions and indicate where each group will meet. The meeting is adjourned for five minutes.

—*curtain*—

Probes

1. Although Jewish practice allowed medical help on the sabbath if life was endangered, Caiaphas seems to be thinking of the law in terms of the debate between Jesus and the authorities in Mark 2:23–3:6. What is the truth that Jesus discloses here?

2. Do you think that the crowd would have actually stoned the woman taken in adultery? Can humiliating words and actions hurt as much as sticks and stones? Discuss the truth in the healing words of Jesus to the woman.

3. Discuss the kind of expediency demonstrated by Pilate that is found in contemporary life. Is truth that which brings success and approval or that which brings ultimate fulfillment?

4. In what ways does falsehood enslave one to sin? In what ways does truth free one for life?

Truth
Audience Participation Drama

SETTING: *The stage is in complete darkness except for a spotlight on a lectern placed on the extreme downstage right of the MODERATOR. He/she is dressed in modern clothing, as are the VOICES which will come from the audience. The other major characters, CAIAPHAS, PILATE, WOMAN, and DISMAS are dressed in biblical garb. Basically, the introductory speeches of the four major characters are dramatic monologues. The rest is a audience participation drama.*

MODERATOR *(enters to polite applause):* Thank you, ladies and gentlemen. It gives me great pleasure to welcome all of you to our annual conference of Truth and Justice. Today we are honored to have with us four well-known persons who have consented to address this question: "Does the truth really make you free?" Joseph Caiaphas will be our first speaker.

(Spotlight comes up center stage right on CAIAPHAS who is seated in an arrogant pose. Pompously he pushes his chair back and stands up. In a condescending voice.)

CAIAPHAS: "Does the truth really make you free?" That is a *good* question. In my many years as high priest I have had numerous opportunities to deal with this problem. I have concluded that truth is that which is found in the *law* and cannot be altered by men. *(Begins to pace back and forth.)* Now—what things are in the law? *(Clears throat.)* I contend that the law is very clear. The rules of behavior on the sabbath, for instance, leave no room for discussion *or* exemption. One does not labor on the sabbath, *ever,* no matter what the circumstances. *(Pointing to audience.)* Oh, I know what you're thinking: What if a man is starving and needs food? What can he do? Can we let him suffer? The answer is *yes!* It's too bad that he's hungry, but we all know that the poor will always be with us. It is God's will. The law is clear and cannot be altered. If we allow every little person who has a complaint to voice it and then *act* on it, what would become of order and tradition? No, truth

lies in the *law!* *(Sits.)*

MODERATOR: Thank you, Joseph Caiaphas; we appreciate your words of introduction. Now, then, for our next speaker we will hear from the Woman. *(Lights go up on stage left on WOMAN who is standing. She makes no move to speak.)* Please, ma'am, you have the floor.

WOMAN *(after a few moments of silence, timidly begins to speak):* I feel a bit out of place among all of you learned people . . . and perhaps it is a bit presumptuous of me to speak directly after the eminent high priest Caiaphas. . . .

CAIAPHAS *(interrupting, but always keeping his back to WOMAN):* It is indeed. Every morning when I wake, I thank God that I am not a woman.

MODERATOR: Please, Mr. Caiaphas, we must have order.

CAIAPHAS *(insincerely):* Of course, let the chattle speak.

(MODERATOR makes move to reprimand CAIAPHAS, but WOMAN stops him.)

WOMAN: Please, sir, it is all right; really it is. I am quite used to it. *(Facing audience.)* The truth is a very hard thing to understand, never mind discuss. Yet it seems to me that the truth must lie somewhere *beyond* the law. I'm not sure how far beyond, but I do know that it was something beyond the law which saved me from the temper of the crowd. I know I sinned, and badly, but when I was about to be stoned by the people, I was rescued by the Teacher. I have always wondered why the man I sinned with was not condemned to the same sentence as I. I certainly didn't sin alone; yet I was expected to carry the weight of guilt alone. Is it true that only *I* was guilty? If not, then why was I the only one punished? Can the truth be one thing for some and another for others? May the rich, for example, call it "truth" when they find ways to pay fewer taxes and "evasion" when the poor do the same? The Teacher seemed to feel that we are all guilty, and yet I did not feel condemnation from him—just cleansing, and an admonition not to sin again.

CAIAPHAS: Young woman, you are misguided. I

have spent my life debunking so-called prophets and self-proclaimed messiahs. Cleansing, indeed ... *(WOMAN meekly bows her head.)*

MODERATOR *(kindly):* Ma'am, is your statement finished?

WOMAN: Yes, sir, that was all I wanted to say.

MODERATOR: Very well then. *(Announcing in a louder voice.)* Our third speaker, His Excellency, Pontius Pilate.

(A young boy rushes in carrying a chair, places it center stage, then rushes out. PILATE enters and sits regally.)

PILATE: Mr.(Ms.) Moderator, ladies and gentlemen. I cannot in good conscience agree with either of the previous speakers. I once asked this same Teacher, "What is truth?" He didn't answer me; he only said that he had come to bear witness to the truth. Can anyone here *really* answer the question? I doubt it. If truth were known, I didn't want to condemn Jesus. I was *forced* to by circumstances. The *circumstances* were the truth in that case, not the guilt or innocence of one man. The "truth" for me was that Caesar had his eye on my work and I could not fail him. That man posed a threat to my career. What else could I do? There is no such thing as "truth," only relative "circumstances."

DISMAS *(calling while he strides in from the rear of auditorium):* I can no longer sit here and listen to this nonsense. *(Continues walking until up on stage. Stage lights are on full now.)*

MODERATOR: Mr. Dismas, you are out of order.

PILATE: Oh, why not allow him to speak, Mr. (Ms.) Moderator? I would like to know what a peasant-thief, whose only claim to fame was death by execution, has to say to learned men about "the truth."

MODERATOR: Very well. Mr. Dismas, you may continue.

DISMAS *(to PILATE):* I may be a thief, an unschooled peasant, and I may even be unwashed, but I have much to say about the truth and salvation. *(Both CAIAPHAS and PILATE begin shouting at him at once, and the MODERATOR has to rap on the table for order.)*

MODERATOR: Gentlemen, please!

DISMAS: It is my turn, sirs, and I mean to have my say. *(To audience.)* I never felt any peace in my life. Growing up in Jerusalem was hard. We were not slaves, but neither were we free. We were taxed beyond endurance. It seemed to me that thieving was the only recourse a man had aside from begging, and that I would *not* do! What can I say to you other than that I always believed that I could waste away and no one would care one way or the other. Truth for me meant living, eating, drinking, and trying to have some fun in my dismal life. Hope was gone, fear was constant, and the future was irrelevant. What about those from whom I stole? What about their freedom from fear? Well, it was every man for himself. I knew what my end was to be, and I wasn't afraid of it. What could be worse than a life full of disease and want? I knew I had earned the cross and was glad of it. Since that was the way I was born to die, I decided to live as I chose. But when Jesus was nailed on the cross next to mine, I knew that there was something wrong. He had done no one any harm. He had loved and healed the afflicted. Jonah, a friend of mine, had heard him speak and had returned to our gang a changed man. He tried to make me change, too, but I wouldn't listen. On the cross I had no choice. I heard his voice and I suddenly understood everything Jonah had been trying to tell me. What this man represented—*that* was the truth. Not *my* way of life *(turning to other characters)*, not yours *(turning to audience)*, and not even *yours!*

CAIAPHAS *(standing, outraged):* Do you, a miserable worm, presume to tell me, a scholar, about the truth?

PILATE *(also angry):* Even your great Teacher didn't presume to answer that question when I, an official of Rome, asked him.

VOICE 1 *(from audience, raises hand and calls out as he or she stands):* Mr.(Ms.) Moderator, may I speak?

MODERATOR: Yes, you may. *(CAIAPHAS sits angrily.)*

VOICE 1: Pontius Pilate, you are wrong. Jesus

did answer that question.

PILATE: When? I certainly don't remember.

VOICE 1: You wouldn't. It was when he was speaking to his disciples that he said, "If you continue in my word, you are truly my disciples, and you will know the truth, and the truth will make you free" (John 8:31-32).

PILATE: So what? Am I a slave that I should seek to be set free?

VOICE 2 *(from another part of the auditorium):* Jesus said, "You are slaves of sin. . . . And slaves don't have rights, but the Son has every right there is! So if the Son sets you free, you will indeed be free" (John 8:34-36, *The Living Bible*).

WOMAN: Of course. *That* is what he did for me. He set me free from sin.

DISMAS *(walking over to WOMAN):* He did more than that. *(Puts arm around her.)* He set us free from sin and *death.*

PILATE: I have a hundred witnesses who saw you die on the cross that afternoon.

DISMAS: My body died, but my soul lives on with Him. Didn't you hear him when he promised me, "Today you will be with me in Paradise"? (Luke 23:43).

CAIAPHAS *(stands):* Mr.(Ms.) Moderator, this is a disgusting display of heresy and sentimentalism. I will not remain here and listen to this. . . . *(Stomps out in disgust.)*

VOICES *(all at once from different parts of the auditorium):* Moderator . . . May I please have the floor? . . . Come back, Mr. Caiaphas. . . . I agree with him. . . . Who does he think he is? . . . Please, I'd like to speak. . . . You don't deserve . . . Is this supposed to be a democratic . . . ? *(Improvise some more noisy statements.)*

MODERATOR *(throughout the confusion, raps on the lectern, looks beseechingly toward CAIAPHAS as he leaves, and finally manages to achieve some semblance of attention):* Ladies and gentlemen, . . . please, your attention. We cannot continue this discussion if we do not remain calm.

PILATE: Mr.(Ms.) Moderator, it is pretty evident that we have not been dealt with in good faith. I, too, must take my departure. It is beyond the dignity of my office to remain under these conditions. *(Stands, nods to audience, and exits. Some boos and jeers are heard from the audience, though it is not as angry as when CAIAPHAS exited.)*

MODERATOR: Order . . . please, ladies and gentlemen, order. *(The audience quiets down.)*

VOICE 3: Mr.(Ms.) Moderator, may I have the floor?

MODERATOR: Yes, but please be brief.

VOICE 3: I don't think this question "Does the truth really make you free?" can be answered properly in this hostile atmosphere. I propose that we divide into smaller groups and discuss this question in a more rational manner. That will give many more an opportunity to air their views, and perhaps later we can all come together in fellowship and share what we have learned.

MODERATOR: That is a fine idea. We will recess for a few minutes. When we reconvene, I will give you instructions and indicate where each group will meet. The meeting is adjourned for five minutes.

—curtain—

Probes

1. Although Jewish practice allowed medical help on the sabbath if life was endangered, Caiaphas seems to be thinking of the law in terms of the debate between Jesus and the authorities in Mark 2:23–3:6. What is the truth that Jesus discloses here?

2. Do you think that the crowd would have actually stoned the woman taken in adultery? Can humiliating words and actions hurt as much as sticks and stones? Discuss the truth in the healing words of Jesus to the woman.

3. Discuss the kind of expediency demonstrated by Pilate that is found in contemporary life. Is truth that which brings success and approval or that which brings ultimate fulfillment?

4. In what ways does falsehood enslave one to sin? In what ways does truth free one for life?

Truth

Audience Participation Drama

SETTING: *The stage is in complete darkness except for a spotlight on a lectern placed on the extreme downstage right of the MODERATOR. He/she is dressed in modern clothing, as are the VOICES which will come from the audience. The other major characters, CAIAPHAS, PILATE, WOMAN, and DISMAS are dressed in biblical garb. Basically, the introductory speeches of the four major characters are dramatic monologues. The rest is a audience participation drama.*

MODERATOR *(enters to polite applause):* Thank you, ladies and gentlemen. It gives me great pleasure to welcome all of you to our annual conference of Truth and Justice. Today we are honored to have with us four well-known persons who have consented to address this question: "Does the truth really make you free?" Joseph Caiaphas will be our first speaker.

(Spotlight comes up center stage right on CAIAPHAS who is seated in an arrogant pose. Pompously he pushes his chair back and stands up. In a condescending voice.)

CAIAPHAS: "Does the truth really make you free?" That is a *good* question. In my many years as high priest I have had numerous opportunities to deal with this problem. I have concluded that truth is that which is found in the *law* and cannot be altered by men. *(Begins to pace back and forth.)* Now—what things are in the law? *(Clears throat.)* I contend that the law is very clear. The rules of behavior on the sabbath, for instance, leave no room for discussion *or* exemption. One does not labor on the sabbath, *ever*, no matter what the circumstances. *(Pointing to audience.)* Oh, I know what you're thinking: What if a man is starving and needs food? What can he do? Can we let him suffer? The answer is *yes!* It's too bad that he's hungry, but we all know that the poor will always be with us. It is God's will. The law is clear and cannot be altered. If we allow every little person who has a complaint to voice it and then *act* on it, what would become of order and tradition? No, truth lies in the *law! (Sits.)*

MODERATOR: Thank you, Joseph Caiaphas; we appreciate your words of introduction. Now, then, for our next speaker we will hear from the Woman. *(Lights go up on stage left on WOMAN who is standing. She makes no move to speak.)* Please, ma'am, you have the floor.

WOMAN *(after a few moments of silence, timidly begins to speak):* I feel a bit out of place among all of you learned people ... and perhaps it is a bit presumptuous of me to speak directly after the eminent high priest Caiaphas....

CAIAPHAS *(interrupting, but always keeping his back to WOMAN):* It is indeed. Every morning when I wake, I thank God that I am not a woman.

MODERATOR: Please, Mr. Caiaphas, we must have order.

CAIAPHAS *(insincerely):* Of course, let the chattle speak.

(MODERATOR makes move to reprimand CAIAPHAS, but WOMAN stops him.)

WOMAN: Please, sir, it is all right; really it is. I am quite used to it. *(Facing audience.)* The truth is a very hard thing to understand, never mind discuss. Yet it seems to me that the truth must lie somewhere *beyond* the law. I'm not sure how far beyond, but I do know that it was something beyond the law which saved me from the temper of the crowd. I know I sinned, and badly, but when I was about to be stoned by the people, I was rescued by the Teacher. I have always wondered why the man I sinned with was not condemned to the same sentence as I. I certainly didn't sin alone; yet I was expected to carry the weight of guilt alone. Is it true that only *I* was guilty? If not, ˙en why was I the only one punished? Can the truth be one thing for some and another for others? May the rich, for example, call it "truth" when they find ways to pay fewer taxes and "evasion" when the poor do the same? The Teacher seemed to feel that we are all guilty, and yet I did not feel condemnation from him—just cleansing, and an admonition not to sin again.

CAIAPHAS: Young woman, you are misguided. I

have spent my life debunking so-called prophets and self-proclaimed messiahs. Cleansing, indeed ... *(WOMAN meekly bows her head.)*

MODERATOR *(kindly):* Ma'am, is your statement finished?

WOMAN: Yes, sir, that was all I wanted to say.

MODERATOR: Very well then. *(Announcing in a louder voice.)* Our third speaker, His Excellency, Pontius Pilate.

(A young boy rushes in carrying a chair, places it center stage, then rushes out. PILATE enters and sits regally.)

PILATE: Mr.(Ms.) Moderator, ladies and gentlemen. I cannot in good conscience agree with either of the previous speakers. I once asked this same Teacher, "What is truth?" He didn't answer me; he only said that he had come to bear witness to the truth. Can anyone here *really* answer the question? I doubt it. If truth were known, I didn't want to condemn Jesus. I was *forced* to by circumstances. The *circumstances* were the truth in that case, not the guilt or innocence of one man. The "truth" for me was that Caesar had his eye on my work and I could not fail him. That man posed a threat to my career. What else could I do? There is no such thing as "truth," only relative "circumstances."

DISMAS *(calling while he strides in from the rear of auditorium):* I can no longer sit here and listen to this nonsense. *(Continues walking until up on stage. Stage lights are on full now.)*

MODERATOR: Mr. Dismas, you are out of order.

PILATE: Oh, why not allow him to speak, Mr. (Ms.) Moderator? I would like to know what a peasant-thief, whose only claim to fame was death by execution, has to say to learned men about "the truth."

MODERATOR: Very well. Mr. Dismas, you may continue.

DISMAS *(to PILATE):* I may be a thief, an unschooled peasant, and I may even be unwashed, but I have much to say about the truth and salvation. *(Both CAIAPHAS and PILATE begin shouting at him at once, and the MODERATOR has to rap on the table for order.)*

MODERATOR: Gentlemen, please!

DISMAS: It is my turn, sirs, and I mean to have my say. *(To audience.)* I never felt any peace in my life. Growing up in Jerusalem was hard. We were not slaves, but neither were we free. We were taxed beyond endurance. It seemed to me that thieving was the only recourse a man had aside from begging, and that I would *not* do! What can I say to you other than that I always believed that I could waste away and no one would care one way or the other. Truth for me meant living, eating, drinking, and trying to have some fun in my dismal life. Hope was gone, fear was constant, and the future was irrelevant. What about those from whom I stole? What about their freedom from fear? Well, it was every man for himself. I knew what my end was to be, and I wasn't afraid of it. What could be worse than a life full of disease and want? I knew I had earned the cross and was glad of it. Since that was the way I was born to die, I decided to live as I chose. But when Jesus was nailed on the cross next to mine, I knew that there was something wrong. He had done no one any harm. He had loved and healed the afflicted. Jonah, a friend of mine, had heard him speak and had returned to our gang a changed man. He tried to make me change, too, but I wouldn't listen. On the cross I had no choice. I heard his voice and I suddenly understood everything Jonah had been trying to tell me. What this man represented—*that* was the truth. Not *my* way of life *(turning to other characters)*, not yours *(turning to audience)*, and not even *yours!*

CAIAPHAS *(standing, outraged):* Do you, a miserable worm, presume to tell me, a scholar, about the truth?

PILATE *(also angry):* Even your great Teacher didn't presume to answer that question when I, an official of Rome, asked him.

VOICE 1 *(from audience, raises hand and calls out as he or she stands):* Mr.(Ms.) Moderator, may I speak?

MODERATOR: Yes, you may. *(CAIAPHAS sits angrily.)*

VOICE 1: Pontius Pilate, you are wrong. Jesus

did answer that question.

PILATE: When? I certainly don't remember.

VOICE 1: You wouldn't. It was when he was speaking to his disciples that he said, "If you continue in my word, you are truly my disciples, and you will know the truth, and the truth will make you free" (John 8:31-32).

PILATE: So what? Am I a slave that I should seek to be set free?

VOICE 2 (from another part of the auditorium): Jesus said, "You are slaves of sin. . . . And slaves don't have rights, but the Son has every right there is! So if the Son sets you free, you will indeed be free" (John 8:34-36, The Living Bible).

WOMAN: Of course. That is what he did for me. He set me free from sin.

DISMAS (walking over to WOMAN): He did more than that. (Puts arm around her.) He set us free from sin and death.

PILATE: I have a hundred witnesses who saw you die on the cross that afternoon.

DISMAS: My body died, but my soul lives on with Him. Didn't you hear him when he promised me, "Today you will be with me in Paradise"? (Luke 23:43).

CAIAPHAS (stands): Mr.(Ms.) Moderator, this is a disgusting display of heresy and sentimentalism. I will not remain here and listen to this. . . . (Stomps out in disgust.)

VOICES (all at once from different parts of the auditorium): Moderator . . . May I please have the floor? . . . Come back, Mr. Caiaphas. . . . I agree with him. . . . Who does he think he is? . . . Please, I'd like to speak. . . . You don't deserve . . . Is this supposed to be a democratic . . . ? (Improvise some more noisy statements.)

MODERATOR (throughout the confusion, raps on the lectern, looks beseechingly toward CAIAPHAS as he leaves, and finally manages to achieve some semblance of attention): Ladies and gentlemen, . . . please, your attention. We cannot continue this discussion if we do not remain calm.

PILATE: Mr.(Ms.) Moderator, it is pretty evident that we have not been dealt with in good faith. I, too, must take my departure. It is beyond the dignity of my office to remain under these conditions. (Stands, nods to audience, and exits. Some boos and jeers are heard from the audience, though it is not as angry as when CAIAPHAS exited.)

MODERATOR: Order . . . please, ladies and gentlemen, order. (The audience quiets down.)

VOICE 3: Mr.(Ms.) Moderator, may I have the floor?

MODERATOR: Yes, but please be brief.

VOICE 3: I don't think this question "Does the truth really make you free?" can be answered properly in this hostile atmosphere. I propose that we divide into smaller groups and discuss this question in a more rational manner. That will give many more an opportunity to air their views, and perhaps later we can all come together in fellowship and share what we have learned.

MODERATOR: That is a fine idea. We will recess for a few minutes. When we reconvene, I will give you instructions and indicate where each group will meet. The meeting is adjourned for five minutes.

—curtain—

Probes

1. Although Jewish practice allowed medical help on the sabbath if life was endangered, Caiaphas seems to be thinking of the law in terms of the debate between Jesus and the authorities in Mark 2:23–3:6. What is the truth that Jesus discloses here?

2. Do you think that the crowd would have actually stoned the woman taken in adultery? Can humiliating words and actions hurt as much as sticks and stones? Discuss the truth in the healing words of Jesus to the woman.

3. Discuss the kind of expediency demonstrated by Pilate that is found in contemporary life. Is truth that which brings success and approval or that which brings ultimate fulfillment?

4. In what ways does falsehood enslave one to sin? In what ways does truth free one for life?

Truth
Audience Participation Drama

SETTING: *The stage is in complete darkness except for a spotlight on a lectern placed on the extreme downstage right of the MODERATOR. He/she is dressed in modern clothing, as are the VOICES which will come from the audience. The other major characters, CAIAPHAS, PILATE, WOMAN, and DISMAS are dressed in biblical garb. Basically, the introductory speeches of the four major characters are dramatic monologues. The rest is a audience participation drama.*

MODERATOR *(enters to polite applause):* Thank you, ladies and gentlemen. It gives me great pleasure to welcome all of you to our annual conference of Truth and Justice. Today we are honored to have with us four well-known persons who have consented to address this question: "Does the truth really make you free?" Joseph Caiaphas will be our first speaker.

(Spotlight comes up center stage right on CAIAPHAS who is seated in an arrogant pose. Pompously he pushes his chair back and stands up. In a condescending voice.)

CAIAPHAS: "Does the truth really make you free?" That is a *good* question. In my many years as high priest I have had numerous opportunities to deal with this problem. I have concluded that truth is that which is found in the *law* and cannot be altered by men. *(Begins to pace back and forth.)* Now—what things are in the law? *(Clears throat.)* I contend that the law is very clear. The rules of behavior on the sabbath, for instance, leave no room for discussion *or* exemption. One does not labor on the sabbath, *ever,* no matter what the circumstances. *(Pointing to audience.)* Oh, I know what you're thinking: What if a man is starving and needs food? What can he do? Can we let him suffer? The answer is *yes!* It's too bad that he's hungry, but we all know that the poor will always be with us. It is God's will. The law is clear and cannot be altered. If we allow every little person who has a complaint to voice it and then *act* on it, what would become of order and tradition? No, truth lies in the *law! (Sits.)*

MODERATOR: Thank you, Joseph Caiaphas; we appreciate your words of introduction. Now, then, for our next speaker we will hear from the Woman. *(Lights go up on stage left on WOMAN who is standing. She makes no move to speak.)* Please, ma'am, you have the floor.

WOMAN *(after a few moments of silence, timidly begins to speak):* I feel a bit out of place among all of you learned people . . . and perhaps it is a bit presumptuous of me to speak directly after the eminent high priest Caiaphas. . . .

CAIAPHAS *(interrupting, but always keeping his back to WOMAN):* It is indeed. Every morning when I wake, I thank God that I am not a woman.

MODERATOR: Please, Mr. Caiaphas, we must have order.

CAIAPHAS *(insincerely):* Of course, let the chattle speak.

(MODERATOR makes move to reprimand CAIAPHAS, but WOMAN stops him.)

WOMAN: Please, sir, it is all right; really it is. I am quite used to it. *(Facing audience.)* The truth is a very hard thing to understand, never mind discuss. Yet it seems to me that the truth must lie somewhere *beyond* the law. I'm not sure how far beyond, but I do know that it was something beyond the law which saved me from the temper of the crowd. I know I sinned, and badly, but when I was about to be stoned by the people, I was rescued by the Teacher. I have always wondered why the man I sinned with was not condemned to the same sentence as I. I certainly didn't sin alone; yet I was expected to carry the weight of guilt alone. Is it true that only *I* was guilty? If not, then why was I the only one punished? Can the truth be one thing for some and another for others? May the rich, for example, call it "truth" when they find ways to pay fewer taxes and "evasion" when the poor do the same? The Teacher seemed to feel that we are all guilty, and yet I did not feel condemnation from him—just cleansing, and an admonition not to sin again.

CAIAPHAS: Young woman, you are misguided. I

have spent my life debunking so-called prophets and self-proclaimed messiahs. Cleansing, indeed ... (WOMAN *meekly bows her head.*)

MODERATOR *(kindly):* Ma'am, is your statement finished?

WOMAN: Yes, sir, that was all I wanted to say.

MODERATOR: Very well then. (*Announcing in a louder voice.*) Our third speaker, His Excellency, Pontius Pilate.

(*A young boy rushes in carrying a chair, places it center stage, then rushes out. PILATE enters and sits regally.*)

PILATE: Mr.(Ms.) Moderator, ladies and gentlemen. I cannot in good conscience agree with either of the previous speakers. I once asked this same Teacher, "What is truth?" He didn't answer me; he only said that he had come to bear witness to the truth. Can anyone here *really* answer the question? I doubt it. If truth were known, I didn't want to condemn Jesus. I was *forced* to by circumstances. The *circumstances* were the truth in that case, not the guilt or innocence of one man. The "truth" for me was that Caesar had his eye on my work and I could not fail him. That man posed a threat to my career. What else could I do? There is no such thing as "truth," only relative "circumstances."

DISMAS (*calling while he strides in from the rear of auditorium*): I can no longer sit here and listen to this nonsense. (*Continues walking until up on stage. Stage lights are on full now.*)

MODERATOR: Mr. Dismas, you are out of order.

PILATE: Oh, why not allow him to speak, Mr. (Ms.) Moderator? I would like to know what a peasant-thief, whose only claim to fame was death by execution, has to say to learned men about "the truth."

MODERATOR: Very well. Mr. Dismas, you may continue.

DISMAS (*to PILATE*): I may be a thief, an unschooled peasant, and I may even be unwashed, but I have much to say about the truth and salvation. (*Both CAIAPHAS and PILATE begin shouting at him at once, and the MODERATOR has to rap on the table for order.*)

MODERATOR: Gentlemen, please!

DISMAS: It is my turn, sirs, and I mean to have my say. (*To audience.*) I never felt any peace in my life. Growing up in Jerusalem was hard. We were not slaves, but neither were we free. We were taxed beyond endurance. It seemed to me that thieving was the only recourse a man had aside from begging, and that I would *not* do! What can I say to you other than that I always believed that I could waste away and no one would care one way or the other. Truth for me meant living, eating, drinking, and trying to have some fun in my dismal life. Hope was gone, fear was constant, and the future was irrelevant. What about those from whom I stole? What about their freedom from fear? Well, it was every man for himself. I knew what my end was to be, and I wasn't afraid of it. What could be worse than a life full of disease and want? I knew I had earned the cross and was glad of it. Since that was the way I was born to die, I decided to live as I chose. But when Jesus was nailed on the cross next to mine, I knew that there was something wrong. He had done no one any harm. He had loved and healed the afflicted. Jonah, a friend of mine, had heard him speak and had returned to our gang a changed man. He tried to make me change, too, but I wouldn't listen. On the cross I had no choice. I heard his voice and I suddenly understood everything Jonah had been trying to tell me. What this man represented—*that* was the truth. Not *my* way of life (*turning to other characters*), not yours (*turning to audience*), and not even *yours!*

CAIAPHAS (*standing, outraged*): Do you, a miserable worm, presume to tell me, a scholar, about the truth?

PILATE (*also angry*): Even your great Teacher didn't presume to answer that question when I, an official of Rome, asked him.

VOICE 1 (*from audience, raises hand and calls out as he or she stands*): Mr.(Ms.) Moderator, may I speak?

MODERATOR: Yes, you may. (*CAIAPHAS sits angrily.*)

VOICE 1: Pontius Pilate, you are wrong. Jesus

did answer that question.

PILATE: When? I certainly don't remember.

VOICE 1: You wouldn't. It was when he was speaking to his disciples that he said, "If you continue in my word, you are truly my disciples, and you will know the truth, and the truth will make you free" (John 8:31-32).

PILATE: So what? Am I a slave that I should seek to be set free?

VOICE 2 (from another part of the auditorium): Jesus said, "You are slaves of sin. . . . And slaves don't have rights, but the Son has every right there is! So if the Son sets you free, you will indeed be free" (John 8:34-36, The Living Bible).

WOMAN: Of course. That is what he did for me. He set me free from sin.

DISMAS (walking over to WOMAN): He did more than that. (Puts arm around her.) He set us free from sin and death.

PILATE: I have a hundred witnesses who saw you die on the cross that afternoon.

DISMAS: My body died, but my soul lives on with Him. Didn't you hear him when he promised me, "Today you will be with me in Paradise"? (Luke 23:43).

CAIAPHAS (stands): Mr.(Ms.) Moderator, this is a disgusting display of heresy and sentimentalism. I will not remain here and listen to this. . . . (Stomps out in disgust.)

VOICES (all at once from different parts of the auditorium): Moderator . . . May I please have the floor? . . . Come back, Mr. Caiaphas. . . . I agree with him. . . . Who does he think he is? . . . Please, I'd like to speak. . . . You don't deserve . . . Is this supposed to be a democratic . . . ? (Improvise some more noisy statements.)

MODERATOR (throughout the confusion, raps on the lectern, looks beseechingly toward CAIAPHAS as he leaves, and finally manages to achieve some semblance of attention): Ladies and gentlemen, . . . please, your attention. We cannot continue this discussion if we do not remain calm.

PILATE: Mr.(Ms.) Moderator, it is pretty evident that we have not been dealt with in good faith. I, too, must take my departure. It is beyond the dignity of my office to remain under these conditions. (Stands, nods to audience, and exits. Some boos and jeers are heard from the audience, though it is not as angry as when CAIAPHAS exited.)

MODERATOR: Order . . . please, ladies and gentlemen, order. (The audience quiets down.)

VOICE 3: Mr.(Ms.) Moderator, may I have the floor?

MODERATOR: Yes, but please be brief.

VOICE 3: I don't think this question "Does the truth really make you free?" can be answered properly in this hostile atmosphere. I propose that we divide into smaller groups and discuss this question in a more rational manner. That will give many more an opportunity to air their views, and perhaps later we can all come together in fellowship and share what we have learned.

MODERATOR: That is a fine idea. We will recess for a few minutes. When we reconvene, I will give you instructions and indicate where each group will meet. The meeting is adjourned for five minutes.

—curtain—

Probes

1. Although Jewish practice allowed medical help on the sabbath if life was endangered, Caiaphas seems to be thinking of the law in terms of the debate between Jesus and the authorities in Mark 2:23–3:6. What is the truth that Jesus discloses here?

2. Do you think that the crowd would have actually stoned the woman taken in adultery? Can humiliating words and actions hurt as much as sticks and stones? Discuss the truth in the healing words of Jesus to the woman.

3. Discuss the kind of expediency demonstrated by Pilate that is found in contemporary life. Is truth that which brings success and approval or that which brings ultimate fulfillment?

4. In what ways does falsehood enslave one to sin? In what ways does truth free one for life?

Truth
Audience Participation Drama

SETTING: *The stage is in complete darkness except for a spotlight on a lectern placed on the extreme downstage right of the MODERATOR. He/she is dressed in modern clothing, as are the VOICES which will come from the audience. The other major characters, CAIAPHAS, PILATE, WOMAN, and DISMAS are dressed in biblical garb. Basically, the introductory speeches of the four major characters are dramatic monologues. The rest is a audience participation drama.*

MODERATOR *(enters to polite applause):* Thank you, ladies and gentlemen. It gives me great pleasure to welcome all of you to our annual conference of Truth and Justice. Today we are honored to have with us four well-known persons who have consented to address this question: "Does the truth really make you free?" Joseph Caiaphas will be our first speaker.

(Spotlight comes up center stage right on CAIAPHAS who is seated in an arrogant pose. Pompously he pushes his chair back and stands up. In a condescending voice.)

CAIAPHAS: "Does the truth really make you free?" That is a *good* question. In my many years as high priest I have had numerous opportunities to deal with this problem. I have concluded that truth is that which is found in the *law* and cannot be altered by men. *(Begins to pace back and forth.)* Now—what things are in the law? *(Clears throat.)* I contend that the law is very clear. The rules of behavior on the sabbath, for instance, leave no room for discussion *or* exemption. One does not labor on the sabbath, *ever,* no matter what the circumstances. *(Pointing to audience.)* Oh, I know what you're thinking: What if a man is starving and needs food? What can he do? Can we let him suffer? The answer is *yes!* It's too bad that he's hungry, but we all know that the poor will always be with us. It is God's will. The law is clear and cannot be altered. If we allow every little person who has a complaint to voice it and then *act* on it, what would become of order and tradition? No, truth

lies in the *law! (Sits.)*

MODERATOR: Thank you, Joseph Caiaphas; we appreciate your words of introduction. Now, then, for our next speaker we will hear from the Woman. *(Lights go up on stage left on WOMAN who is standing. She makes no move to speak.)* Please, ma'am, you have the floor.

WOMAN *(after a few moments of silence, timidly begins to speak):* I feel a bit out of place among all of you learned people ... and perhaps it is a bit presumptuous of me to speak directly after the eminent high priest Caiaphas. ...

CAIAPHAS *(interrupting, but always keeping his back to WOMAN):* It is indeed. Every morning when I wake, I thank God that I am not a woman.

MODERATOR: Please, Mr. Caiaphas, we must have order.

CAIAPHAS *(insincerely):* Of course, let the chattle speak.

(MODERATOR makes move to reprimand CAIAPHAS, but WOMAN stops him.)

WOMAN: Please, sir, it is all right; really it is. I am quite used to it. *(Facing audience.)* The truth is a very hard thing to understand, never mind discuss. Yet it seems to me that the truth must lie somewhere *beyond* the law. I'm not sure how far beyond, but I do know that it was something beyond the law which saved me from the temper of the crowd. I know I sinned, and badly, but when I was about to be stoned by the people, I was rescued by the Teacher. I have always wondered why the man I sinned with was not condemned to the same sentence as I. I certainly didn't sin alone; yet I was expected to carry the weight of guilt alone. Is it true that only *I* was guilty? If not, then why was I the only one punished? Can the truth be one thing for some and another for others? May the rich, for example, call it "truth" when they find ways to pay fewer taxes and "evasion" when the poor do the same? The Teacher seemed to feel that we are all guilty, and yet I did not feel condemnation from him—just cleansing, and an admonition not to sin again.

CAIAPHAS: Young woman, you are misguided. I

199

have spent my life debunking so-called prophets and self-proclaimed messiahs. Cleansing, indeed ... (WOMAN *meekly bows her head.*)

MODERATOR (*kindly*): Ma'am, is your statement finished?

WOMAN: Yes, sir, that was all I wanted to say.

MODERATOR: Very well then. (*Announcing in a louder voice.*) Our third speaker, His Excellency, Pontius Pilate.

(*A young boy rushes in carrying a chair, places it center stage, then rushes out. PILATE enters and sits regally.*)

PILATE: Mr.(Ms.) Moderator, ladies and gentlemen. I cannot in good conscience agree with either of the previous speakers. I once asked this same Teacher, "What is truth?" He didn't answer me; he only said that he had come to bear witness to the truth. Can anyone here *really* answer the question? I doubt it. If truth were known, I didn't want to condemn Jesus. I was *forced* to by circumstances. The *circumstances* were the truth in that case, not the guilt or innocence of one man. The "truth" for me was that Caesar had his eye on my work and I could not fail him. That man posed a threat to my career. What else could I do? There is no such thing as "truth," only relative "circumstances."

DISMAS (*calling while he strides in from the rear of auditorium*): I can no longer sit here and listen to this nonsense. (*Continues walking until up on stage. Stage lights are on full now.*)

MODERATOR: Mr. Dismas, you are out of order.

PILATE: Oh, why not allow him to speak, Mr. (Ms.) Moderator? I would like to know what a peasant-thief, whose only claim to fame was death by execution, has to say to learned men about "the truth."

MODERATOR: Very well. Mr. Dismas, you may continue.

DISMAS (*to PILATE*): I may be a thief, an unschooled peasant, and I may even be unwashed, but I have much to say about the truth and salvation. (*Both CAIAPHAS and PILATE begin shouting at him at once, and the MODERATOR has to rap on the table for order.*)

MODERATOR: Gentlemen, please!

DISMAS: It is my turn, sirs, and I mean to have my say. (*To audience.*) I never felt any peace in my life. Growing up in Jerusalem was hard. We were not slaves, but neither were we free. We were taxed beyond endurance. It seemed to me that thieving was the only recourse a man had aside from begging, and that I would *not* do! What can I say to you other than that I always believed that I could waste away and no one would care one way or the other. Truth for me meant living, eating, drinking, and trying to have some fun in my dismal life. Hope was gone, fear was constant, and the future was irrelevant. What about those from whom I stole? What about their freedom from fear? Well, it was every man for himself. I knew what my end was to be, and I wasn't afraid of it. What could be worse than a life full of disease and want? I knew I had earned the cross and was glad of it. Since that was the way I was born to die, I decided to live as I chose. But when Jesus was nailed on the cross next to mine, I knew that there was something wrong. He had done no one any harm. He had loved and healed the afflicted. Jonah, a friend of mine, had heard him speak and had returned to our gang a changed man. He tried to make me change, too, but I wouldn't listen. On the cross I had no choice. I heard his voice and I suddenly understood everything Jonah had been trying to tell me. What this man represented—*that* was the truth. Not *my* way of life (*turning to other characters*), not yours (*turning to audience*), and not even *yours!*

CAIAPHAS (*standing, outraged*): Do you, a miserable worm, presume to tell me, a scholar, about the truth?

PILATE (*also angry*): Even your great Teacher didn't presume to answer that question when I, an official of Rome, asked him.

VOICE 1 (*from audience, raises hand and calls out as he or she stands*): Mr.(Ms.) Moderator, may I speak?

MODERATOR: Yes, you may. (*CAIAPHAS sits angrily.*)

VOICE 1: Pontius Pilate, you are wrong. Jesus

did answer that question.

PILATE: When? I certainly don't remember.

VOICE 1: You wouldn't. It was when he was speaking to his disciples that he said, "If you continue in my word, you are truly my disciples, and you will know the truth, and the truth will make you free" (John 8:31-32).

PILATE: So what? Am I a slave that I should seek to be set free?

VOICE 2 *(from another part of the auditorium):* Jesus said, "You are slaves of sin. . . . And slaves don't have rights, but the Son has every right there is! So if the Son sets you free, you will indeed be free" (John 8:34-36, *The Living Bible*).

WOMAN: Of course. *That* is what he did for me. He set me free from sin.

DISMAS *(walking over to WOMAN):* He did more than that. *(Puts arm around her.)* He set us free from sin and *death.*

PILATE: I have a hundred witnesses who saw you die on the cross that afternoon.

DISMAS: My body died, but my soul lives on with Him. Didn't you hear him when he promised me, "Today you will be with me in Paradise"? (Luke 23:43).

CAIAPHAS *(stands):* Mr.(Ms.) Moderator, this is a disgusting display of heresy and sentimentalism. I will not remain here and listen to this. . . . *(Stomps out in disgust.)*

VOICES *(all at once from different parts of the auditorium):* Moderator . . . May I please have the floor? . . . Come back, Mr. Caiaphas. . . . I agree with him. . . . Who does he think he is? . . . Please, I'd like to speak. . . . You don't deserve . . . Is this supposed to be a democratic . . . ? *(Improvise some more noisy statements.)*

MODERATOR *(throughout the confusion, raps on the lectern, looks beseechingly toward CAIAPHAS as he leaves, and finally manages to achieve some semblance of attention):* Ladies and gentlemen, . . . please, your attention. We cannot continue this discussion if we do not remain calm.

PILATE: Mr.(Ms.) Moderator, it is pretty evident that we have not been dealt with in good faith. I, too, must take my departure. It is beyond the dignity of my office to remain under these conditions. *(Stands, nods to audience, and exits. Some boos and jeers are heard from the audience, though it is not as angry as when CAIAPHAS exited.)*

MODERATOR: Order . . . please, ladies and gentlemen, order. *(The audience quiets down.)*

VOICE 3: Mr.(Ms.) Moderator, may I have the floor?

MODERATOR: Yes, but please be brief.

VOICE 3: I don't think this question "Does the truth really make you free?" can be answered properly in this hostile atmosphere. I propose that we divide into smaller groups and discuss this question in a more rational manner. That will give many more an opportunity to air their views, and perhaps later we can all come together in fellowship and share what we have learned.

MODERATOR: That is a fine idea. We will recess for a few minutes. When we reconvene, I will give you instructions and indicate where each group will meet. The meeting is adjourned for five minutes.

—curtain—

Probes

1. Although Jewish practice allowed medical help on the sabbath if life was endangered, Caiaphas seems to be thinking of the law in terms of the debate between Jesus and the authorities in Mark 2:23–3:6. What is the truth that Jesus discloses here?

2. Do you think that the crowd would have actually stoned the woman taken in adultery? Can humiliating words and actions hurt as much as sticks and stones? Discuss the truth in the healing words of Jesus to the woman.

3. Discuss the kind of expediency demonstrated by Pilate that is found in contemporary life. Is truth that which brings success and approval or that which brings ultimate fulfillment?

4. In what ways does falsehood enslave one to sin? In what ways does truth free one for life?

Truth
Audience Participation Drama

SETTING: *The stage is in complete darkness except for a spotlight on a lectern placed on the extreme downstage right of the MODERATOR. He/she is dressed in modern clothing, as are the VOICES which will come from the audience. The other major characters, CAIAPHAS, PILATE, WOMAN, and DISMAS are dressed in biblical garb. Basically, the introductory speeches of the four major characters are dramatic monologues. The rest is a audience particiption drama.*

MODERATOR *(enters to polite applause):* Thank you, ladies and gentlemen. It gives me great pleasure to welcome all of you to our annual conference of Truth and Justice. Today we are honored to have with us four well-known persons who have consented to address this question: "Does the truth really make you free?" Joseph Caiaphas will be our first speaker.

(Spotlight comes up center stage right on CAIAPHAS who is seated in an arrogant pose. Pompously he pushes his chair back and stands up. In a condescending voice.)

CAIAPHAS: "Does the truth really make you free?" That is a *good* question. In my many years as high priest I have had numerous opportunities to deal with this problem. I have concluded that truth is that which is found in the *law* and cannot be altered by men. *(Begins to pace back and forth.)* Now—what things are in the law? *(Clears throat.)* I contend that the law is very clear. The rules of behavior on the sabbath, for instance, leave no room for discussion *or* exemption. One does not labor on the sabbath, *ever,* no matter what the circumstances. *(Pointing to audience.)* Oh, I know what you're thinking: What if a man is starving and needs food? What can he do? Can we let him suffer? The answer is *yes!* It's too bad that he's hungry, but we all know that the poor will always be with us. It is God's will. The law is clear and cannot be altered. If we allow every little person who has a complaint to voice it and then *act* on it, what would become of order and tradition? No, truth lies in the *law! (Sits.)*

MODERATOR: Thank you, Joseph Caiaphas; we appreciate your words of introduction. Now, then, for our next speaker we will hear from the Woman. *(Lights go up on stage left on WOMAN who is standing. She makes no move to speak.)* Please, ma'am, you have the floor.

WOMAN *(after a few moments of silence, timidly begins to speak):* I feel a bit out of place among all of you learned people . . . and perhaps it is a bit presumptuous of me to speak directly after the eminent high priest Caiaphas. . . .

CAIAPHAS *(interrupting, but always keeping his back to WOMAN):* It is indeed. Every morning when I wake, I thank God that I am not a woman.

MODERATOR: Please, Mr. Caiaphas, we must have order.

CAIAPHAS *(insincerely):* Of course, let the chattle speak.

(MODERATOR makes move to reprimand CAIAPHAS, but WOMAN stops him.)

WOMAN: Please, sir, it is all right; really it is. I am quite used to it. *(Facing audience.)* The truth is a very hard thing to understand, never mind discuss. Yet it seems to me that the truth must lie somewhere *beyond* the law. I'm not sure how far beyond, but I do know that it was something beyond the law which saved me from the temper of the crowd. I know I sinned, and badly, but when I was about to be stoned by the people, I was rescued by the Teacher. I have always wondered why the man I sinned with was not condemned to the same sentence as I. I certainly didn't sin alone; yet I was expected to carry the weight of guilt alone. Is it true that only *I* was guilty? If not, then why was I the only one punished? Can the truth be one thing for some and another for others? May the rich, for example, call it "truth" when they find ways to pay fewer taxes and "evasion" when the poor do the same? The Teacher seemed to feel that we are all guilty, and yet I did not feel condemnation from him—just cleansing, and an admonition not to sin again.

CAIAPHAS: Young woman, you are misguided. I

have spent my life debunking so-called prophets and self-proclaimed messiahs. Cleansing, indeed ... (WOMAN meekly bows her head.)

MODERATOR (kindly): Ma'am, is your statement finished?

WOMAN: Yes, sir, that was all I wanted to say.

MODERATOR: Very well then. (Announcing in a louder voice.) Our third speaker, His Excellency, Pontius Pilate.

(A young boy rushes in carrying a chair, places it center stage, then rushes out. PILATE enters and sits regally.)

PILATE: Mr.(Ms.) Moderator, ladies and gentlemen. I cannot in good conscience agree with either of the previous speakers. I once asked this same Teacher, "What is truth?" He didn't answer me; he only said that he had come to bear witness to the truth. Can anyone here really answer the question? I doubt it. If truth were known, I didn't want to condemn Jesus. I was forced to by circumstances. The circumstances were the truth in that case, not the guilt or innocence of one man. The "truth" for me was that Caesar had his eye on my work and I could not fail him. That man posed a threat to my career. What else could I do? There is no such thing as "truth," only relative "circumstances."

DISMAS (calling while he strides in from the rear of auditorium): I can no longer sit here and listen to this nonsense. (Continues walking until up on stage. Stage lights are on full now.)

MODERATOR: Mr. Dismas, you are out of order.

PILATE: Oh, why not allow him to speak, Mr.(Ms.) Moderator? I would like to know what a peasant-thief, whose only claim to fame was death by execution, has to say to learned men about "the truth."

MODERATOR: Very well. Mr. Dismas, you may continue.

DISMAS (to PILATE): I may be a thief, an unschooled peasant, and I may even be unwashed, but I have much to say about the truth and salvation. (Both CAIAPHAS and PILATE begin shouting at him at once, and the MODERATOR has to rap on the table for order.)

MODERATOR: Gentlemen, please!

DISMAS: It is my turn, sirs, and I mean to have my say. (To audience.) I never felt any peace in my life. Growing up in Jerusalem was hard. We were not slaves, but neither were we free. We were taxed beyond endurance. It seemed to me that thieving was the only recourse a man had aside from begging, and that I would not do! What can I say to you other than that I always believed that I could waste away and no one would care one way or the other. Truth for me meant living, eating, drinking, and trying to have some fun in my dismal life. Hope was gone, fear was constant, and the future was irrelevant. What about those from whom I stole? What about their freedom from fear? Well, it was every man for himself. I knew what my end was to be, and I wasn't afraid of it. What could be worse than a life full of disease and want? I knew I had earned the cross and was glad of it. Since that was the way I was born to die, I decided to live as I chose. But when Jesus was nailed on the cross next to mine, I knew that there was something wrong. He had done no one any harm. He had loved and healed the afflicted. Jonah, a friend of mine, had heard him speak and had returned to our gang a changed man. He tried to make me change, too, but I wouldn't listen. On the cross I had no choice. I heard his voice and I suddenly understood everything Jonah had been trying to tell me. What this man represented—that was the truth. Not my way of life (turning to other characters), not yours (turning to audience), and not even yours!

CAIAPHAS (standing, outraged): Do you, a miserable worm, presume to tell me, a scholar, about the truth?

PILATE (also angry): Even your great Teacher didn't presume to answer that question when I, an official of Rome, asked him.

VOICE 1 (from audience, raises hand and calls out as he or she stands): Mr.(Ms.) Moderator, may I speak?

MODERATOR: Yes, you may. (CAIAPHAS sits angrily.)

VOICE 1: Pontius Pilate, you are wrong. Jesus

did answer that question.

PILATE: When? I certainly don't remember.

VOICE 1: You wouldn't. It was when he was speaking to his disciples that he said, "If you continue in my word, you are truly my disciples, and you will know the truth, and the truth will make you free" (John 8:31-32).

PILATE: So what? Am I a slave that I should seek to be set free?

VOICE 2 (from another part of the auditorium): Jesus said, "You are slaves of sin. . . . And slaves don't have rights, but the Son has every right there is! So if the Son sets you free, you will indeed be free" (John 8:34-36, The Living Bible).

WOMAN: Of course. That is what he did for me. He set me free from sin.

DISMAS (walking over to WOMAN): He did more than that. (Puts arm around her.) He set us free from sin and death.

PILATE: I have a hundred witnesses who saw you die on the cross that afternoon.

DISMAS: My body died, but my soul lives on with Him. Didn't you hear him when he promised me, "Today you will be with me in Paradise"? (Luke 23:43).

CAIAPHAS (stands): Mr.(Ms.) Moderator, this is a disgusting display of heresy and sentimentalism. I will not remain here and listen to this. . . . (Stomps out in disgust.)

VOICES (all at once from different parts of the auditorium): Moderator . . . May I please have the floor? . . . Come back, Mr. Caiaphas. . . . I agree with him. . . . Who does he think he is? . . . Please, I'd like to speak. . . . You don't deserve . . . Is this supposed to be a democratic . . . ? (Improvise some more noisy statements.)

MODERATOR (throughout the confusion, raps on the lectern, looks beseechingly toward CAIAPHAS as he leaves, and finally manages to achieve some semblance of attention): Ladies and gentlemen, . . . please, your attention. We cannot continue this discussion if we do not remain calm.

PILATE: Mr.(Ms.) Moderator, it is pretty evident that we have not been dealt with in good faith. I, too, must take my departure. It is beyond the dignity of my office to remain under these conditions. (Stands, nods to audience, and exits. Some boos and jeers are heard from the audience, though it is not as angry as when CAIAPHAS exited.)

MODERATOR: Order . . . please, ladies and gentlemen, order. (The audience quiets down.)

VOICE 3: Mr.(Ms.) Moderator, may I have the floor?

MODERATOR: Yes, but please be brief.

VOICE 3: I don't think this question "Does the truth really make you free?" can be answered properly in this hostile atmosphere. I propose that we divide into smaller groups and discuss this question in a more rational manner. That will give many more an opportunity to air their views, and perhaps later we can all come together in fellowship and share what we have learned.

MODERATOR: That is a fine idea. We will recess for a few minutes. When we reconvene, I will give you instructions and indicate where each group will meet. The meeting is adjourned for five minutes.

—curtain—

Probes

1. Although Jewish practice allowed medical help on the sabbath if life was endangered, Caiaphas seems to be thinking of the law in terms of the debate between Jesus and the authorities in Mark 2:23–3:6. What is the truth that Jesus discloses here?

2. Do you think that the crowd would have actually stoned the woman taken in adultery? Can humiliating words and actions hurt as much as sticks and stones? Discuss the truth in the healing words of Jesus to the woman.

3. Discuss the kind of expediency demonstrated by Pilate that is found in contemporary life. Is truth that which brings success and approval or that which brings ultimate fulfillment?

4. In what ways does falsehood enslave one to sin? In what ways does truth free one for life?

Woodman, Spare That Tree
A Stinger

APPLICATION: To help people gain an appreciation for the world of nature and to discern the interrelationship among the various parts of God's creation.

SETTING: *Ideally, VOICE 1 should be taller than VOICE 2, though this is not absolutely necessary. If possible, position VOICE 1 directly behind VOICE 2. VOICE 2's voice should be higher or younger in sound than VOICE 1's voice.*

VOICE 1 *(calling downstage):* Hey, down there, what do you think you're doing? Cut it out; that hurts!

VOICE 2: Can't we have a little quiet around here? What's all the noise about?

VOICE 1: Can't you see? He's pushing me so hard my leaves won't stop shaking. *(To someone below.)* Hey, I said stop it!!!

VOICE 2: I can't believe it. "Mr. Big" is all upset. Where's that 300-year-old "cool" you're always putting on?

VOICE 1: Look, you sap-ling! *(Pointing.)* That idiot down there is cutting nicks into my bark. OUCH!

VOICE 2: Good! Maybe he'll whittle you down to size.

VOICE 1: What do you mean, whittle? . . . I think he's planning to chop me down!

VOICE 2: Well, I hate to say it, but it serves you right. You've been rather uppity ever since I've known you.

VOICE 1: I can't help being older and taller than you are. *(To unseen chopper.)* I said cut it out—NO—I mean STOP IT!!

VOICE 2 *(to audience):* It's about time he got his comeuppance. Now I'll be king of the hill.

VOICE 1: You really are stupid, aren't you? Have you any idea what it will mean to this forest if persons indiscriminately keep chopping down perfectly good, healthy trees?

VOICE 2: I know what it will mean to you. I think you'd make a great chest of drawers.

VOICE 1: Have your joke, but remember that we have other uses. Right now we supply the air with oxygen, help prevent erosion and floods, and provide homes for the birds and animals that live in the forest.

VOICE 2: My goodness, I never thought of it that way. I'm sorry I was flippant, Big Tree. Big Tree—what's the matter? What's happening?

OFFSTAGE: TIMBER!!! *(VOICE 1 turns and gives back to the audience.)*

VOICE 2: Gosh, I really feel awful about Big Tree. He was an OK guy, really. *(Pause.)* OUCH—Hey, what are you doing down there? Cut it out—NO—I mean—STOP IT!

OFFSTAGE: TIMBER!!! *(VOICE 2 turns and gives back to audience.)*

Probes

1. Why should we be concerned about what happens to trees?

2. If so-called human values and environmental values are in conflict, which should be given preference? Is there a difference?

3. How does this problem apply to the direct gift of God to Adam when he said, "Behold, I have given you every plant yielding seed which is upon the face of all the earth, and every tree with seed in its fruit; you shall have them for food. And to every beast of the earth, and to every bird of the air, and to everything that creeps on the earth, everything that has the breath of life, I have given every green plant for food" (Genesis 1:29-30)?

4. To what extent does the destruction of any particular individual person diminish the human race?

Woodman, Spare That Tree
A Stinger

APPLICATION: To help people gain an appreciation for the world of nature and to discern the interrelationship among the various parts of God's creation.

SETTING: *Ideally, VOICE 1 should be taller than VOICE 2, though this is not absolutely necessary. If possible, position VOICE 1 directly behind VOICE 2. VOICE 2's voice should be higher or younger in sound than VOICE 1's voice.*

VOICE 1 *(calling downstage):* Hey, down there, what do you think you're doing? Cut it out; that hurts!

VOICE 2: Can't we have a little quiet around here? What's all the noise about?

VOICE 1: Can't you see? He's pushing me so hard my leaves won't stop shaking. *(To someone below.)* Hey, I said stop it!!!

VOICE 2: I can't believe it. "Mr. Big" is all upset. Where's that 300-year-old "cool" you're always putting on?

VOICE 1: Look, you sap-ling! *(Pointing.)* That idiot down there is cutting nicks into my bark. OUCH!

VOICE 2: Good! Maybe he'll whittle you down to size.

VOICE 1: What do you mean, whittle? . . . I think he's planning to chop me down!

VOICE 2: Well, I hate to say it, but it serves you right. You've been rather uppity ever since I've known you.

VOICE 1: I can't help being older and taller than you are. *(To unseen chopper.)* I said cut it out—NO—I mean STOP IT!!

VOICE 2 *(to audience):* It's about time he got his comeuppance. Now I'll be king of the hill.

VOICE 1: You really are stupid, aren't you? Have you any idea what it will mean to this forest if persons indiscriminately keep chopping down perfectly good, healthy trees?

VOICE 2: I know what it will mean to you. I think you'd make a great chest of drawers.

VOICE 1: Have your joke, but remember that we have other uses. Right now we supply the air with oxygen, help prevent erosion and floods, and provide homes for the birds and animals that live in the forest.

VOICE 2: My goodness, I never thought of it that way. I'm sorry I was flippant, Big Tree. Big Tree—what's the matter? What's happening?

OFFSTAGE: TIMBER!!! *(VOICE 1 turns and gives back to the audience.)*

VOICE 2: Gosh, I really feel awful about Big Tree. He was an OK guy, really. *(Pause.)* OUCH— Hey, what are you doing down there? Cut it out—NO—I mean—STOP IT!

OFFSTAGE: TIMBER!!! *(VOICE 2 turns and gives back to audience.)*

Probes

1. Why should we be concerned about what happens to trees?

2. If so-called human values and environmental values are in conflict, which should be given preference? Is there a difference?

3. How does this problem apply to the direct gift of God to Adam when he said, "Behold, I have given you every plant yielding seed which is upon the face of all the earth, and every tree with seed in its fruit; you shall have them for food. And to every beast of the earth, and to every bird of the air, and to everything that creeps on the earth, everything that has the breath of life, I have given every green plant for food" (Genesis 1:29-30)?

4. To what extent does the destruction of any particular individual person diminish the human race?

Woodman, Spare That Tree
A Stinger

APPLICATION: To help people gain an appreciation for the world of nature and to discern the interrelationship among the various parts of God's creation.

SETTING: *Ideally, VOICE 1 should be taller than VOICE 2, though this is not absolutely necessary. If possible, position VOICE 1 directly behind VOICE 2. VOICE 2's voice should be higher or younger in sound than VOICE 1's voice.*

VOICE 1 *(calling downstage):* Hey, down there, what do you think you're doing? Cut it out; that hurts!

VOICE 2: Can't we have a little quiet around here? What's all the noise about?

VOICE 1: Can't you see? He's pushing me so hard my leaves won't stop shaking. *(To someone below.)* Hey, I said stop it!!!

VOICE 2: I can't believe it. "Mr. Big" is all upset. Where's that 300-year-old "cool" you're always putting on?

VOICE 1: Look, you sap-ling! *(Pointing.)* That idiot down there is cutting nicks into my bark. OUCH!

VOICE 2: Good! Maybe he'll whittle you down to size.

VOICE 1: What do you mean, whittle? . . . I think he's planning to chop me down!

VOICE 2: Well, I hate to say it, but it serves you right. You've been rather uppity ever since I've known you.

VOICE 1: I can't help being older and taller than you are. *(To unseen chopper.)* I said cut it out—NO—I mean STOP IT!!

VOICE 2 *(to audience):* It's about time he got his comeuppance. Now I'll be king of the hill.

VOICE 1: You really are stupid, aren't you? Have you any idea what it will mean to this forest if persons indiscriminately keep chopping down perfectly good, healthy trees?

VOICE 2: I know what it will mean to you. I think you'd make a great chest of drawers.

VOICE 1: Have your joke, but remember that we have other uses. Right now we supply the air with oxygen, help prevent erosion and floods, and provide homes for the birds and animals that live in the forest.

VOICE 2: My goodness, I never thought of it that way. I'm sorry I was flippant, Big Tree. Big Tree—what's the matter? What's happening?

OFFSTAGE: TIMBER!!! *(VOICE 1 turns and gives back to the audience.)*

VOICE 2: Gosh, I really feel awful about Big Tree. He was an OK guy, really. *(Pause.)* OUCH—Hey, what are you doing down there? Cut it out—NO—I mean—STOP IT!

OFFSTAGE: TIMBER!!! *(VOICE 2 turns and gives back to audience.)*

Probes

1. Why should we be concerned about what happens to trees?

2. If so-called human values and environmental values are in conflict, which should be given preference? Is there a difference?

3. How does this problem apply to the direct gift of God to Adam when he said, "Behold, I have given you every plant yielding seed which is upon the face of all the earth, and every tree with seed in its fruit; you shall have them for food. And to every beast of the earth, and to every bird of the air, and to everything that creeps on the earth, everything that has the breath of life, I have given every green plant for food" (Genesis 1:29-30)?

4. To what extent does the destruction of any particular individual person diminish the human race?